INTERNATIONAL BUSINESS
CASES AND EXERCISES, SECOND EDITION

Charles A. Rarick

authorHOUSE®

AuthorHouse™
1663 Liberty Drive
Bloomington, IN 47403
www.authorhouse.com
Phone: 1-800-839-8640

First published by AuthorHouse 6/29/2009

ISBN: 978-1-4389-8276-2 (sc)

Printed in the United States of America
Bloomington, Indiana

This book is printed on acid-free paper.

PREFACE

This book acts as a supplement to the traditional text in international business and is considered appropriate for both an undergraduate and a graduate audience. The cases and exercises can be utilized as in-class activities or assigned as homework; whichever is deemed most appropriate by the instructor. Case length and time required for analysis varies in order to utilize the book in a variety of ways.

The casebook provides a more application-oriented approach to the teaching of international business. Students apply what they have read in the textbook or in class to problems relevant to global business activities.

The cases ask students to solve a problem related to various aspects of international business, and the discussion questions are provided as a guide to this analysis. The experiential exercises provide for either individual or group learning, and some of the exercises can be completed outside of class. The Web-based exercises are especially good assignments for individual, outside-of-class work. Many of the cases can be effectively conducted during class time in a small group setting. Most of the cases have been written so as not to require too much class time. The longer cases can be used for group projects and/or presentations.

Cases and exercises are grouped into basic themes regarding international business; however, many of the cases can be used to teach a variety of topics, and users should feel free to assign them in the course where they seem most appropriate. Problems in international business do not always fit into just one topical area, and cross-fertilization of ideas can be a useful to the learning experience.

About the Author

Charles A. Rarick is Professor of International Business in the School of Management at Purdue University Calumet. Previously he was the Director of International Business in the Andreas School of Business, Barry University in Miami, Florida. He has also lectured at the University of the Philippines, Instituto Tecnologico y Estudios Superiores de Monterrey ITESM in Mexico, Romanian-American University in Bucharest, EAFIT in Colombia, Asian Institute of Technology in Thailand, the Asian Institute of Management in Manila, the International University of Business and Economics in Beijing, and the Yangon Institute of Economics, where he served as a Fulbright Senior Specialist to Myanmar in 2005. He was also the 2006-2007 Fulbright Distinguished Lecturer in Business Administration to the Philippines.

Dr. Rarick received his Ph.D. from Saint Louis University and he is certified as a Senior Professional in Human Resource Management. He is a member of the Academy of International Business, International Case Studies Academy, and the Society for the Advancement of Management, and has published numerous articles in academic journals including: *The Journal of Management Research, Advanced Management Journal, Journal of Business Perspective, Journal of Strategic E-Commerce, International Journal of Business Disciplines, International Journal of Value-Based Management, Journal of International Case Studies, Journal of International Business Research, Journal of Educational Leadership, Journal of International Management Studies*, and the *Journal of Business Strategy*. Dr. Rarick is on the editorial review board *Advanced Management Journal*, is Associate Editor of the *Journal of the International Academy of Case Studies*, and is Editor of the *Academy of Strategic Management Journal*. In addition to this book, he is the author of *Cases and Exercises in International Management*, and *The Confucian Advantage*. Dr. Rarick has made professional presentations in India, Taiwan, Hong Kong, Ireland, Mexico, Myanmar, Malaysia, Thailand, Japan, China, Jamaica, Puerto Rico, Romania, Bermuda, Austria, Greece, Slovakia, Colombia, Australia, Venezuela, Costa Rica, Egypt, and throughout the United States and Canada.

Contributors

Arifin Angriawan, Ph.D. (Southern Illinois University) is an Assistant Professor of Management in the School of Management at Purdue University Calumet.

Martine Duchatelet, Ph.D. (Stanford University) is Dean and Professor of Economics in the School of Management, Purdue University Calumet.

Lori Feldman, Ph.D. (University of Michigan) is Chair and Professor of Marketing in the School of Management at Purdue University Calumet.

Anne Fiedler, Ph.D. (Florida International University) is Professor of Management in the Andreas School of Business, Barry University.

Kasia Firlej, MBA (Purdue University Calumet) is a Continuing Lecturer in the School of Management at Purdue University Calumet and has had extensive experience working in Russia and Europe.

Charles Hill, Ph.D. (University of Manchester Institute of Science and Technology) is the Hughes M. Blake Professor of International Business at the University of Washington.

Lawrence Hudack, Ph.D., C.P.A. (University of North Texas) is Professor of Accounting at Troy University.

Jack Kleban, MBA (University of Toledo) is a lecturer in the Andreas School of Business, Barry University and Florida International University, in addition to being a successful entrepreneur.

Suzanne Lowensohn, Ph.D., C.P.A. (University of Miami) is Assistant Professor of Accounting at Colorado State University.

Stephen O. Morrell, Ph.D. (Virgina Polytechnic Institute) is Professor of Economics and Finance in the Andreas School of Business, Barry University.

Inge Nickerson, DBA (Louisiana Tech University) is Professor of Management in the Andreas School of Business, Barry University.

Charles A. Rarick, Ph.D. (Saint Louis University) is Professor of International Business in the School of Management, Purdue University Calumet.

Michael Wilcox, MBA (Barry University) is a retired manager and local entrepreneur.

Gregory Winter, Ph.D. (University of Illinois) is Associate Professor of Management at St. Leo University.

CONTENTS

PART ONE

THE ENVIRONMENT OF INTERNATIONAL BUSINESS

Cases:
Jollibee Foods Corporation
McDonald's in India
Russian LUKOIL's Global Reach
Gambling on China
Colas with a Mission
Ted and Harry's Goes International
Major League Baseball in Mexico?
International Healthcare Tourism

Exercise:
Multinational Corporations

JOLLIBEE FOODS CORPORATION

Jollibee Foods Corporation operates a number of different concept restaurants in the Philippines, and beyond. From its core business, a McDonald's-like concept restaurant, Jollibee has expanded into a pizza chain, fast food Chinese restaurants, bakeries, breakfast bars, and a tea house. The company competes well with multinationals in the Philippines, and has begun a large expansion into the international market, including China and the United States. The flagship brand, Jollibee, with its distinctive company mascot, a large red and yellow bumble bee and additional product concepts, dreams of becoming a global powerhouse in the restaurant industry.

The Republic of the Philippines is a country in Southeast Asia consisting of over 7,000 islands. The Philippines was "discovered" by Ferdinand Magellan in 1521, who claimed the islands for Spain. While Magellan met his death soon after arriving in the Philippines, the country was under Spanish control for a number of years. The Philippines came under the rule of the United States in 1898 when Admiral Dewey defeated the Spanish, and Spain ceded the islands under the Treaty of Paris. While Tagalog, or Filipino, is the official language of the Philippines, English is widely spoken, especially among educated Filipinos. In 1935, the Philippines became a self-governing commonwealth and gained complete independence in 1946. After a number of different administrations, strongman Ferdinand Marcos ruled the country for a number of years and maintained strong ties with the United States. With the increasing discontentment of the Filipino people, a "people's revolution" occurred, and Marcos was forced to leave the country. Political instability resulted for a time, however, democracy quickly took a firm hold in the Philippines. The democracy could be described as somewhat fragile, suffering from a number of cases of political corruption and attempted coups.

The population of the Philippines is approximately 91 million, with an estimated population growth rate of a little under 2% per year. The Filipino people are a mix of Malay, Indonesian, and Spanish, with a significant Chinese ancestry population. The ethnic Chinese have been very influential in the Filipino economy. Filipino culture is a mix of Asian, Spanish, and American cultural values. Total GDP for 2007 was $144.1 billion, with a growth rate of 7.3%. Per capita GDP is $1,624. The currency of the Philippines is the peso (PHP) and has traded in an approximate range of 53 to 40 PHP per U.S. dollar during the past five years.

What would eventually become Jollibee Foods began as an ice cream parlor named Magnolia, started by Tony Tan in 1975 as a family-based business. Eventually the company began offering hot meals and sandwiches, and from this operation the concept of a fast food hamburger business was developed. From these humble beginnings, Jollibee has expanded over the years, both in terms of revenue, and concentric diversification. In 1978, the company began a bakery, and by 1986 Jollibee opened its first international operation in Taiwan. With the acquisition and development of additional restaurant concepts, Jollibee moved into the pizza business, breakfast cafes, Chinese fast food, and the teahouse business. Much of this diversification has come in recent years. While mostly known for its Jollibee hamburger franchise, the company has diversified into many additional fast food areas and has expanded significantly in terms of outlets and geographical coverage.

The mission of Jollibee Foods is stated as: *To serve great tasting food, bringing the joy of eating to everyone.* Jollibee has a vision statement which not only expresses its current values, but also addresses its aspirations.

VISION
We are the best QSR...
The most endearing brand ...
that has ever been ...
We will lead in product taste at all times ...
We will provide FSC excellence
in every encounter
Happiness in every moment ...
By year 2020, with over 4,000 stores worldwide,
Jollibee is truly a GLOBAL BRAND

Jollibee makes itself well-known in the Philippines through extensive advertising, hiring of celebrity endorsers with wholesome images, and through its charitable works.

Jollibee Foods Corporation (JFC) consists of a number of SBUs which cut across different food groups. At the core of JFC is Jollibee, the McDonald's-like hamburger restaurant. The unit sells a standard fare of lunch and breakfast items, but adds a local touch with products such as the Amazing Aloha Burger (slice of pineapple on top of a burger), the Jolly Hotdog Taco Style, Chickjoy with Rice, and Palabok (noodles with a spicy sauce, boiled egg, shrimp, ground pork). Jollibee competes with McDonald's on the basis of price, local product offerings, and national identity. JFC also owns Chow King, a Chinese fast food restaurant chain with operations in a number of countries. The firm has a pizza restaurant chain called Greenwich. In addition, JFC owns a bakery chain called Red Ribbon, and a breakfast cafe called Delifrance.

JFC is looking internationally to increase sales and recently acquired Yonghe King, a "contemporary Chinese fast food" restaurant chain in China. Also in China, JFC has established its first teahouse, called Chun Shui Tang, to serve upscale Chinese consumers. JFC operates restaurants in the Philippines, China, Brunei, Vietnam, Saipan, Indonesia, Dubai, and the United States. The units in the U.S. are located in areas with large Filipino-American populations. JFC feels that international expansion is important not only to grow the company, but because: "Being open to different cultures widens one's spectrum of tastes, style, and ways of seeing food." JFC feels that international expansion provides for organizational learning, and the leveraging of this learning into new markets. JFC is always searching for new product concepts, including its new pilot store called Tio Pepe Karinderia. This new restaurant concept serves very low-priced typical Filipino dishes and seeks to compete with street vendors by offering a more hygienic and cost-efficient operation.

As Jollibee looks to the future, it seeks greater expansion opportunities. The company plans on opening more stores and in more markets, including the Indian market in 2009. Jollibee has experienced great success in its relatively short history, but it now faces a number of challenges. Rising food and fuel prices are putting pressure on the company to raise prices. Consumer spending in the Philippines is starting to show weakening, especially among lower income consumers, as their disposable income has started to decline. In addition, the flagship brand is coming under attack from McDonald's as it continues to open more new stores in the Philippines. According to Tony Lopez of the *Manila Times*, McDonald's beats Jollibee in revenue per store, and has been gaining ground through better customer service, better kid's meals, and better cost and supply chain management. Undeterred, Jollibee looks ahead with the pioneering spirit that established the first ice cream shop in 1975.

Discussion Questions

1. What advantages does a domestic firm have over a MNC in its local market?

2. Can Jollibee Foods Corporation continue to leverage its brands and products in other geographic markets successfully, including the United States? Explain.

3. What strategic direction would you suggest for Jollibee Foods Corporation?

Sources:
Chae, S. *Jollibee serves up fast food, Filipino-style: Chicken, rice noodles a nice change.* Tribune Business News, November 8, 2007; Cuevas-Miel, L. *Fast-food giant plans new round of price hikes.* Tribune Business News, May 15, 2008; Jollibee Foods Corporation Annual Report 2006; Lopez, T. *McDo vs. Jollibee.* The Manila Times, August 14, 2007; Rubio, R. *Jollibee ventures into karinderia concept.* BusinessWorld, July 25, 2007; http://www.jollibee.com.ph. Accessed on May 23, 2008; http://www.state.gov. Country Background Notes: Philippines. Accessed on June 3, 2008; http://finance.yahoo.com/currency/convert?from=USD&to=PHP&amt=1&t =5y. Accessed June 5, 2008.

Case prepared by Charles A. Rarick

CASE 2

MCDONALD'S IN INDIA

In 1954, a milkshake mixer salesman named Ray Kroc traveled to San Bernardino, California, to see why one restaurant had ordered so many of his Multimixers. The McDonald brothers had invented a new concept in the restaurant business and Kroc wanted to see for himself why the business was so popular. Dick and Mac McDonald had pioneered fast food based on high volume, low prices, limited menu, and quick service. The restaurant was a success and Ray Kroc wanted it. He negotiated an agreement with the McDonald brothers in which he would become the exclusive franchiser of the McDonald name.

In 1955, the first McDonald's franchise opened in Des Plaines, Illinois. The McDonald's empire would be based on four core values providing customers with *quality, service, cleanliness,* and *value* (QSCV). Kroc believed that consistency in these core values would allow McDonald's to build a strong brand image throughout the United States. He was right. The concept was a success, and by 1963 McDonald's was selling one million hamburgers a day.

The first international McDonald's opened in Canada in 1967. McDonald's continued its international expansion into Japan, Germany, Australia, France, and England in the 1970s. Additional outlets were established in Latin America, the Middle East, Central and Eastern Europe, Russia, and China. The motive for McDonald's international

8

expansion was the realization that most potential sales existed outside the United States. As Kroc said in 1954, when he witnessed the McDonald brothers' original restaurant concept, "This idea can sell anywhere." Based on the need for additional sales growth and the belief that the concept could be exported, McDonald's embarked on an aggressive international expansion effort beginning in the 1970s. Today, McDonald's has restaurants in over 100 countries and derives approximately 60% of its profits from sales overseas. On average, the company opens a new restaurant somewhere in the world every five hours, and McDonald's can be found on every continent, except Antarctica.

Prior to 1996, McDonald's did not have a restaurant anywhere on the Indian subcontinent. With a population of over one billion, India is viewed by many as a market with enormous potential. India's population is second only to that of China, and, with differing birth rates, India will become the most populated country in the world by 2020, according to some estimates.

India represented a big challenge to McDonald's because most Indians could not eat the main menu item: the beef hamburger. Over 80% of the Indian population is Hindu and this religion prohibits the consumption of cow products. Also, approximately 40% of Indians are strict vegetarians and eat no meat of any kind. A significant percentage of the Indian population is Muslim, which also prohibits the consumption of pork products.

India is a federal republic which gained its independence from Great Britain in 1947. After many years of British rule, Mahatma Gandhi led a mass movement for independence. Since that time, India has been, as its constitution states, a "sovereign, socialist, secular, democratic republic." The economic self-reliance or "swadeshi" begun under Gandhi influenced public policy in India for over 40 years. India finally began to liberalize economic policy after experiencing a severe foreign currency crisis. In 1991, major changes occurred that made foreign investment easier, including reduced tariffs, removal of non-tariff barriers to trade, and loosened foreign investment restrictions and currency controls.

India still remains a poor country and a difficult market for Western companies. Per capita GDP is $909, and many Indians live on less than a dollar a day. Yet the economy, with a high growth rate in recent years, has raised many out of poverty and produced widespread income gains. The government recognizes eighteen languages, with Hindi being the most widely spoken. English is also spoken, especially in urban areas and among the better-educated component of the population. Violent religious clashes occur between Hindus and Christians and between Hindus and Muslims and there is a current movement to establish an all-Hindu India. The religious and social class tolerances advocated by Gandhi do not seem to be as well accepted by many in India today. India is a country divided by languages, religion, and caste.

In 1996, McDonald's opened its first restaurant in India. The first McDonald's in India was located in Delhi and was the only McDonald's outlet worldwide not to offer beef on its menu. Due to dietary restrictions imposed by religion, McDonald's had to be creative in its product offerings. Without the possibility of serving beef or pork, McDonald's offered the lamb patty and a veggie burger. The Big Mac was named the Maharaja Mac and substituted ground lamb for beef. After opening its second restaurant in India, this one in Mumbai (Bombay), McDonald's had invested $14 million, yet the company was not completely sure of the potential of the Indian market. Although business was brisk at both locations, some concerns were raised.

Some consumers complained about the bland taste of the food. Accustomed to the spicy traditional Indian food, McDonald's meals seemed too plain for some consumers. There was also a concern about the political stability of the country and long-term acceptance of McDonald's in India. The Indian government did not support the entry of McDonald's into the country and some Indians protested the arrival of the American multinational. Previous American franchises have been the target of vandalism in India in the past. KFC, Dominos Pizza, and Pizza Hut all have several locations in India, and some of the restaurants have experienced difficulties with political mobs. McDonald's is perhaps in an even more vulnerable position because its primary product worldwide (beef) is viewed by many Hindus as not appropriate for consumption. As one protestor remarked "They are the chief killers of the cow." Other protestors see McDonald's as a symbol of the exploitation of the world's poor by rich American multinationals. In 2005, McDonald's settled a $10 million lawsuit brought by vegetarians in the United States who had charged McDonald's with misleading advertising. McDonald's had been using a beef flavoring for its French fries without telling consumers. The news of this culinary process caused protest in India and some store vandalism, however, McDonald's had been careful not to use the beef flavoring in India.

McDonald's of India is a 50/50 partnership between the McDonald's Corp. and two Indian businessmen, who have divided the market into Northern and Western India. McDonald's faces stiff competition from Yum! Brands Inc., which operates KFC, Pizza Hut, and Taco Bell. Yum has the advantage of having its product offerings more consistent with the requirements of a Hindi diet. At present, there are over 120 McDonald's restaurants in India. Faced with the difficulties of product acceptance, low purchasing power among consumers, and the ever-present potential of political conflict, McDonald's, nevertheless, has decided to triple the number of restaurants in India with an investment of 3 billion Indian rupees in the next few years. With a large and growing population, and increasing incomes, McDonald's feels that Indians will embrace the product offerings and make India a very good growth market for the company.

Discussion Questions:

1. What approach to international business is McDonald's following: ethnocentric, polycentric, or geocentric? Explain.

2. Does the movement into the Indian market represent any risks for McDonald's?

3. Do you think McDonald's will be a success in India? Explain.

Sources: McDonald's corporate web site (www.mcdonalds.com); S. Mohanty, "India's Maharaja Mac Has No Beef" Reuters Business Report, October 11, 1996; S. Mohanty "Where's the Beef: India's McDonald's Eschews Chuck" Reuters, October 11, 1996; "McDonald's Goes to India Without Beef" Dallas Morning News, October 12, 1996; K. Cooper, "Where's the Beef: McDonald's Menu in India Culturally Correct,

But Company's Presence Cooks up Controversy" <u>Dallas Morning News</u>, November 10, 1996; "Big in Bombay: The Maharaja Mac is One Hot Item" <u>The Philadelphia Inquirer</u>, April 22, 1998; "Background Notes: India" <u>U.S. Department of State</u>, January 20, 2009; S. Dutta, "Domino Theory" <u>Business India</u>, May 1, 2000; L. Kadaba, D. Gardner, "India's Elusive Reforms" <u>Financial Times</u>, August 4, 2000; C. Raghatta, "McDonald's Pays Up Hindu Veggie Group in US" <u>The New Times of India</u>, July 12, 2005. McDonald's Finds Unique Way to Beef Up Its Presence in India. <u>www.moneymorning.com</u>. October, 27, 2007; <u>www.mcdonaldsinindia.com</u>. Accessed on January 21, 2009.

Case prepared by Charles A. Rarick

CASE 3

RUSSIAN LUKOIL'S GLOBAL REACH

Lukoil is Russia's largest vertically integrated oil company. It not only deals with the exploration of oil, but also its distribution, refining and retail distribution. The company was a state entity under the Soviet Union, but was privatized in the 1990's. Lukoil supplies close to 19% of Russia's oil production and approximately 2% of world oil supplies. In addition to aggressive oil exploration, the company has formed a strong alliance with GAZPROM, the state owned gas company and most recently has expanded into petro-chemicals in order to further diversify its portfolio.

The oil giant has invested in exploration ventures in the Caspian region, South America, Europe, and the Middle East. Lukoil's diversification strategy also prompted it to invest in oil processing and gasoline retail outlets in the countries of Ukraine, Romania, Bulgaria, Finland, Belarus, the Baltic states, former Yugoslavia, the United States. Not only is Lukoil seeking to spread its influence throughout Europe, the firm has also established a separate arm to focus on investment in North and South America called LUKOIL AMERICAS. Through the purchase of the Getty retail chain, American consumers in the New England area now are purchasing some of their gasoline and fuel oil directly from this Russian company's over 1,800 retail outlets. The rebranded Lukoil gas stations even offer American consumers a Lukoil credit card.

Lukoil is a truly global company with a base in a transitioning country marked by unpredictable policies and failed reforms. The United States and other developed countries rely heavily on oil to grow their economies. As the world's appetite for oil continues to grow, Russia will continue to emerge as an important player in the global energy market; it has the seventh largest oil reserves in the world. Interestingly, Russia is the greatest oil producer that does not belong to the Organization of Oil Producing Countries (OPEC) and has a strong impetus for selling that precious resource to the rest of the world; its economy depends on it. It has been estimated that over half of Russia's state budget revenues are tied to the oil and gas industry.

With the expansion of the Indian and Chinese economies, global demand for energy has risen faster than production, causing prices to increase and allowing Russian oil companies to reap the benefits of these rising commodity prices. Russian oil output has exceeded domestic demand and is expected to continue to do so for a number of years to come. The abundance of excess energy allows Russia and firms like Lukoil to increase their standing in the global community. Some see this situation as an opportunity for foreign investment, others express concerns about the safety of such investments.

The price of a barrel of crude oil has been wildly fluctuating over the past decade based on supply and demand. One thing is for certain, the rising appetite for modernization and increasing oil prices are driving governments and oil companies to push for new field exploration. In the case of Lukoil, foreign fields constitute only five percent of the total output, but in the long term, the firm's CEO, Vagit Alekperov, has publicly committed to increasing this proportionately to twenty percent. This is yet another sign of Lukoil's commitment to diversification and demonstrates that Lukoil is a truly global firm with a decentralized business strategy.

Lukoil's CEO, Vagit Alekperov is the largest individual shareholder owning over 20% of the company stock. Mr. Alekperov, has made public statements that an American investor might view as nationalistic. "The efficient development of reserves directly linked to national security…it preserves the economic integrity of the country…it strengthens national positions in the international arena. The concept has always been the same: in the Russian Empire, the Soviet Union and Russian Federation. It will remain this way, until the 'oil era' is over." (Vagit Alepkerov speech on National Oilmen's Day, September 2005).

Lukoil's aim has been to behave as a decentralized company that is both free of Russia's political influence and eager to attract foreign investment. Some would argue that this is not possible. Lukoil was the largest taxpayer in the Russian Federation in the year 2008. The firm lists its shares on the London Stock Exchange and the NYSE through American Depositary Receipts (ADRs). The value of the ADRs has done well over the past five years, however, it can be argued that the stock is underperforming due to the political risk investors see in Russia today. It may be reassuring to American investors that ConocoPhillips has had a 20% stake in Lukoil since 2005. The acquisition of a fifth of Lukoil's shares by a US owned company and LUKOIL's openness to scrutiny by an independent outside accounting commission should indicate that LUKOIL is making a great effort to shed the image of being a corrupt Soviet style national oil giant. Russia's oil fields are vast and there are many waiting to be explored in Western Siberia and the Sakhalin region. What is troubling to some is the unpredictability of actions undertaken by the Russian government in terms of the confiscation of another private Russian oil company (Yukos), for example, and its aggressive stand with foreign investors. Furthermore, some might also find worrisome that TNL-BP, the joint venture between BP and Lukoil produces 20% of BP's output, yet yields only 10% of the profits to the foreign investor.

Discussion Questions:

1. What are the geopolitical implications of the rising prominence of Russian oil companies such as Lukoil?
2. Do you feel that Lukoil is a good investment for American investors? Explain your answer.

3. What can Lukoil do to attract foreign investment it needs in order to further its oil exploration?

SOURCES:

Bary, A. (2008). *Personal Wealth: Georgia Conflict makes Russian stocks cheap but dangerous.* The Edge. August 25; Gorst, Isabel. (2007) *Lukoil: Russia's Largest Oil Company.* The James Baker III Institute for Public Policy at Rice University; The Economist. (2008) *Russia's Oil Industry : Trouble in the Pipeline.* May 8; Henderson J., Radosevic S. (2003). *The influence of Alliances on Corporate Growth in the Post-Soviet Period:LUKoil and Yukos.* University College of London; McCarthy S., Campbell M., (2008). *Russia's Energy Card has upped the ante in a real-world game of Risk. Valuable access to the region's pipeline's hangs in the balance.* The Globe and Mail . August 16; King, Byron. (2008) *Special Report: Russian Oil for the Welfare of Russia.*; www.whiskeyandgunpowder.com. Retrieved September 14, 2008; www.Eia.doe.gov. Retrieved September 11, 2008; www.LUKOIL.com. Retrieved January 20, 2009; LUKOIL Annual Report, 2007; www.lukoilamericas.com. Retrieved September 10, 2008; www.ogj.com. Retrieved September 12, 2008.

Case prepared by Kasia Firlej

CASE 4

GAMBLING ON CHINA: IS MACAU A GOOD BET FOR THE INTERNATIONAL GAMING INDUSTRY?

Macau has become a large rival to Las Vegas as the gambling capital of the world. For a short period of time, the former Portuguese colony did surpass Las Vegas in gambling revenue. The Cotai Strip (concentration of casinos in Macau) was believed by some to be able to outperform the Las Vegas Strip and to become the gaming center of the world, however, circumstances have recently changed unfavorably for Macau.

Macau is a small area with only a little over 29 sq. km of territory and a population of around 550,000. The state sits on a peninsula connected to mainland China. Macau was returned to China in 1999 and became a Special Administrative Region (SAR), operating much like Hong Kong, with some degree of autonomy. Macau is the only place in China where gambling is permitted. Gambling was denounced by the Communists in 1949 as evil human behavior and all gambling establishments were closed. Macau, being a colony of Portugal, was able to set different rules and allowed gaming. For over 40 years, gambling in Macau was controlled by Stanley Ho, with his historic Lisboa Casino being one of the trademark properties. In 2002, the Chinese government opened up gaming opportunities to outsiders and the Sands became the first American-owned casino in Macau. Soon, others would follow. By 2008, Macau had 28 casinos, some as impressive as the most expensive properties of Las Vegas.

With the opening of the gaming industry to foreigners, Macau experienced tremendous growth in gambling. Gaming revenues exceeded $10 billion in 2007, which was a significant increase over the previous year. Casino revenue growth peaked in early 2008 and revenues began to fall sharply. Three factors contributed to the rapid decline in revenue: 1) a global economic slowdown, 2) factory closings in southern China, and 3) Chinese policy changes relative to the issuance of visas. Mainland Chinese were allowed to travel to Macau to gamble twice a month but the Chinese government changed its policy to allow visits only once every two months. Macau was receiving about 27 million visitors a year, the vast majority of them coming from mainland China or Hong Kong. Only about 200,000 Americans visit Macau each year. There are no direct flights to Macau from the U.S., however, tourists can arrive in Hong Kong and take one of the many ferries that cross between Hong Kong and Macau. The ferry is relatively inexpensive and short ride of approximately one hour makes travel between the two places easy for tourists. One of the reasons for the low tourist turnout is that besides visiting a few historical sites, Macau offers few alternatives attractions, other than gambling and the entertainment offered by the mega-casinos. Only about 25% of the visitors to Macau book a hotel room. Many simply gamble during the day and leave at night, or spend the evening at massage parlors. Unlike Las Vegas, Macau has yet to develop a complete entertainment infrastructure.

One source of nongaming entertainment is the $2.4 billion Venetian complex which opened in 2007. With over 3,000 rooms and a 565,000 sq. ft. casino, the Venetian Macau is the largest casino in the world. In addition to the casino, the Venetian offers a Las Vegas style show called Zaia, and many shops and restaurants all under one roof. By offering elegant Italian frescos and architecture, marble floors, and guest rooms of the highest quality, the Venetian hopes to attract tourists who will stay longer and spend more money. The Venetian is operated by the Las Vegas Sands Corp. and has been one of the hardest hit by the gaming slowdown in Macau. Las Vegas Sands (LVS) has seen its share price fall by more than 90% in the past year. Other casino stocks have fallen as well, but none as drastically as LVS. The company faces bankruptcy as its debt load has become difficult to manage. It has stopped construction on additional properties in Macau and has had to reduce staff. Las Vegas Sands is continuing to develop a casino in Singapore as a safer alternative to Macau.

While the situation in Macau seems very uncertain to many, some see the long term prospects as bright, and are hopeful that the current situation will change soon. One of the more hopeful casino operators is Steve Wynn. Wynn built some of the more impressive structures in Las Vegas, including the Mirage, Treasure Island, and The Bellagio, and was responsible for changing the face of Las Vegas. While he has taken a more cautious approach in Macau, Wynn feels that the long term opportunities are very promising. As he has stated: "The pent-up demand for the good life in China is extraordinary." With a rising middle class and a culture that enjoys gambling as form of entertainment, China may be a good bet for the international gaming industry. With foreign firms either retrenching or remaining cautious, the Ho family is moving forward. It has announced plans to develop a mega-casino and hotel with the help of a Dubai partner.

Facing a global economic downturn, difficulties in the capital markets, and unpredictable Chinese policies, Macau appears not to offer great potential in the short term for foreign investors. Some have even proposed that the change in visa restrictions by the Chinese was intended to drive out foreign investors after they had to make significant investments in Macau. This would allow local businesspeople to acquire those assets at distressed prices, when the foreign firms decide Macau is no longer a good bet. After the foreign investors have left, China would then ease the visa restrictions. Over a short period of time Macau has gone from a winning hand to an uncertain hand for foreign investors.

Discussion Questions:

1. Looking at both the short and long term prospects, do you see Macau as a good place to invest in the gaming industry? Explain.
2. Does the change in visa restrictions represent a form of political risk? If so, what can be done to reduce this risk?
3. What advice would you offer foreign casino operators in Macau?

Sources:: J. Cheng. (2008). *Las Vegas Sands cuts 500 jobs in Macau*. The Wall Street Journal, December 24; J. Chidley. (2008). *Dreaming in Macau*. Canadian Business, November 25-December 8; CNN. (2008). *Steve Wynn: Casino mogul moves on Macau*, September 2; M. Cohen. (2008). *No sure thing*. Macau Business, January 12; C. Simons. (2008). *Macao outshines Vegas as next gambling Mecca*. AJC Travel News, October 17; H. Stutz. (2008). *Gambling beyond Nevada: Macau's gaming win: $10.3 billion*. Las Vegas Review Journal, January 23; The Economist. (2008). *Casino operators have taken some big gambles*: Who will clean up? November 15; www.state. gov. Country background notes – Macau. Accessed on December 12, 2008 Personal visit to Macau, December 8-9, 2008.

Case prepared by Charles A. Rarick

1) No government changes it's mind all the top - yes if government wouldn't intervene

2)

COLAS WITH A MISSION

In November 2002, French political activist, Tawfik Mathlouthi, began selling a new brand of cola in France. Mathouthi called his cola Mecca, after the city in Saudi Arabia where Muhammad was born. Some religious leaders question the use of Islam's holiest city for a brand name. Mecca, the site of the Great Mosque and the yearly hajj, or pilgrimage, holds a very significant meaning to followers of Islam. Mathlouthi hopes the name can have an equally significant meaning for consumers of soft drinks.

Mathlouthi hoped to capitalize on the rising tide of anti-Americanism in the Arab world and beyond. He has fashioned his product on Zamzam Cola, an Iranian Coca-Cola substitute sold in Iran, Saudi Arabia, and Bahrain. Mecca Cola sponsored a large peace rally in London to promote opposition to America's war in Iraq and the Mecca brand. The company gave out 36,000 bottles of Mecca Cola, and 10,000 shirts with the Mecca logo and the words "Stop the War" and "Not in my Name." The product uses phrases such as "No more drinking stupid" and "Drink with commitment" to sell the brand and makes no apologies for its political position. Mathouthi, who was born in Tunisia and moved to Paris in 1997 to start a radio station, admits that his product is political in nature. He states that it is an attempt to fight "American imperialism and Zionism by providing a substitute for

American goods and increasing the blockade of countries boycotting American goods."

A particularly strong appeal of the product for some consumers appears to be the fact that twenty percent of the company's net profit goes to charities, including ten percent to Palestinian charities. One consumer in Paris, Youssef, age 26, states "The product is very good too. It has a taste somewhat between Coke's and Pepsi's." In certain markets it appears that Mecca Cola has begun eating into Coca-Cola's popularity. A storeowner in a Muslim part of Paris states, "Since I started selling Mecca Cola, consumption of Coca-Cola has fallen 80%. People are attracted to the idea of supporting the Palestinians." Mathlouthi defends the charge that the company may be funding terrorism by claiming that money is not given directly to the Palestinians, but rather, the company provides the Palestinians with food, clothing, and the construction of buildings. Mecca Cola also uses proceeds from its sales to support some European non-government organizations (NGOs).

Mecca Cola, with packaging which looks much like the product it is attempting to replace (Coca-Cola), gained distribution in over 28 countries, including a number of Western European countries. At first the product was only sold in small ethnic shops in Muslim areas, however, the product later found in large grocery stores in the Arab world and in France, Britain, Italy, Spain, Belgium, and Germany. Mecca Cola hoped to have a rapid expansion into the European market and even enter the United States as a competitor to Coca-Cola.

Mecca Cola is not alone in attempting to beat the American Coca-Cola brand. Qibla Cola (Qibla refers to the direction in which Muslims pray) began operating in the United Kingdom in 2003. Matching much of the marketing strategies of Mecca Cola, Qibla saw sales increase and distribution expand, however, the company soon went into receivership. The Qibla brand is now bottled and sold in British Colombia and exported to Pakistan and Malaysia. Zam Zam Cola of Iran has begun to expand into Southeast Asia in countries with large Muslim populations.

Discussion Questions:

1. If you saw Mecca Cola or Qibla Cola on a store shelf would you consider purchasing it? Why or why not?
2. What should be the response of Coca-Cola to these brands?
3. Will protest products do long-term harm to American brands?

Sources: **Anonymous. (2002).** *Mecca Cola to Finance Palestinian Charity Work.* <u>Arabic News</u>. October 5; Anonymous. (2003); *Mecca Cola Gaining Ground.* <u>Monday Morning</u>. www.mmorning.com. Accessed March 31, 2003; Britt, B. (2003); *Coca-Cola Mimics Coke.* <u>AdAge</u>. February 24; Hood, J. (2003); *US Companies Need to be Locally Minded Overseas.* <u>PRWeek</u>. February 24; Murphy, V. (2003); *Mecca Cola Challenges US Rival.* <u>BBC News</u>. January 8. *Fashionable New Drink in Malaysia is Iran's Zam Zam Cola.* Payvand's Iran News, June 12, 2003. <u>www.qibla-cola.com</u> accessed on January 29, 2009.

Case prepared by Charles A. Rarick

Case 6

TED & HARRY'S GOES INTERNATIONAL

In 1975, Ted Cooper and Harry Greenberg began selling ice cream in a converted church in Little Rock, Arkansas. The two young men, who had recently completed a correspondence course in ice cream making, seemed an unlikely pair to eventually lead a multimillion-dollar enterprise, which would challenge corporate America's sense of social responsibility. The company began to manufacture, and sell on the retail level, a premium ice cream line with unusual sounding names such as Silly Strawberry Surprise and Harry's Very Berries. The pair sold their product through retail shops, which they called Ted & Harry's Ice Cream Factory, and consumers could order ice cream by the scoop, or in packaged form for home consumption.

By 1985, Ted & Harry's was a publicly traded company with over 50 retail operations in the United States. Gross sales were in excess of $35 million and the company had taken a very proactive stance in the area of social responsibility. The company employed disadvantaged members of society and donated 15% of its pretax profit to various charities. Ted and Harry were also actively involved in a worldwide peace movement and openly supported the bilateral disarming of the United States and the Soviet Union.

In 1989 Ted Cooper visited Russia and decided that international peace could be promoted through cooperative business ventures. Since domestic sales growth was still very strong, Ted & Harry's had not branched out into any foreign markets. In 1992 it was decided that Ted & Harry's would establish foreign direct investment in Russia. Although promotion of peace was a main objective, it was intended that the Russian venture would make a profit and provide a return on invested capital. It was hoped that profit from the operation would allow for further campaigns for peace and generate an entrepreneurial spirit in the Russian people. Ted & Harry's developed a manufacturing and distribution capacity in Russia that included six ice cream shops.

Ted & Harry's Russia sold its regular products, such as Whitewater Crunch and Kookie Chocolate, along with products unique to Russia, such as a vodka-laced ice cream, called Russian Holiday. Most of the products sold in Russia were identical to the products sold in the United States, including identical product packaging. Although Russian labels were placed over some of the packaging, the product was essentially the same product sold in the United States. The product was unique to Russian consumers, who were used to smooth ice cream as opposed to the "chunky" variety sold by Ted & Harry's.

Originally Ted and Harry planned on hiring a bilingual American to head the Russian operation. An external recruiting effort was undertaken, and recent business school graduates were interviewed from some of America's best business schools. Ted and Harry had hoped that a bright M.B.A. who spoke Russian, possessed significant business experience, and shared the vision of the company in terms of social responsibility could be hired. It was felt that someone with good business training and a strong sense of social accountability could spark an entrepreneurial spirit in the Russian people and be a good role model for others. When no suitable candidate could be found, the search shifted to internal recruiting.

The internal search resulted in the selection of Billy Bob Whitson. Billy Bob had been with Ted & Harry's for nine years, moving up from factory worker to production manager. Billy Bob did not speak Russian, and he had not received any business training other than on-the-job training at Ted & Harry's. He had never lived outside Arkansas; however, he did have a strong interest in Russia, and his enthusiasm impressed the selection team. He was appointed general manager of Ted & Harry's Russia, and the selection team was confident that he could handle the responsibility. There was a general belief that experience with product quality and acceptance of corporate values were more important than experience with Russian culture. Billy Bob was technically well qualified to supervise the making of ice cream and he possessed the character Ted sought for the position.

The Russian operation was established as a joint venture between Ted & Harry's and three Russian partners. Although the local partners had originally presented themselves as active members of the Russian business community, they were in fact very inexperienced and lacked connections. The three men impressed Ted Cooper with their intelligence, friendliness, and entrepreneurial spirit. Ted also found them appealing in that they represented the average Russian citizen.

The arrangement established an equal partnership between the two parties, with Billy Bob Whitson acting as general manager. It was agreed, however, that decisions would be made jointly between Billy Bob and the Russian partners. Ted & Harry's provided almost all of the capital required to establish the venture, and the Russian partners agreed to provide the necessary experience and effort required to establish the new business.

The Russian partners flew to Arkansas to learn how to make ice cream and Billy Bob moved his family to Russia to begin building the business. While the Russian partners learned the science of ice cream making, Billy Bob was learning how to conduct business in Russia. From the start Billy Bob experienced numerous problems with permits, construction crews, supplier agreements, and employee recruitment. The Russian business environment was more difficult than expected, and it appeared at times that it would be impossible to ever establish Ted & Harry's Russia. Billy Bob discovered that it was quite common for bribes to be paid to Russian officials to expedite the needed permits, and that the Russian mafia was deeply involved in the transportation and construction industries.

Since it was against Ted & Harry's corporate culture (and illegal under the Foreign Corrupt Practices Act) to pay bribes or engage in other questionable business practices, Billy Bob felt very frustrated with his inability to quickly get the business up and running. With the help of a Russian attorney and much patience, Ted & Harry's Russia finally began operation in 1996. Although it had taken much longer than anticipated, Billy Bob was content in the knowledge that the business had been established without the use of bribes or other forms of payoff.

Ted & Harry's entered the Russian market at a very difficult time. As the political and economic environment rapidly changed, the firm constantly experienced difficulties. Supplier relationships were unreliable, product quality was inconsistent, transportation was a nightmare, and it was often unclear who was really in charge of many government functions. Russia was also becoming a dangerous place to do business, and it was not uncommon for foreign expatriates to hire bodyguards for personal protection.

Product sales were lower, and costs were higher, than expected. Additional capital had to be supplied by Ted & Harry's in order to keep the operation functioning. The relationship between Ted & Harry's and the Russian partners was becoming strained as the local partners pushed for more growth. The Russian partners had envisioned becoming wealthy in a short period of time, and were becoming dissatisfied with the progress of Billy Bob and the management team back in Arkansas. Lacking any signs of near-term profitability, Ted & Harry were not inclined to entertain any suggestions of a growth strategy. Billy Bob felt that he could not manage any further expansion at this time, and he began to question the integrity of the local partners.

By 1998 the business had lost so much money, and the relationship between the joint venture partners had deteriorated to such an extent that it was decided to end the partnership. Ted & Harry's would pull out of Russia, leaving the investment and equity interest to the local partners. Ted Cooper stated in a press release that the decision was made jointly, and that a mutual agreement had been reached to end the Russian venture. Both parties had "parted on good terms and the experiment had been a success." Cooper stated that the objective of the joint venture was to bring entrepreneurship to Russia, and that by turning over the operations to the Russians "that objective had been accomplished." The business would continue with Russian ownership and the name of Ted & Harry's would not be used by the local partners. While admitting that some unexpected problems had occurred, Ted continued to defend the operation as an experiment and proclaim it a success.

Discussion Questions:

1. Do you think Ted & Harry's Russia was a success? Explain.
2. Do you think that Ted & Harry's made any mistakes in either country, partner, or management selection?
3. What, if anything, could Ted & Harry's have done more effectively?

Note: This case is fictional; however, it is based on an actual situation. It is not an actual account of this real case and no representation is implied.

Sources: Berdrow and Lane, "Iceverks," <u>University of Western Ontario Cases</u>, 1993; Kurtis, "World Full of Trouble: Fraud Comes in Many Flavors," <u>International Business</u>, 1997; Liesman, "Ben & Jerry's Reaches a Fork in its Rocky Russian Road", <u>The New York Times</u>, 1994.

Case prepared by Charles A. Rarick

CASE 7

MAJOR LEAGUE BASEBALL IN MEXICO?

In March 2004, the World Series Florida Marlins played the Houston Astros in a preseason goodwill game in Mexico City. The game ended in a 2-2 tie and many of the 11,000 fans in attendance pelted the field with debris as the game came to an undecided end. While professional basketball and American football have begun to see significant increases in international interest, baseball's interest globally has remained flat. With the failure of the Montreal Expos franchise, Major League Baseball (MLB) had to find a new city for the team, and one serious contender was a city in Mexico.

Baseball, as played in the United States, dates back to the mid-1700s and evolved from a very similar British game called rounders. Rounders, or "base" as it was sometimes called, was played on a diamond-shaped field and had many of the characteristics of modern day baseball. Credit for the invention of baseball often goes to Abner Doubleday, a general in the U.S. Civil War. Historians now doubt Doubleday's invention of the sport and generally believe that the legend was created by A.G. Spalding in an attempt to make baseball "America's Pastime" and to sell more baseball equipment. Having a Civil War hero as the invention of an American game was good for his business.

It can be argued that American baseball was really created by Alexander Cartwright in 1845 when he created the rules of the modern game. In 1846 the first game was played between two amateur teams in Hoboken, New Jersey. It was amateurs who enjoyed the sport enough to play without compensation who first played baseball in America. As amateur teams multiplied in the U.S., travel and other expenses increased, which required the charging of an admission fee to view a game. In 1869, Harry and George Wright organized the first team of paid players, the Cincinnati Red Stockings. The brothers were able to recruit the best players and won many games. The era of professional baseball had arrived.

In 1875 the National League was formed to set standards for ticket prices and to regulate player contracts. In 1901 a rival league was formed called the American League. Over time the two leagues learned to work together and to successfully defend against new entrants. In 1922 the United States Supreme Court decided in their favor and ruled that baseball was exempt from anti-trust legislation. The National and American Leagues no longer had to worry about competition. The game grew in popularity in the U.S. and was played on a limited basis in other countries as well. Mexico was quick to follow the U.S. in appreciating the sport.

The origins of baseball in Mexico are somewhat unclear, however, it is generally believed that the game arrived sometime between 1870 and 1890. Many areas of Mexico claim to have been the birthplace of baseball in the country, including Mazatlan, Veracruz, and Nuevo Leon. Monterrey, Mexico, in the Mexican state of Nuevo Leon developed a strong interest in baseball in the early years, and has maintained that interest up to the present. Monterrey today boasts a popular team called the Sultanes, is home to the Baseball Hall of Fame for Mexico, and is proud of the fact that its Little League team was the first non-United States team to win the Little League World Series. In 1957 Jose "Pepe" Maiz Garcia was the star player for the Monterrey Little Giants which won the World Series. Maiz is still actively involved in Mexican baseball.

The relationship between Mexico and the United States in terms of baseball goes back even earlier than the Little League World Series. In the 1940s eighteen Major League players accepted higher salaries to play for Mexican teams. Liquor dealer Jorge Pasqual offered many Major League players salaries that were often as high as five times their normal salary if they would play for Mexican teams. A number of players from the Negro Leagues accepted Pasqual's offer, as did some players from the Major Leagues. Baseball Commissioner, A.B. "Happy" Chandler did not like Major League players defecting to Mexico and threatened to ban any players who made the move. The few players who did play in Mexico found conditions to be difficult, including one playing field that consisted of a railroad track running through the outfield. Most of the players soon returned to the U.S. and attempted to get their jobs back. All the players were blacklisted and not allowed to play until they challenged the League in court and the League rescinded its ban.

By 1955 the Mexican League was struggling for survival and Anuar Canavati, president of the Monterrey Sultanes, created a plan to begin working with the Major Leagues. The Mexican Leagues prospered and grew to twenty teams. Today the Mexican League consists of 16 summer teams and 8 winter teams. Roughly half of the Major League teams have working relationships with Mexican teams. In addition, a number of Mexican players have gone on to the Major Leagues.

Mexican baseball teams do not draw the same attendance figures as the Major Leagues and are closer to the Minor Leagues in revenues. Attendance for the 16 summer teams can be seen below.

Mexican League Average Attendance

Saltillo Sarape Makers	11,387
Monterrey Sultanes	9,301
Yucatan Lions	4,424
Monclova Stealers	4,053
Luguna Cowboys	3,559
Puebla Parrots	3,024
Angelopolis Tigers	2,732
Cancun Lobstermen	2,604
Oaxaca Warriors	2,430
Cordoba Coffeegrowers	2,044
Reynosa Broncos	1,643
Mexico City Red Devils	1,559

Tabasco Carrlemen	1,540
Veracruz Reds	1,475
Two Laredo Owls	1,351
Campeche Pirates	1,225

In 2002 the Montreal Expos were purchased by the other 29 Major League teams due to the team's inability to attract a sizable fan base in Montreal. The decision was made to relocate the team to a city that would be more supportive of a Major League team. A number of cities had expressed an interest in being the new home of the Expos including Washington, D.C, Portland, San Antonio, Las Vegas, and San Juan Puerto Rico. Monterrey, Mexico was also a strong contender for selection. Monterrey is located in Northern Mexico which puts the city within a few hours by air of many U.S. cities. The city is relatively clean, economically viable, and safe. With 3.5 million inhabitants, Monterrey exceeds the population of some U.S. cities with successful baseball programs.   Monterrey has a desert climate, making it a good choice for outdoor sports. Currently the city has a 27,000-seat stadium which is considered by many to be the best in Latin America. The stadium has an impressive view of the Cerro de la Silla Mountains and residents are excited about the prospects of Major League baseball coming to Monterrey. The MLB relocation committee visited Monterrey and declared that the stadium was suitable for Major League play. Some modifications would have to be made including the addition of 3,000 more seats. The Commissioner of Baseball, Bud Selig, stated, however, that the city chosen for the Expos would have to be willing to build a new stadium within five years.

Monterrey has a very supportive ownership group headed by wealthy financier Carlos Bremer and Jose Maiz of World Little League fame and the owner of the Monterrey Sultanes. MLB has been eyeing the international market since 1999, playing 60 games in Mexico, Cuba, Venezuela, Japan, Puerto Rico, and the Dominican Republic. MLB plans to start playing some games in Europe next season. The Mexican League is a member of the National Association of Professional Baseball Leagues which regulates the Minor Leagues in the United States. Mexican baseball is at present considered the equivalent of America's Triple A League. Attendance at Mexican League games increased by 4.2% in 2003. Some observers worried that moving a team to Mexico would lead to many difficulties due to language barriers and the volatility of the Mexican peso. Others felt that since over 40% of players under MLB contract are from Latin America, that it is perhaps time for a Mexican team. As Jose Maiz states: "If we had the team here (Monterrey), 104 million Mexicans could follow the team, plus 25 million Mexicans working in the States."

While some had predicted that Monterrey would be selected as the new home of the Expos, on September 29, 2004, it was announced that Washington, D.C. had won the bid to host the team. The mayor of Washington, Anthony Williams, made the announcement by stating: "After 30 years of waiting, and waiting, and waiting, and a lot of hard work and more than a few prayers, there will be baseball in Washington in 2005." The team will play its first three seasons in R.F.K. Stadium until a new $400 million stadium is built. Baseball Commissioner Bud Selig released a statement justifying the selection of Washington by stating "There has been tremendous growth in the Washington, D.C. area over the last 33 years and we in Major League Baseball believe that baseball will be welcomed there and will be a great success." Selig praised the city of Washington, D.C. for its tenacity and dedication to having baseball return to the city. Washington has been home to previous Major League teams. From 1901 to 1960, the Senators played in Washington before moving to Minnesota to become the Twins. From 1961 to 1971, Washington hosted another team called the Senators, but this team also moved, this time to Texas to become the Rangers. The Washington, D.C. area has a wealthy and growing population, however, it is only 35 miles from another Major League team, the Baltimore Orioles. Concerns have been raised about the possibility of Washington eroding the fan base of the Orioles.

As MLB eyes competing markets, the organization must not only consider the sale of pennants and hats, but also television revenue and the possible expansion into other cities and markets. While other American sports have been successfully exported to the global market, baseball has experienced limited international appeal. As MLB baseball ponders international expansion, the people of Monterrey are still hopeful that they too will soon be able to host a Major League Baseball team.

Discussion Questions:

1. Did MLB make a mistake in selecting Washington, D.C. over Monterrey, Mexico?
2. Should MLB establish a Mexican franchise?
3. How important is internationalization to the success of MLB?

Sources:
Baxter, K. (2004). MLB eyes Mexico. *Miami Herald,* March 14; Baxter, K. (2004). Extra-disappointed fans litter field with debris. *Miami Herald,* March 15; Beyer, R. (2004). *The greatest stories never told.* New York: HarperCollins Publishers; Dellios, H. (2004). Monterrey makes a pitch for the Expos. *Chicago Tribune,* February 10; Lahman, S. (1996). *A brief history of baseball.* Retrieved March 14, 2004 from www.baseball.com; Sanchez, J. (2004). *History of baseball in Mexico.* Retrieved March 14, 2004 from www.mlb.com; Sandomir, R. (2004). Baseball returns to Washington as Expos move from Montreal. *The New York Times.* September 29; Tayler, L. (2004). From Montreal to Monterrey? *Cincinnati Post,* March 12 Ward, G. & K. Burns. (1994); B*aseball: An illustrated history.* New York: Alfred A. Knopf.

Case prepared by Charles A. Rarick, Inge Nickerson, and Gregory Winter

INTERNATIONAL HEALTH CARE TOURISM

Amy, a thirty-nine year-old American, wanted a chin implant, eyelid surgery, and an exotic vacation. She found all three at the Half Moon Golf, Tennis, and Beach Club in Montego Bay, Jamaica. The facility's medical center is only three years old, is considered state-of-the-art, and is doing well catering to Americans and Europeans who want to combine a vacation with cosmetic surgery. While the Half Moon Resort is not a particularly inexpensive option, it does offer the advantage of more privacy for its patients and the option of combining the recovery period with a relaxing vacation.

Many international health care travelers, however, are opting for low-cost options and increasingly are choosing locations such as India, Thailand, Costa Rica, Cuba, Mexico, and South Africa. One of the better-known programs for cosmetic surgery is called *Surgery and Safari*, which began operating in 2000 in South Africa. The medical treatment combines cosmetic and/or orthopedic surgery, and an African safari. The entire cost of the surgical procedures and vacation can be much lower than a patient would pay back home just for the surgery alone. For example, the cost of a full-body liposuction procedure in the U.S. can cost $19,000, compared to *Surgery and Safari's* cost of $8,500, which includes lodging and the safari.

Patients seeking low-cost care without a safari can choose a number of less adventurous options. Thailand has increasingly become the location of choice for many traveling patients. Patients first receive a video consultation before they travel to Thailand, are met at the airport by limousine, and are treated to a luxury spa and recovery facility after their surgery. The cost of most procedures is a fraction of the cost of the same procedure in the United States. For example, a hip replacement procedure in the United States can cost up to $35,000, where the same procedure can be performed in Thailand for less than $8,000. The additional costs associated with travel are small compared to the savings from the medical procedures. In addition, most of the medical facilities offer longer hospital stays, and additional amenities not typically found in the U.S., such as luxury hospital rooms, massages, cafes, and adjoining rooms for family members. American patients are selecting Thailand for a variety of medical procedures including orthopedic, cosmetic, and heart operations. Many patients returning from Thailand report high levels of satisfaction with the facilities and the quality of services.

Many of the countries that are capitalizing on the increasing global market for medical care are doing so to increase foreign exchange. Cuba has leveraged its well-respected health care industry into a global enterprise and caters mainly to other Latin American consumers. Because of the legal restrictions on travel to Cuba for Americans, the Cuban medical industry has not grown as rapidly as Thailand's, but is well known for its treatment programs in certain areas such as cosmetic surgery, and treatments for vitiligo, psoriasis, and long-term care of HIV patients. Funds from international patients are channeled back into medical research on the island.

Much of the promotion of offshore medical services is conducted via the Internet and word-of-mouth advertising. Satisfied consumers can be a good source of additional patients for the clinics, and most of the clinics have Web pages promoting their services. Dentistas de Tijuana. Com, for example, provides potential dental patients with a list of Mexican dentists who provide services ranging from orthodontics and dental implants to cosmetic dentistry and root canals. Web viewers can see the qualifications of the dentists and get directions and travel trips from the Web pages.

Not all foreign medical travel is to less-developed countries. Due to a surplus of doctors in Germany, the German government has been promoting the country as an alternative medical shopping destination. With a declining general population and an increasing number of physicians, Germany has experienced an unusual unemployment situation in its medical services. The primary foreign markets for German medical services include wealthy consumers in the Middle East, Africa, and Russia, and also patients tired of waiting for treatment in Scandinavian countries. German officials are now planning on establishing hospitals in China where consumers are impressed with the quality of German engineering. It is hoped that medical services can reap spillover benefits from the increasing sales of German automobiles in China.

While the advantages of international health care are primarily in cost savings and/or more luxurious care facilities, many potential international consumers have reservations about traveling abroad for medical treatment. One of the major disadvantages consumers may see in foreign medical services is the difficulty of after-surgery care and potential complications. Another disadvantage is the lack of insurance coverage. While some American insurers have paid for foreign surgery, the incentive to travel for surgery is reduced for consumers who have health insurance. The majority of the international patients either do not have health care insurance, or they are electing to have a procedure such as cosmetic surgery that is not covered by their policies. Still other potential consumers are concerned about the quality of care and the potential for disease. Thailand has lost some patients due to the outbreak of avian flu and the SARS virus in the region.

Regardless of the disadvantages, consumers are increasingly electing to travel abroad to receive medical treatment and to take in the sun or a safari. With rising health care costs in the United States and an increasing percent of the population becoming uninsured, it is likely that even more patients will be returning from a visit from their doctors with suntans and a photo album filled with adventure.

Discussion Questions:

1. Would you travel abroad to have a surgical procedure? Explain.
2. What do you see as the potential impact on the medical industry of developed countries to this approach to global medicine?
3. How might the medical industry of developed countries change its marketing strategies to compete against this international threat?

Sources: Author Unknown. (1997). *Health Care Booms in Cuba.* <u>NACLA Report on the Americas</u>, January-February; Author Unknown. (2002). *Sun, Fun, and Plastic Surgery?* <u>Forbes Travel Feature</u>, November 17; Balfour, F., M. Kripalani, K. Capell, L. Cohn. (2004). *Sand, Sun, and Surgery.* <u>Business Week</u>, February 16; Louis, M. (2000); *Germans Lure Patients to Hospitals.* <u>Wall Street Journal</u>, December 6.

Case prepared by Charles A. Rarick

EXERCISE 1

MULTINATIONAL CORPORATIONS:
GLOBAL REACH

Purpose: The purpose of this exercise is to test your knowledge of global companies and their impact on you.

Procedure: Following are 15 companies from *Fortune's* 500 Global Company list. These companies represent some of the biggest companies in the world.

See if you can identify each company's nationality and its principal products.

The second part of this exercise asks you to think about ways in which global business affects your daily life. This component utilizes small group discussion.

Companies:

Ericsson	Pemex	Bayer
Samsung	LUKOIL	Siemens
Lenovo	Nestle	HSBC
Canon	Cemex	Bridgestone
Michelin	Philips	Christian Dior

Company	Nationality	Products
Ericsson	Switherland	
Pemex	Mexico	
Bayer	Germany	Asprin
Samsung	Korean	
LUKOIL	Russian	oil
Siemens	Germany	Electronic
Lenovo	China	CP
Nestle	Swiss	Chocolate
HSBC	Brittish	BANK
Canon	Japan	Comera
Cemex	Mexico	Construct
Bridgestone	Japan	Tire
Michelin	France	Tire
Philips	Dutch / Brith	electronic
Christian Dior	French	Perfume

Company Influence:

Working in small groups, brainstorm ways in which global companies affect the lives of individuals. List the group's conclusions below.

Influence 1 _____

Influence 2 _____

Influence 3 _____

Influence 4 _____

PART TWO

INTERNATIONAL TRADE ISSUES

Cases:

NAFTA is Destroying the Family Farm
Boca to Beijing
Outsourcing Jobs to India
Levi Strauss: No Longer Made in USA
No Business with Burma

Exercises:

The European Union
U.S. Trade Representative
World Trade Organization

CASE 9

NAFTA IS DESTROYING THE FAMILY FARM

Sunshine Farms, Inc. is a fourth-generation family business located in South Florida. Sunshine began as a small farm devoted to citrus fruits and vegetables, and over the years the company has prospered. Sunshine Farms now grows and markets limes, lemons, mangos, snap beans, tomatoes, and other "row crops." Sunshine Farms has endured hurricanes, tropical flooding, freezes, and plant diseases; however, its most recent challenge appears to be its greatest.

Since the passage of the North American Free Trade Agreement (NAFTA), a number of Florida farms have been closed. With the reduction of tariffs on agricultural products, farmers have had difficulty competing with Mexican producers. Many Mexican farm products are imported into the United States and sold at a price that is considerably below the cost of domestic products. Row crop farmers, as compared to nurseries, have been particularly hard hit by the Mexican competition.

Domestic producers complain that lower labor costs, and fewer environmental regulations in Mexico, allow Mexican farmers to export their products into the United States at a price that will not allow American farmers to make a profit. Without tariffs on these goods, and given the inability to differentiate their products, some American farms have not been able to make a profit and stay in business.

Sunshine Farms possessed a strong competitive advantage prior to NAFTA. Florida weather allows for a growing season that is much longer than that in other parts of the United States. Florida farmers were able to grow products in December and January when much of the country was experiencing frigid temperatures. Mexican farmers were exporting agricultural products into the United States prior to NAFTA; however, the tariffs assessed on those products made Sunshine's prices competitive. With lower production costs, longer growing seasons, and the elimination of tariffs, Mexican farm products have become a significant threat to the survival of some domestic farmers.

Ben McDonald, CEO of Sunshine Farms, is worried not only about the survival of his business, but the survival of the entire Florida farming community. "In 20 years you won't have a single row crop farmer left in Florida," McDonald predicts. Since farm products are commodities, it is difficult to brand the products and extract a premium price. "Consumers are usually not aware of where their tomatoes come from, and in most cases they simply don't care. All they care about is price," says McDonald. He has stated on several occasions that "We should learn from the country's dependence on foreign oil and the disruptions in supply. Just wait until this happens in food production."

Some have recommended that Ben and others shift their focus toward the nursery business. The nurseries of South Florida have been doing very well with the construction increases in the U.S., and they seem less vulnerable to foreign imports. Others have recommended that American farmers begin to brand their products or place a "Grown in the USA" label on them in order to charge a higher price. Few row crop farmers have successfully made the shift into nurseries or seem willing to brand their products. As more farms continue to close each year, Ben wonders if Sunshine Farms can survive in a free-trade environment.

Discussion Questions:

1. Is NAFTA unfair to American farmers? Explain.
2. Could Sunshine Farms differentiate its products by placing a "Grown in the USA" label on them in order to charge a premium price?
3. What would you recommend to Ben McDonald in order to save the farm?

This case is fictional; however, it is based on actual situations as reported in "Farming on Faith." <u>Miami Herald</u>, January 1, 2001.

Case prepared by Charles A. Rarick

BOCA TO BEIJING:
THE RISE AND FALL OF IBM'S
PERSONAL COMPUTER BUSINESS

The company that would become IBM was incorporated in 1911 as the Computing-Tabulation-Recording Company (CTR). The origins of the company can, however, be traced back to Herman Hollerith and his punch card tabulating machine. Hollerith, a Census Bureau statistican invented a card with holes that could be read by an electric current. Hollerith began the Tabulating Machine Company in 1896. It was Charles Flint who merged the Tabulating Machine Company with two other companies to create the Computing-Tabulating-Recording Company.

Flint hired an executive from NCR named Thomas Watson, Sr. as the general manager of the new company. Watson soon became president of CTR and developed his famous slogan, "THINK" for the emerging company. In 1924 the company's name was changed to International Business Machines (IBM) to reflect the company's expanded product offerings. By the 1940s IBM was moving into computing with the development of the Mark I. In 1952 the company introduced the IBM 701, the first large computer to use vacuum tubes. In the 1950s the company also developed the FORTRAN computer language. The 1960s saw the introduction of the very successful IBM 360 series computer. IBM was a very successful company during the 1950s, 1960s, and 1970s, however, as the company grew, it developed into a large bureaucratic organization.

The late 1970s saw the beginning of a radical transformation in the computer industry. Earlier in the decade Intel had developed the first microprocessor, and Altair had begun selling a kit computer for less than $400. The age of personal computing had begun. In 1976 Steve Jobs and Steve Wozniak built the first Apple computer, and later Commodore and Radio Shack began offering inexpensive personal computers. IBM saw the market changing from large systems to smaller units, and in 1980 began to plan its introduction into personal computers. Five years earlier IBM had developed the IBM 5100, the company's first personal computer, but at a price of over $8,000 it was not a big seller and quickly faded from consumer awareness.

IBM decided that to be successful in the personal computer industry, it would have to establish a new business unit away from IBM headquarters. John Opel, IBM's CEO at the time created a team of engineers and selected Boca Raton, Florida as the location of its new PC business. In a facility designed to withstand hurricanes, and almost any other unforeseen disaster short of a direct hit by a nuclear bomb, the Boca facility was poised to become a leading business unit for IBM. The code name for the new product was called "Acorn" and it was headed by IBMer Don Estridge. Estridge and his team created the IBM 5150 in 1981. IBM announced its entry to the PC market with great fanfare at the Waldorf Astoria in New York City. To gain widespread distribution of the unit, IBM would sell its PC through retailers such as Computerland and Sears. The model retailed for $2,880 and had 64K Ram, one 5 ¼" floppy disk drive, and used the Intel 8088 central processing unit.

With a sense of urgency to rush a product to market, the 5150 was developed using an open design and off-the-shelf parts. IBM also outsourced its operating system (OS) to a little known company called Microsoft, who at the time really had no operating system to sell IBM. Microsoft acquired rights to an OS called QDOS from Seattle Computer and resold the OS to IBM on a nonexclusive basis. The nonexclusive use of the OS and the open design of the PC would eventually lead to competitors who would offer "IBM PC clones." IBM developed other PC models such as the IBM PC Junior, but sales were disappointing. IBM was operating in an environment where entry barriers were low and competitors were quick to develop new technologies and exploit cost advantages. IBM's PC unit got off to a good start, but quickly began to struggle. Boca Raton had for a short time been the PC capital of the world, but in the 1990s, IBM began moving its PC operations to Raleigh, North Carolina and Austin, Texas. Many former IBM employees at the Boca facility chose to remain in Florida and started new companies such as Citrix Systems, Cybergate, and Inprimis. The business unit that was created in South Florida would eventually have a new owner, one located half a world away.

In the summer of 2002, IBM began to look for a buyer for its PC unit that was now losing $400 million a year. IBM sent its chief financial officer to China to make a pitch to the Legend Group, China's leading PC manufacturer. Legend wasn't interested in purchasing the money-losing business, but eighteen months later the situation was different. IBM had cut costs by outsourcing most of its production, making the unit a most desirable acquisition. In 2004, at a press conference in Beijing, it was announced that Legend, now called the Lenovo Group, was purchasing IBM's Personal Computing Division for $1.75 billion and an 18.9 percent stake in Lenovo.

It was announced that Lenovo would be the preferred supplier of PC's to IBM, and that Lenovo would be allowed to use the IBM brand name for five years. IBM would provide Lenovo with warranty service and customer leasing and financing. Lenovo would have the right to sell the IBM ThinkPad and ThinkCenter desktop computers. A new company, also called Lenovo, was created to capitalize on the PC unit acquisition. The new company would be headquartered in Purchase, New York, five miles from IBM's headquarters. Lenovo announced that its CEO would be Stephen Ward, a former head of IBM's PC operations, and that its chairman would be Yang Yuanqing, CEO of the Lenovo Group.

The Lenovo Group (Legend) was founded in Beijing in 1984 by eleven Chinese scientists in a small one-story building. By 1994 the company was trading on the Hong Kong Stock Exchange, and by 1998 it had sold its one-millionth personal computer. The company now employs over 19,000 and is China's largest PC manufacturer. The name Lenovo comes from its previous name Legend (Le), and the Latin word for new (novo). Lenovo also produces servers, handheld computers, mobile headsets, and imaging equipment. The company seeks to be a leader in what it calls the "3C Era" - meaning computers, communications, and consumer electronics.

The newly established business unit seeks to be an innovator in personal computers. While the Legend Group had not been strong in research and development, the new unit is expected to become a leader in new product development. The company describes its values by the following pronouncement:

> *We reject the status quo*
> *We reject mediocrity*
> *We choose not to follow*
> *We choose to INNOVATE*

Lenovo makes a point of emphasizing the importance of an innovative and entrepreneurial spirit for the long-term success of the new company. Lenovo is hoping to leverage the IBM acquisition and to move into a more leading edge capacity in the industry.

The merging of the Lenovo Group and the IBM Personal Computing Division gives Lenovo a stronger position in terms of market share. Dell is the world's leading PC seller with 16.4% of the global market, followed by HP with 13.9%. Lenovo will be in the third position with an estimated 7.2% of global sales. The merger will also facilitate Lenovo's drive to expand outside of China. The Lenovo Group has a proven track record in developing countries (China) and personal computer demand is expected to be greatest in developing countries such as China, India, Russia, and Brazil. Unlike Dell, Lenovo sells almost all of its computer products through retail outlets. In developing countries it is sometimes important for consumers to have hands-on experience with products before purchasing them. Many consumers in developing markets also do not have credit cards, which makes on-line purchasing more difficult. Lenovo is more familiar with the nuances of marketing in less developed countries.

The wisdom of IBM's sale, and Lenovo's purchase, has been questioned by some observers. Some have argued that by selling its PC unit, IBM has, in effect, admitted defeat in an important segment of the industry. Also, past experience with mergers and acquisitions in the computer industry shows a poor track record of success. Michael Dell, chairman of Dell Computers, said when referring to the IBM-Lenovo merger: "We're not a big fan of the idea of taking companies and smashing them together. When was the last time you saw a successful acquisition or merger in the computer industry?" A noted computer industry analyst was even more direct in his assessment of the merger by saying: "This has all the earmarks of a train wreck of biblical proportions." Others feel that IBM made the correct decision to unload its PC unit and to focus on its core competency – big systems and big customers. That component of the industry is more profitable and moves IBM out of the "commodity" computer business. Lenovo feels that with its rock bottom $3 per unit labor cost, and newly acquired research competency, it will be able to challenge the efficiencies and innovation of industry leaders.

Discussion Questions:

1. Do you think IBM's decision to sell its PC unit was a good decision?
2. Do you think Lenovo will be able to leverage its purchase of IBM's PC unit and challenge companies like Dell and HP?
3. Does the sale of IBM's PC unit to a Chinese company represent a threat to the economy of the United States?

Sources: Cox, J. (2005). *IBM employees have a new boss.* <u>Knight Ridder Tribune Business News</u>, **May 2; Enderle, R. (2004).** *Big Blue's departure from the PC biz.* <u>Mac News World</u>, **December 9; Kanellos, M. (2004).** *IBM sells PC group to Lenovo.* <u>C/Net News</u>, **December 8; Robets, D. and L. Lee. (2005)** *East meets West, big-timeLenovo deal forIBM's PC unit led to merger of talent – and threat to Dell.* <u>Business Week</u>, **May 9; Scott-Joynt, J. (2004).** *PC pioneer leaves its history behind.* <u>BBC News</u>, **December 8; Winter, C. (2001).** *IBM alumni* *founded many of S. Florida's high-tech companies.* <u>Sun-Sentinel</u>, August 10; <u>www.hoovers.com</u>. Accessed on May 25, 2005; <u>www.IBM.com</u>. Accessed on May 25, 2005; <u>www.lenovo.com</u>. Accessed on May 25, 2005.

Case prepared by Charles A. Rarick

CASE 11

OUTSOURCING JOBS TO INDIA

After independence from Great Britain in 1947, India established a socialist-oriented government that discouraged foreign investment. Major industries were state-owned and government heavily regulated private businesses. Westerners viewed India as a very poor country with little to offer the international business community. In 1991, India experienced a currency crisis and was forced to fly its remaining stock of gold to London as collateral for an IMF loan. Faced with a very difficult situation, India then began to reform its economy. Since the early 1990s the Indian economy has transformed itself into a very competitive global competitor. With an abundance of workers and very low wage levels, India is attractive to international companies for low-end manufacturing and service delivery. Of special interest is the recent outsourcing of service jobs that can be performed over satellite and fiber optics communication channels.

India produces over 3 million college graduates a year. With high unemployment, companies have no difficulty in finding young college graduates who are content to handle customer service for American and European companies, at a fraction of the cost of their American and European counterparts. Typical of this new approach is AOL which now employs 1,500 people in India to answer its calls for customer service. Even though AOL is not available in India, AOL customers in the U.S. and elsewhere call an 800 number and may never realize that they are talking with someone half way around the world. AOL reports much lower operating costs, and lower turnover in its Indian call center than it experiences in the United States. Costs are lower, even though training costs are higher, and the company must provide employees with transportation to and from work.

Like AOL, other well-known American companies have beaten a path to India to outsource their back-office services. Recently, Microsoft announced that it was moving some of its customer service jobs to India. Microsoft joins a long list of American companies already operating back-office operations in India, such as: Oracle, IBM, Intel, and HP. Lloyds TSB, the UK's fourth largest bank, has announced the closing of its call center in England, and its movement to India. Lloyds TSB call center workers earn on average ten times the wages to be paid to their Indian substitutes. Even the World Bank has moved its accounting function from Washington to India. American businesses are realizing that almost any back-office or service job can be moved overseas.

While the call center and other lower-level service jobs which have moved to India are becoming commonplace, India is also embarking on a much more ambitious approach to job creation. India has attracted work from the United States and Europe in software development, chip design, IT consulting, financial services, and drug research. An estimated 20,000 U.S. tax returns were prepared in India last year, and the number is expected to skyrocket to 200,000 this year. The returns are prepared by Indian accountants familiar with the U.S. tax code and are signed by CPAs in the United States. Indians now process mortgage applications, do legal and medical transcription, and book travel reservations. The management consulting firm, McKinsey, now outsources to India the design of its PowerPoint presentations that it shows its clients.

The skill level of jobs being outsourced is increasing. GE has established the Jack Welch Technology Center in India and employs 1,800 engineers, many with doctoral degrees, to conduct basic research. The relatively new center has already earned 95 patents in the United States. India has an abundance of well-trained engineers and scientists, and MNCs are beginning to realize the potential of this human capital. According to the managing director of the Welch Center, it isn't about saving money on labor costs. "The game here really isn't about saving costs but to speed innovation and generate growth for the company." Nevertheless, a top of the line electrical engineer in India earns only about $10,000 USD a year, a fraction of the salary of an American or European with the same qualifications.

While GE may not be primarily concerned with cost-savings, most companies moving, or establishing operations in India are doing so because of the labor rate differential. One UK travel agency has put a different spin on the outsourcing concept. Ebookings is moving both its work, and workers to India. The London-based travel agency is not only moving the jobs of selling and booking travel, but is also moving workers to India, and paying the prevailing Indian wage level. Ebookings is selling the idea of living in India as an adventure and a way to sell the world. The firm's employees in India, both European and Indian will be paid about $6,000 USD a year, resulting in a significant cost savings to the company. While most companies that have moved their back-office operations to India are American or British, India is seeking additional jobs from other English speaking countries such as Australia, and non-English speaking countries in which customer service is conducted in English.

India has the advantage of having an educated workforce that can speak English and is willing to work for a fraction of the wage level of developed country workers. India, however, does have a number of disadvantages to consider when companies decide to outsource work. India has experienced very impressive economic growth in the years since economic liberalization; however, India is still very much a less developed country. An estimated one-third of the population is illiterate and only the higher classes speak English well. The official language of India is not English but Hindi. And India still possesses a very poor infrastructure with unreliable power sourcing and frequent flooding. Government bureaucracy is still very much a factor in business activity, and presently India's fiscal deficit is running at over 10% of GDP. While India has made great strides in eliminating excessive government, much improvement needs to be made. In addition to concerns over budget deficits, political tensions are also troublesome. India has an uneasy relationship with its neighbor, Pakistan, and the tension between Muslims and Hindus produces violent conflict at times.

While educated Indians speak English, it is considered to be the "Queens English" and has a different accent from American English. Although many Indians are enrolling in accent reduction classes, some American customers have complained about the ability to communicate with Indian customer service personnel. Indians tend to speak rapidly, averaging 180 words a minute, compared to 120 for Americans and 90 for the British. Dell recently announced that it was moving its call center operations out of Bangalore, India and back to Texas because it "had issues with differing Indian accents." GE, while investing heavily in research in India, nevertheless, moved its appliance call center from India back to the United States. GE had discovered that many Indian employees could not relate well to the concerns of GE's customers because many did not own, or were not familiar with the appliances they were discussing.

At the present time, India is the lead country in attracting service outsourcing, however, other countries are now beginning to compete with India. Like India, the Philippines is an English speaking country with a low wage level. Unlike India, the Philippines, a former colony of the United States, is closer to the U.S. in language and culture. While the number of jobs outsourced to the Philippines is currently much lower, estimated to be around 30,000, the number is expected to grow rapidly. Currently, Filipinos work in the Philippines for American companies doing medical and legal transcription, answering call centers, and providing technical support. In addition to the Philippines, a number of Eastern European countries may rival India for job outsourcing. One indication is the bidding process on a web site for programmers called Rent-A-Coder. Companies, mostly small and medium sized firms from the United States and Europe, post jobs for free-lancing software developers. Indians still are able to solicit most of the programming jobs from the site, however, Romania is the second most popular country for this outsourcing. Under Soviet domination, Romania like many Eastern European countries, emphasized science, math, and engineering instruction and now has an abundance of technically qualified people who are willing to work at low wage levels. Like Romania, the Czech Republic has an abundance of technically qualified workers who are available at a lower wage level. The Czech Republic has the advantage of membership in the European Union and a more developed economy.

Recently, DHL announced a 500 million euro investment that will employ Czechs to track shipments, provide customer service, and perform billing operations. The Czech Republic has a strong telecommunication infrastructure, workers who are proficient in many languages, and a skilled and inexpensive labor force.

An additional factor which may slow the growth of outsourcing to India is political backlash caused by job loss in the United States and Great Britain. In the United States, the state of Indiana recently cancelled a $15 million contract with the software arm of large Indian company, Tata Group, over fears of unemployment in the United States. Protection of domestic jobs is a very strong political motive and one that will likely be raised as more and more jobs are outsourced to India. Many will argue the costs and benefits of overseas outsourcing. A study by the McKinsey Global Institute found that for every dollar invested in overseas outsourcing, $1.25 returned to the United States. Supporters of foreign outsourcing argue the benefits of free trade and comparative advantage, while critics argue that foreign workers are taking jobs and potentially destroying the country's technical competitive advantage.

Discussion Questions:

1. From the perspective of American and European companies, analyze the advantages and disadvantages of outsourcing work to India.
2. What would you recommend to Indian government officials to ensure continued job creation?
3. Is it fair to workers of developed countries when companies shift work to lower wage countries? Explain.

Sources: Andress, M. (2003). *You're Speaking to Prague*. <u>Financial Times</u>, November 19; Angwin, J. (2003). *AOL's Tech Center in India is Money Saver*. <u>Wall Street Journal</u>, August 7; Delaney, K. (2003). *Outsourcing Job and Workers to India*. <u>Wall Street Journal</u>, October 13; Fox, M. (2003). *Where Your Job is Going*. <u>Fortune</u>, November 24; Gomes, L. (2003). *Romanians Become Latest*

Tech Rivals for Off-Shore Jobs. <u>Wall Street</u> Journal, November 17; Hagenbaugh, B. (2003). *Moving Work Abroad Tough for Some Firms.* <u>USA Today</u>, December 2; Kripalani, M. and P. Engardio. (2003). *The Rise of India.* <u>Business Week</u>, December 8; Luce, E. and K. Merchant. (2003). *Dell Cuts Back Indian Customer Service Center.*; <u>Financial Times</u>, November 26; Merchant, K. (2003). *India's Call Centers Drop Fake Accents.* <u>Financial Times</u>, December 8; Slater, J. (2001). *Back-Office Bonanza.* <u>Far Eastern Economic Review</u>, August 30; Teves, O. (2003). *A Faraway Wakeup Call.* <u>Miami Herald</u>, December 9; Vina, G. and T. Mudd. (2003). *Call Centers Migrate to India, and North of England Loses Jobs.* <u>Wall Street Journal</u>, November 5.

Case prepared by Charles A. Rarick

LEVI STRAUSS & COMPANY: NO LONGER MADE IN THE USA

Levi Strauss & Company (LS&C) of San Francisco, California has been in the clothing business for 150 years. The company developed, and set the standard for denim jeans and has been manufacturing them for over 130 years. Throughout most of LS&C's existence its clothing has been manufactured, at least in part, in the United States. The firm recently announced that it will no longer manufacturer its products in North America, shutting down its one remaining plant in the United States and two in Canada. For most of its history, the company founded by Levi Strauss proudly manufactured clothing in the United States.

Levi Strauss was born in Bavaria in 1829. He immigrated to the United States with his mother to join other family members in a dry goods business in New York. At age 24 Strauss moved to San Francisco to open a west coast branch of the family business. While the dry goods business was successful, Strauss stumbled upon a product line that would make Levi's a household name in the United States, and much of the rest of the world.

Jacob Davis, a tailor in Reno, Nevada was a customer of Levi Strauss. Davis wrote Strauss in 1872 telling him of an invention in which he might be interested. Davis had developed a new way of insuring that men did not rip the pockets of their pants. He had installed metal rivets at the corners of the pants pockets to strengthen them, and he found that customers liked the new product. Davis sought a patent on this process; however, he did not have the money required for the legal protection of his invention, so he sought the financial aid of Strauss. Realizing that riveted pants might have potential, Strauss provided the $68 needed to obtain the patent. Using denim to create work pants, the partnership of Strauss and Davis created the "original, authentic jeans."

Today Levi Strauss & Company is privately owned by the Haas family, descendents of Levi Strauss. LS&C sells its products in over 100 countries. The firm continues to sell its traditional product under the Levi brand, and has added the successful Dockers brand of khaki-type products to its product offerings. LS&C also sells a value-oriented brand called Signature that it markets through mass merchandisers such as Wal-Mart. While the company enjoyed enormous success throughout many years of its existence, it has suffered in recent years as competitors have significantly eroded market share. The company, once the premier supplier of clothing for America's youth, has witnessed sizable decreases in sales and earnings over the past few years. A new strategy of product development is underway in an effort to recapture the loyalty of the youth market. At the same time, LS&C is attempting to reduce its costs through a change in its product sourcing.

In the past, LS&C relied on its own manufacturing capability to source its product. The company operated many manufacturing facilities in the United States. Eventually foreign manufacturing was established and production capability began to shift to lower cost countries. The company also began to contract the manufacturing of its products to independent producers. The decision in 2003 to end all North American production caused some to question the ethical orientation of a company well-known for being a socially responsible organization. The change in strategy will allow LS&C to focus on product design and marketing, and to free resources previously devoted to manufacturing.

LS&C was built on four core values: empathy, originality, integrity, and courage. The company feels that these core values have served the organization well, and they continue to be the driving forces for change at LS&C. Levi Strauss has been a pioneer not only in clothing design, but also in other areas of business as well. The firm's progressive employment policies predated the civil rights movement in the United States, and LS&C has been listed as one of "America's 50 Best Companies for Minorities" by *Fortune* magazine. LS&C has been awarded the Excellence in Ethics designation by *Business Ethics* magazine, and the company was a pioneer in establishing and supporting employee volunteers through its Community Involvement Teams. In addition, the Levi Strauss Foundation awards $15 million annually to community-based organizations. LS&C was an early supporter of ethical guidelines for contractors. In 1991 the Company created the Global Sourcing and Operating Guidelines that regulate its contractors in areas of worker health and safety, environmental standards, and general employment practices.

Critics of the company contend that LS&C is simply following other American companies in outsourcing its production to lower labor cost countries. This practice reduces the employment opportunities available in the United States and further erodes the industrial base of the country. It is felt by some that the company relies on the important U.S. market for sales, however, the company does not provide employment opportunities to support those sales. LS&C has responded to these charges by stating that outsourcing of production is necessary in order for the company to survive. As CEO Phil Marineau states, "We're in a highly competitive industry where few apparel brands own and operate manufacturing facilities in North America." The company also counters its critics with the fact that a Community Trust Fund has been established by the company to aid the communities affected by the plant closures, and that comprehensive separation packages will be offered to the terminated employees. Some critics feel that Levi, an American icon, has a greater responsibility in stopping the deindustralization of America.

Discussion Questions:

1. Do you feel that LS&C is acting in a responsible manner in closing its North American production operations? Explain.

2. Do American companies like LS&C that transfer production to lower wage countries hurt or help the economy of the United States?
3. Evaluate the soundness of the strategic shift away from production and towards a focus on design and marketing.

Sources: Foster, L. (2003). *Levi to End North America Production.* Financial Times. September 26; Matthews, S. (2003). *Levi to Fire 1,980, Shut Plants.* Miami Herald. September 26; www.hoovers.com. Accessed on September 29, 2003; www.levistrauss.com. Accessed on September 26, 2003.

Case prepared by Charles A. Rarick

NO BUSINESS WITH BURMA

While most American businesspeople may think that the entire world is available for conducting business, there are a number of countries and individuals who are off-limits for American business transactions. The government of the United States has imposed a number of economic sanctions on a number of countries and individuals as a tool of its foreign policy. This foreign policy tool reduces opportunities for American businesspeople, but is defended by policy makers as necessary to bring about desired changes in countries, without the use of more serious action such as military intervention. Economic sanctions are administered by the U. S. Department of the Treasury through its Office of Foreign Assets Control.

One country in which the United States has imposed economic sanction is Myanmar, better known in the U.S. by its former name, Burma. Burma, once under British control, became independent from Great Britain after World War II. Burma held its first democratic election in 1951, but by 1962, ethnic conflict and internal rivalry resulted in a military coup. The military government nationalized businesses and proceeded along the road to "the Burmese way of socialism." In the 1980s, a democratic movement began in Burma, resulting in mass protests and what is believed to have been the death of thousands of citizens. Free elections were held in 1990, with the National League for

Democracy winning a majority of the votes. The ruling military junta refused to accept the election results and ordered the house arrest of the party's leader, Aung San Suu Kyi. With just brief moments of freedom, she has remained under house arrest since that time. Aung San Suu Kyi was awarded the Nobel Peace Prize for her efforts to bring democracy to her country. In addition to its disregard for democracy, the ruling junta also holds a number of political prisoners, and is accused of violating basic human rights of its citizens. Protests are usually met with military force, there is no free press in the country, and the Internet is restricted and monitored. Burma is also a major producer of illicit opium.

In response to the lack of democracy and the civil rights violations in Burma, the U.S. Congress has passed legislation and the Executive Branch has issued executive orders, essentially banning business in Burma for American companies and citizens. Penalties for violating these regulations include significant fines, and imprisonment of up to ten years. While the Burmese government acts in ways inconsistent with good governance, Burma, however, is not alone in possessing a government considered less than ideal. Some have challenged the U.S. sanctions imposed on Burma while it supports other non-democratic regimes such as China and Saudi Arabia. Others point out the ineffective nature of economic sanctions and the difficulties these sanctions cause the people they are intended to help. While there have been cases in which sanctions have resulted in governmental change (most notably South Africa), most sanctions do not produce their intended outcomes. In addition, economic sanctions often hurt the people the sanctions were intended to help by making their economic lives more difficult.

Economic sanctions aimed at the government of Burma have resulted in closed factories and high unemployment for the citizens of Burma. Per capita GDP in Burma now stands at only $239 (2007 IMF estimate) - in a country rich in natural resources such as oil and gas, timber, tin, copper, zinc, and precious stones. While other countries have imposed limited sanctions on Burma, the widespread sanctions imposed by the world's largest economy have increased the suffering of the Burmese people. The banking sector has collapsed, healthcare is deplorable, and child malnourishment is rising. The junta has survived by doing business with China, India, and other countries which have not imposed any business restrictions on their firms. As the economy and people of Burma continue to suffer, American business and investment opportunities are blocked in the belief that economic pain will bring about a change in government.

Discussion Questions:

1. Do you feel that economic sanctions unfairly interfere with international business? Explain your answer.
2. Is it hypocritical for the United States to promote free trade to other countries, while imposing economic sanctions on so many countries?
3. Given the difficulties caused to citizens of countries such as Burma, do you feel economic sanctions are ethical? Explain.

Sources: Case based on two articles published by the author of the case: *Destroying a Country in Order to Save It: The Folly of Economic Sanctions Against Myanmar*. Economic Affairs, June 2006; *Economic Sanctions: Failed Foreign Policy Tool and a Cost to American Business*. Economic Affairs, September 2007; www.state.gov. Country Background Notes, November 14, 2008; U.S. Department of the Treasury, Office of Foreign Asset Control. What You Need to Know About U.S. Sanctions Against Burma, August 16, 2005.

Case prepared by Charles A. Rarick

EXERCISE 2

WEB-BASED EXERCISE:
THE EUROPEAN UNION

Purpose: To gain a fundamental understanding of the European Union, the currency of the European Monetary Union, and the importance of the EU in matters of trade.

Procedure: Using search engines, such as Google, Yahoo, or others, find answers to the questions below. You may also find the Web site http://europa.eu/ useful in this exercise.

Questions:

1. What is the European Union (EU)?
2. How many countries are members of the EU?
3. Which countries have substituted their national currencies for the euro?
4. What important treaties led to the creation of the European Union?
5. What are the pros and cons of a single European currency?
6. How has the establishment of the European Union changed international trade?

EXERCISE 3

OFFICE OF THE UNITED STATES TRADE REPRESENTATIVE

WEB ADDRESS: www.ustr.gov

Purpose: To gain a better understanding of the important functions of the Office of the U.S. Trade Representative, and to become familiar with current free trade agreements (FTAs) currently in force.

Procedure: Visit the website listed above and answer the following questions:

1. What is the purpose of the Office of the U.S. Trade Representative?
2. What is a Trade and Investment Framework Agreement (TIFA) and what countries have one with the United States?
3. Which countries does the United States currently have bilateral free trade agreements (FTAs) with?
4. Select one country with a FTA with the United States. Briefly explain that agreement.

EXERCISE 4

WEB-BASED EXERCISE:
THE WTO

Web Address: www.wto.org

Purpose: To gain a fundamental understanding of the World Trade Organization and its function in international trade.

Procedure: Visit the Web page of the World Trade Organization and find the answers to the following questions.

Questions:

1. What is the WTO?
2. When was it established?
3. Where is it headquartered?
4. How many countries are members of the WTO?
5. Explain the benefits of the WTO trading system.
6. What are the common misunderstandings about the WTO? Do you agree with any of these misunderstandings?

PART THREE

THE GLOBAL MONETARY SYSTEM

Cases:
Islamic Finance
Zimbabwe's Hyperinflation
Global Trade Blues
The Mouse That Roared

Exercises:
The Foreign Exchange Market
International Monetary Fund
The World Bank

ISLAMIC FINANCE
A VIABLE ALTERNATIVE IN THE GLOBAL FINANCIAL MARKET?

It is estimated that over $500 billion in assets are managed around the world in accordance with Islamic principles. With an estimated 1.3 billion followers of Islam, many in areas of the world where excess funds have been recently accumulating, increased interest has been generated in Islamic finance. Islamic banking centers have been developed in places such as Dubai, London, Kuala Lumpur, Singapore, and Bahrain. According to Standard and Poor's, Islamic banking has been growing by about 10% per year for the past decade. A number of the world's largest banks and financial institutions have begun to offer Islamic financial services, including Citigroup and HSBC. Dow Jones has even created the Dow Jones Islamic Market Index, signifying the importance of this growing financial niche.

According to *The Economist* magazine, about 20% of the world's population is Muslim, but Islamic finance represents only 1% of the world's financial instruments. This gap is seen as an opportunity for growth. Islamic finance based on *sharia*, or Islamic law, prohibits the payment of interest, or usury. Also prohibited are investments in certain industries such as those tied to alcohol, pornography, pork production, tobacco, and gambling. Bonds based on *sharia*, called *sukuk*, do not pay interest, but rather pay the investor based on the profit generated from the asset which underlies the bond. Islamic finance mandates a degree of risk sharing not found in traditional finance.

After the terrorists' attack in the United States on September 11, 2001, the U.S. government froze the bank accounts of certain wealthy Muslims. This caused capital flight by others fearful of having their assets confiscated. Much of this money ended up in places like Malaysia where the assets were deemed safer. Rising oil prices increased the cash position of a number of Muslim countries, and a rising middle class in many Muslim countries created the need for an alternative financial system. A financial system consistent with Islamic principles became more necessary, and lucrative. Even business schools have taken note of the trend and have begun offering courses and seminars in Islamic finance.

(Not charging interest on loans is a central element of Islamic finance. According to Sheikh Nizam Yaquby, a noted advisor to Western investment firms: "There is no sin the Koran, not even drinking, not even fornicating, not even homosexuality, which could be as abhorrent and serious as dealing in riba (interest)." The prohibition of charging interest is not just linked to Islam. Early Christians prohibited usury, however, over time the definition changed to allow interest to be charged for loans, but not at an excessive rate. (Not being able to charge interest on loans has forced Islamic bankers to be more creative in their business. Loans are typically made by adding a profit to the balance, and then dividing the sum by equal payments. Variable rate interest loans are generally not permitted under Islamic finance. Since interest cannot be charged borrowers, other arrangements can be made such as when a house is financed by a bank. The bank may buy the house and value it at its expected appreciated price when the loan has ended. The inflated price is then divided into equal payments over the life of the loan. No interest is paid by the borrower. Shared risk is an important part of Islamic finance. Some business loans are made on the basis of *mudharaba*. A *mudharaba* is a partnership between the lender and the borrower. In this case, no interest is charged the person, or business, needing the loan. Instead, the borrower shares in the profit generated

as opposed to a market or industry Rate

by the loaned funds. The borrower and lender become partners, sharing in the profit or loss of the enterprise.

Islamic finance prohibits the selling of something which one does not own. Short-selling, for example is not allowed under Islamic finance, as well as a number of other more risky Western investment practices such as derivates. Some have proposed that the financial crisis which began in 2008 would have been avoided if the world's financial institutions had followed *sharia.* As a result of the requirement of an underlying asset base, however, Islamic finance is more concentrated in property assets and subject to the market fluctuations of those assets.

Oversight of Islamic finance, and the determination of the appropriateness of investments, is of some concern. Some Islamic banks operate in countries with few regulations, such as in North Africa, and only a handful of people determine what is a proper investment under Islamic law. The availability of religious scholars who also have training in finance and a good command of the English language is limited. The shortage of such individuals means that the price of investment advice is quite high, reported to be in the six figure range for each *fatwa*, or investment decision. With the limited number of skilled Islamic advisors, many of the advisors work for competing firms, creating the perception of a conflict of interest in the minds of some.

Even with the limited number of qualified advisors, and other concerns, Islamic finance is, nevertheless, expected to continue to grow in the years ahead. Islamic finance may appeal to non-Muslims as well, in that some socially responsible investors may like the idea of avoiding investing in "sinful" industries, and feel that their investments are safer in an Islamic style investment arrangement.

Discussion Questions:

1. Do you feel that Islamic finance is a safer alternative to Western finance? Explain.
2. Some critics feel that Islamic finance is only a disguise for traditional finance and the process "rent-a-sheikh" allows for

possible manipulation of financial decisions. What is your opinion?

3. Do you feel that Islamic finance can grow beyond its current small niche in the financial market?

Sources: Black, J. (2008). *An unhealthy interest?* The Middle East, July; Bremner B. and S. Assif. (2007). *The ties that bind the Middle East and Asia.* Business Week Online, May 21; DiMeglio, F. (2007). *A fresh take on Islamic finance.* Business Week Online, March 27; Eaves, E. (2008). *Good and mammon.* Forbes, April 21; The Economist. (2008). *Savings and souls.* September 6; Modi, V. (2007). *Writing the rules: The need for standardized regulation of Islamic finance.* Harvard International Review, Spring; Power, C. (2009). *Faith in the market.* Foreign Policy, January-February; Quinn, B. (2008). *London warms to Islamic finance.* Christian Science Monitor, November 11; Ram, V. (2008). *The enforcers.* Forbes, April 21.

Case prepared by Charles A. Rarick

CASE 15

ZIMBABWE'S HYPERINFLATION WHO WANTS TO BE A TRILLIONAIRE?

Speaking before an audience of concerned citizens and international spectators in July of 2008, Gideon Gono, Governor of the Reserve Bank of Zimbabwe, tried to reassure the crowd that the government of Zimbabwe had its monetary policy under control. "This time, we will make sure that those zeros that would come knocking on the governor's window will not return." Not everyone believed that Mr. Gono had things under control.

When Zimbabwe gained its independence in 1980, the Zimbabwe dollar (ZWD) was worth more than the U.S. dollar (USD). By September 2008, it took 60,000,000,000,000,000 Zimbabwe dollars to buy one USD (without the thirteen zeros removed) and devaluation is continuing at a rapid pace. Inflation is accelerating so rapidly that it is hard to estimate its rate. It was thought to be 98% per day in December 2008 and growing. This means that prices were doubling from day to day. Bank notes of 100 billion dollars were succeeded by banknotes of 200 million dollars in a matter of weeks. In January 2009, residents of the country carry stacks of 100 trillion Zimbabwe banknotes (dollars) to pay for basic commodities. Increasingly residents have had to resort to bartering and using U.S. dollars, or South African rands for commercial transactions while the government struggles to print enough of its own currency. In Zimbabwe, everyone can be a billionaire, yet still be poor.

While Zimbabwe's stock market led the world in 2007 in performance, with a gain of over 12,000 percent, the performance was illusory in that stock prices are driven by its hyperinflation, and not based on economic performance. In the past seven years industrial output has fallen by 47%, agricultural output by 51%, and natural resource output by 35%. People struggle for their basic necessities and well over 25% of the population has fled the country. Millions of Zimbabweans eke out a living just across the border in neighboring Zambia, Botwsana, South Africa and Mozambique. Items like milk, meat, and fresh fruit are considered luxury items to most residents. Life expectancy at birth is the lowest in the world, estimated at 44 years, and dropping fast. HIV/AIDS reigns endemic and a recent outburst of cholera is unfolding. Attempts by the government to stop inflation have not worked, including a then bold move of the government in 2007 to cut retail prices by 50%. The result was a thriving black market and empty shelves in retail stores.

Zimbabwe's inflation and devaluation, while extreme, are not without precedent. Similar situations occurred in Germany in the early 1920s, and more recently in the former Yugoslavia between 1992 and 1994 (see chart below). However, Germany was an economically developed country at the time with a large industrial infrastructure and a very educated population. Former Yugoslavia was a strong emerging economy with large markets within Eastern Europe and the USSR. Its population was very educated following the model of communist regimes that place a strong emphasis on general education.

Zimbabwe is in a wholly different economic situation; it used to be able to rely on exporting its agricultural products (maize and tobacco) to secure hard currencies. Zimbabwe possesses vast natural resources including gold, silver, platinum, coal, copper, nickel, and iron ore. The country had a rich agricultural tradition, and with Victoria Falls, the Great Zimbabwe stone ruins, and diverse wildlife, great tourism potential exists in the country. Many blame Zimbabwe's economic troubles on one man, Robert Mugabe. Once seen as a liberator of his country, Mugabe who has ruled Zimbabwe since its independence is now seen by many as an incompetent and corrupt leader moving his country towards collapse. Zimbabwe, previously the Southern part of Rhodesia, was controlled by Great Britain until its independence. Mugabe gained independence for his people and was seen as a progressive and inclusive leader in the earlier days of his rule. Today the international community sees the 84 year old Mugabe as divisive and dictatorial. Many of the citizens of Zimbabwe share this viewpoint. Recent elections have resulted in charges of election fraud. The United States and the European Union have placed sanctions on Zimbabwe and its top government officials.

Zimbabwe's worse economic problems began in 2000, when white-owned farms were allowed to be confiscated by black Zimbabweans resulting in the collapse of the country's agricultural output of maize and tobacco). Many of the white Zimbabweans families had owned their large, efficient farms for generations. Mugabe justified the land confiscation on the basis of redistributing land taken by British settlers many years ago. Inexperienced and feuding new land owners could not match the farm output of the previously experienced and skilled white owners.

Zimbabwe faces a monetary and economic crisis. With a government quoted inflation rate of 230 million percent in December 2008, and a more realistic independent estimate of over one billion percent, residents of the country struggle to survive. In addition, foreign investors are staying away with their badly needed capital.

Other developing countries have been afflicted by instances of hyperinflation in the two decades, although much less spectacularly than Zimbabwe, for example, the Democratic Republic of Congo, Angola, Bolivia, and Croatia, to name only a few. Researches of the IMF point out that in all cases, a disciplined stabilization policy has been able to reign in hyperinflation within a matter of months, just as was the case for emerging economies, such as Brazil, Argentina, Peru, Nicaragua, Armenia, and Ukraine to name only a few. Stabilization measures include institutional reforms, control of quasi-fiscal activities (cases where the central bank bails out state-owned companies), fiscal responsibility (reduction of government spending), deregulating prices, and removing restrictions on exchange rates and international payments. Above all, reestablishing confidence in the currency, and maintaining interest rate stability in order to reduce inflationary expectations, is needed. Steve Hanke of the CATO Institute has suggested three possible options to reestablish confidence in the currency. First, Zimbabwe could scrap its currency and use the currency of another country such as the United States dollar, the South African rand, or the European Monetary System's euro. Zimbabwe could instead keep its currency, but create a currency board, whereby its currency would be backed by foreign reserves and fully convertible into those foreign currencies upon demand. Lastly, Zimbabwe could privatize its currency by allowing commercial banks to issue their own currency.

Discussion Questions:

1. What is the relationship between hyperinflation and currency devaluation?
2. What problems does hyperinflation create for MNCs operating in countries with such rapidly rising prices?
3. Do traditional methods of reducing exchange rate risk work for companies operating in an environment such as that being experienced in Zimbabwe today? Explain your answer.
4. What should Zimbabwe do re-establish confidence in its currency?

Sources: Associated Press: "Zimbabwe gives in to U.S. dollar." International Herald Tribune, January 29, 2009; Berger, S. "Final humiliation for Zimbabwe dollar as foreign currency legalized." Telegraph, September 11, 2008; Burgis, T. "Zimbabwe to lop zeros off worthless currency." Financial Times, July 28, 2008; Coorey, S. et al. "Lessons from high inflation episodes for stabilizing the economy in Zimbabwe." IMF Working Paper 07/99, April 2007; Ehlers, M. "Mugabe's land redistribution brings inflation, food scarcity." McClatchy-Tribune News, October 19, 2008; Hanke, S. "Hyperinflation: Mugabe versus Milosevic." CATO Institute, July 21, 2008; Hawkins, T. "Zimbabwe inflation exceeds 66,000%." Financial Times (Asian Edition), February 15, 2008; Stevenson, D. "Zimbabwe's inflation hides a few hopes." Financial Times, March 8, 2008; Tupy, Marion: "The spiral of Zimbabwe." CATO

Institute , June 23 008; www.cnn.com. Zimbabwe issues $100 million bills as inflation soars, November 3, 2008; www.cnn.com. Zimbabwe issues $200 million notes. December 7, 2008 ;www.state.gov. Country Background Notes: Zimbabwe. Accessed November 2, 2008

Case prepared by Charles A. Rarick and Martine Duchatelet

CASE 16

GLOBAL TRADE BLUES

Anthony Richardson and Diego Velasquez were sitting at a bar in South Beach, Miami. They had both graduated from a local university with a B.S. in international business three years before and had remained friendly. Anthony, a native of Jamaica, carried a green card thanks to his mother's remarriage to an American citizen several years ago. Diego, a native of Spain, had come to the U.S. on a student visa and had been one of the few lucky ones to win a green card in one of U.S.'s periodic lotteries for all comers without regard to national origin. Both were ambitious and possessed entrepreneurial spirit. Both had started their own businesses about fifteen months prior to this meeting. Both were taking advantage of their cultural backgrounds and their connections in their homelands to foster their business endeavors.

Anthony was exporting sports equipment to Jamaica and Diego was exporting travel services to Western European countries by organizing exclusive, luxury tours for small groups of wealthy Europeans interested in seeing the sights in the U.S. They both felt they had discovered a promising niche in which their businesses could grow and prosper, but, fueled by beer, they both started bemoaning the adverse effects of currency devaluations on their profits.

Anthony has a cousin in Montego Bay, Jamaica, who acts as his agent. He secures contracts for sports equipment (swimming goggles, swimming fins, snorkels and masks, scuba gear, tennis rackets, etc.) with the various resorts and fancy retail shops all over the island. His cousin is successful at acquiring new customers and Anthony is confident that his business is growing. However, as a middleman (he does not manufacture the sporting goods), he pays in U.S. dollars for the goods he exports while he receives payment in Jamaican dollars for the goods he brings to Jamaica. Anthony earns his profit from undertaking the tasks of selecting the goods, organizing for their transport to Jamaica, paying all necessary taxes and tariffs, selecting appropriate clients, and mostly from accepting the risk of exchange-rate fluctuations between the U.S. and the Jamaican currencies. He keeps close watch on the valuation of the U.S. dollar in relationship to the Jamaican dollar.

Exchange Rates – Jamaican Dollars per U.S. Dollar

January 1, 1997	35.03
June 1, 1997	35.09
January 1, 1998	36.59
June 1, 1998	36.47
January 1, 1999	37.16
June 1, 1999	38.80
January 1, 2000	41.37
June 1, 2000	42.24
October 17, 2000	44.00

When he started his business in June 1999, Anthony had priced his goods to realize a net profit margin of 50%, without taking into account the vagaries of the currency exchange rate. He has attempted to reduce uncertainty by locking his suppliers, his transporters, and his Jamaican clients into two-year contracts. These two-year contracts do not allow him to adjust flexibly to the changes in the currency exchange rate, and Anthony feels that his profits are being squeezed out. Furthermore, another cousin, a talented artist in Kingston, the capital of Jamaica, is pestering him. She calls him a "fat cat" and demands that he help struggling Jamaican artists by purchasing their artwork (mostly paintings and wood carvings of all styles). She even insists that she is doing him a favor because Jamaican art is so well appreciated in the

U.S. that it could be sold in art stores in Miami, Fort Lauderdale, and the Palm Beaches for ten times its worth in Jamaica.

Diego's woes are different. He deals with several travel agencies in Western Europe that cater to the discerning wealthy tourist who seeks to discover unusual destinations. Egyptian tombs, Greek or Roman temples, gothic cathedrals, and medieval castles are run of the mill for such travelers. Diego, as an upper-middle-class, educated Spaniard, understands his clients' taste for a different experience quite well. He offers several successful packages: New York City (museums and Broadway), San Francisco and the wine country, Chicago and the Great Lakes country, the American Southwest (Taos, Mesa Verde, Santa Fe, Albuquerque, Bryce and Zion canyons), the American West (Colorado Rockies, Yellowstone and Grand Tetons national parks), and so on. Because his customers come from various European countries, he formulates his prices in the common currency, the euro. He has observed with great trepidation the recent, accelerated slide of the euro against the U.S. dollar.

Exchange Rates – U.S. Dollars per Euro

January 4, 1999	1.1812
June 1, 1999	1.0449
January 3, 2000	1.0155
June 1, 2000	0.9307
July 3, 2000	0.9526
August 1, 2000	0.9228
October 2, 2000	0.8806
October 17, 2000	0.8499

Diego's profits are threatened by the fact that all his expenses are incurred in U.S. dollars while his revenues are collected in euros. Marketing considerations suggest to Diego that he should keep the tours' prices steady rather than adjust them to reflect the slide of the euro. Diego is aware that he could perform operations on the forward market for the euro to mitigate the effects of exchange rate-risk. The *Financial Times* of the day (October 18, 2000) published the following information for October 17, 2000:

Euro	Spot	1month	3 months	1 year
U.S. $	0.8499	0.8512	0.8523	0.8621

Anthony and Diego are feeling too mellow to try and sort out their currency exchange rate woes. They both feel good about having shared their global trade blues with a kindred spirit and they part with the intention of remaining in contact and meeting periodically over a couple of "cold ones."

Discussion Questions:

1. How could Diego use the forward market to protect himself from further devaluations of the euro?
2. Why doesn't Diego consider the futures market?
3. Could Anthony also protect himself by hedging on the forward market?

4. How threatening is the devaluation of the dollar to Anthony's profits?
5. Is there an obvious solution to Anthony's worsening situation?

Sources: JMD to USD: www.patriot.net/~bernkopf; Spot Exchange Rate, Euro Area: www.bog.frb.us/releases/H10/hist/dat96 eu.txt; "Currencies and Money," Financial Times, October 18, 2000; "Euro Markets," Financial Times, October 18, 2000.

Case prepared by Martine Duchatelet

CASE 17

THE MOUSE THAT ROARED

The world's smallest country, the Duchy of Grand Fenwick, is only 16 square miles. Located on mountainous slopes, it enjoys favorable climactic conditions for the cultivation of grapes. The country is mostly unspoiled by modern standards and wine making is a time-honored tradition, developed into an art. Like most economically backward small countries, Grand Fenwick exports its main agricultural product and imports rudimentary machinery. Its sole trading partner is the United States to which it exports its famous wine, "Pinot Grand Fenwick." Grand Fenwick's official currency is the ecu (E): one ecu is equal to one dollar.

Table 1 summarizes the situation in the U.S. and Grand Fenwick. Inside the table appears the value expressed in Ecus of the resources each country must expand to produce a case of Pinot wine and a machine, respectively. Grand Fenwick's exceptional climate gives it the edge in wine production while the United States' size allows for mass production and economies of scale realized in the machinery production.

Table 1

	Pinot Wine (By case)	Machinery (By machine)

| U.S. | E 25 | E 200 |
| Grand Fenwick | E 20 | E 500 |

A price for each product established itself on the world markets so that Grand Fenwick was able to subsist on the export of its Pinot wine to the U.S. as long as the conditions in Table 1 prevailed. But, in the 1950s, wine production in the U.S. underwent major restructuring. Investors poured money into the Napa and Sonoma valleys in California, buying large ranches, planting healthy grapes, and building large cellars and large bottling facilities that Grand Fenwick could not match.

Modern technology allowed for new cost reductions in California wine production. Furthermore, extensive marketing efforts launched a "Pinot Grand Enwick," which for most American wine drinkers was undistinguishable from the foreign "Pinot Grand Fenwick." As a result, the amount of resources needed for the U.S. to produce one case of Pinot wine fell dramatically.

Table 2
Resources Required to Produce 1 Case of Wine and 1 Machine

	Pinot Wine (By case)	Machinery (By machine)
U.S.	E 10	E 200
Grand Fenwick	E 20	E 500

The Duke of Grand Fenwick and his advisors saw bankruptcy looming over their beloved country and decided to declare war on the U.S. This seemingly foolhardy move was actually quite devious: Grand Fenwick counted on losing the war to the U.S. and benefiting thereafter from all the economic aid this generous nation has historically showered on the countries it had defeated.

Discussion Questions:

Looking at Table 1, the initial situation:

1. What rate of exchange between the two goods might prevail?
2. How is an actual exchange rate established on the global market?
3. Which country will likely end up selling its export goods on the global market at the most favorable price?
4. Assuming the actual international prices are E 50 per case of wine and E 600 per machine, what is the exchange rate between the two goods?
5. Show that both nations benefit from trade. Assume that Grand Fenwick has 2,500 ecus worth of resources per year and needs 5 new machines per year.

Looking at Table 2, the subsequent situation:

6. Is there any rationale for the two countries to engage in trade?
7. Would the previous exchange rate established in the initial situation still be acceptable?
8. Assume the new international prices are E 600 per machine, as before, but E 26 per case of wine, knowing that Grand Fenwick needs 5 new machines per year and that, all other things being equal, the annual value of Grand Fenwick's resources is 2,500 ecus, why does Grand Fenwick feel hard-pressed?

Note: Grand Fenwick is a fictional country immortalized in the satirical novel, The Mouse that Roared, by Leonard Wibberley, and in the 1958 classic British movie, directed by Jack Arnold, which starred Peter Sellers in three major roles, plus Leo McKern and Jean Seberg.

Case prepared by Martine Duchatelet

EXERCISE 5

THE FOREIGN EXCHANGE MARKET:
CONVERTING WORLD CURRENCIES

Purpose: To develop skill in determining the value of one currency relative to another. An ability to determine a currency's forward premium or discount is also established through this exercise.

Procedure: Complete the exercise either individually or in small groups. Answer the five questions that follow using the currency exchange rates below.

EXCHANGE RATES

<u>Country</u>	<u>U.S. $ equiv.</u>	<u>Currency per U.S. $</u>
Britain (Pound)	1.4266	.7010
Euro Area (Euro)	1.2855	.7779
Japan (Yen)	.011007	90.85
1 month forward	.011011	90.82
3 month forward	.011027	90.69
6 month forward	.011055	90.46
Saudi Arabia (Riyal)	.2666	3.7509

Questions:

1. How many American dollars can be purchased with 100 British pounds?
2. How many Saudi riyals can be purchased with 100 American dollars?
3. How many euros can be purchased with 1 million Japanese yen?
4. How many American dollars would it take to purchase 2 million Japanese yen for a 90-day delivery?
5. Is the forward contract in question 4 selling at a premium or discount? What is the annual premium or discount?

EXERCISE 6

WEB-BASED EXERCISE:
THE IMF

Web Address: www.imf.org

Purpose: To increase your understanding of the mission of the International Monetary Fund and how the organization functions.

Procedure: Visit the Web site of the IMF and answer the following questions.

Questions:

1.   What is the stated purpose of the IMF?
2.   Where is the IMF located?
3.   What is a special drawing right (SDR) and a quota?
4.   How are quotas determined?
5.   Provide your opinion of the statement "The IMF cannot coerce its members to do much of anything."

EXERCISE 7

WEB-BASED EXERCISE:
THE WORLD BANK

Web Address: www.worldbank.org

Purpose: To further your understanding of the mission of the World Bank and its role in the global economy.

Procedure: Visit the Web page of the World Bank and answer the following questions.

Questions:

1. What is the mission of the World Bank?
2. Who runs the World Bank?
3. What is the difference between the World Bank and the World Bank Group?
4. Briefly explain the role of each of the five agencies within the World Bank Group.
5. Locate two separate World Bank projects in two separate countries and describe these projects.

PART FOUR

INTERNATIONAL STRATEGY AND ALLIANCES

Cases:

Wal-Mart or Carrefour?
Great Wall Motor Company
The International Diamond Industry
San Miguel Corporation
Bahamasair
Café Britt: Costa Rican Coffee

Exercise

Competitive Advantage of Nations

WAL-MART OR CARREFOUR: WHO WILL BE MASTER OF PLANET RETAIL?

Sam Walton began Wal-Mart, the world's largest retailer, in 1962. Headquartered in Bentonville, Arkansas, Wal-Mart was built on the policies of "everyday low prices" and a 100% customer satisfaction guarantee. Walton provided the lowest prices, on average, among American retailers, and directed the organization to achieve superior customer satisfaction. He had previously worked for the JC Penney Company and it has been reported that Mr. Penney once told Sam that he did not have a future in retailing. Walton's views on retailing were iconoclastic and industry-defining in the United States.

With over 3,000 stores in the United States, Wal-Mart has begun an aggressive expansion into the international marketplace and is currently present in 13 markets outside the United States. Wal-Mart has over 3600 stores in Argentina, Brazil, Canada, Mexico, UK, India, China, Japan and Central America. It also operates a small number of stores in a few other countries through joint ventures, most notably in India, where Wal-Mart's chief international rival, Carrefour, has failed to make inroads. Wal-Mart's primary retail format is supercenters, discount stores and neighborhood markets, as well as the wholesale warehouse format named Sam's Club.

Wal-Mart's attempts to enter the European market were unsuccessful with the exception of the UK market. Most recently, Tesco, the fourth largest retailer came to the offensive by entering the US market, but Carrefour still has not ventured into the North American world of retail. Wal-Mart's sales figures are larger than its major competitors Carrefour, Metro AG, and Tesco, combined. Many contend that Wal-Mart's primary strength lies in its centralized distribution network – a formula that the retailer hopes to copy in all of the markets that it enters.

Carrefour, the second-largest retailer in the world, was started in France in 1957 when two brothers, Jacques and Denis Deforey, who were in the grocery business, partnered with Marcel Fournier, who owned a department store. The name Carrefour, means "crossroads". Carrefour is known for their extreme attention to detail and the ability to cater to local tastes by sourcing and hiring locally. Carrefour established itself as the major retailer in Europe and it now has over 87,000 stores in Europe, Asia and Latin America. It is important to note that Carrefour has not dared to encroach on the turf of Wal-Mart, its formidable competitor, it does not have a presence in North America. Likewise, Wal-Mart has left Europe untouched outside of the United Kingdom. The retailing mix of Carrefour varies from that of Wal-Mart. Carrefour has ventured into cash and carry operations, hypermarkets, and supermarkets, but also owns a huge number of smaller convenience stores and banking and travel centers. Carrefour's focus has strayed away from the hypermarket format and has focused on smaller sized outlets, adding to the retailer's versatility, but subtracting from its bottom line.

Carrefour's global strategy involves careful study of local markets and careful attention to local customs. The retailer insists on hiring domestic employees at all levels of operations in order to best meet the local tastes. Carrefour failed to follow that policy in South Korea and was swiftly forced out of that country's retail landscape. Despite this policy, Carrefour was dealt a serious blow in China, where it were met with a tremendous amount of resistance because of the company's support of the cause to free Tibet. Carrefour used to be the largest foreign retailer in China and believed the Asian market was critical to its continued success. Carrefour has been a pioneer in the concept of international store clustering internationally, altering its product mix, store facilities, and prices to suit different economic regions. This

European retailer is considered a pioneer in adopting a strategy of differentiation by focusing on locally sourced products. Its strongest success has come from online retail operations and success in the large European markets of Spain and Poland. The variety of store formatting approaches has allowed Carrefour to outpace Wal-Mart in its entry into the promising Chinese market. However, the lack of economies might have hurt it in entering the fragmented Indian market, where Carrefour failed to make a dent. According to the Management Strategies of Global Retailers in the Crisis Report released in March of 2009, Wal-Mart has recorded growth of 1% and Carrefour posted 1.9% growth. Overseas markets are key contributors to that growth. They accounted for over half of the revenue source for Carrefour and 65% for Wal-Mart. However, both retailers have experienced setbacks in terms of international expansion.

Wal-Mart is a much stronger company financially and it has deep pockets for international expansion. Its "everyday low price" concept has been a very viable strategy and Wal-Mart pioneered creative and successful approaches to supplier management and technology integration. In the United States, Wal-Mart has huge economies of scale and world renowned logistical operations. In terms of domestic operations, Wal-Mart has a very impressive 20% return on shareholder equity.

Internationally, Wal-Mart has experienced less success, having failed in South Korea and Germany, and remaining unprofitable in Japan. International sales account for only about 30% of Wal-Mart's total revenue, and its return on assets for international operations has been considerably lower than for its domestic operations. Still, Wal-Mart's profit margins remained higher (3.3%) to that of Carrefour (2.8%) in 2008.

The world's largest retailer hopes to match its domestic success internationally and many analysts believe it has the financial and managerial ability to do so. On the other hand, Wal-Mart lacks the international experience and flexibility of Carrefour and is a late-comer in many markets where Carrefour is well established.

Discussion Questions:

1. Which international strategy does Wal-Mart follow? Which international strategy does Carrefour follow? Which do you feel is a better strategy for global expansion?
2. Why has Wal-Mart avoided the battle for the European retail market (outside of the UK)? Why is Carrefour avoiding the North American market?
3. Which retailer, in your opinion, will win the battle for global retail leadership?

Sources:
www.carrefour.com, Retrieved March 25, 2009; www.walmartstores.com, Retrieved March 25, 2009; Datamonitor, Global Food and Staples Retail, March 2009
Kumar, Nirmalya, Labelled with Love, Business Strategy Review, Summer 2007
Moreau, Raphael, Retail in Practice, Carrefour and Wal-mart's differing expansion strategies in China, Euromonitor International, Retail Digest, March14, 2007
Yoo, Soh-jung, Emerging markets, pricing key to retail ; THE KOREA HERALD, March 20, 2009; Licensemag.com, The top 25 Global Retailers, Retrieved March 25, 2009

Case prepared by Kasia Firjej and Charles A. Rarick

CASE 19
_____

GREAT WALL MOTOR COMPANY ATTEMPTING TO MAKE THE GREAT LEAP IN A COMPETITIVE INDUSTRY

Our nation is at war. This war isn't being fought on foreign soil, but right here at home and most Americans seem to be paying little attention to it."

Kevin Kelly, Senior Editor
Automotive Design & Production

The quote by Mr. Kelly is in response to his concerns about the potential onslaught of automobiles, and auto parts, which are expected to be coming from China in the near future. While auto parts are currently being exported to the United States, it is the fear of many that China's auto manufacturers will begin to get a foothold in the automobile market soon and that the Chinese will represent yet another strong foreign competitor to domestic manufacturers.

Currently there are over 100 separate automobile manufacturers operating in China, with Chery Automotive being the largest. Geely, China's second largest auto manufacturer, now sells in a number of countries, mainly in Asia, Africa, Russia, and the Middle East and soon plans on building a plant in Mexico to export cars to the United States and Latin America. In addition to cost advantages, Chery and Geely are quickly moving onto the hybrid, electric, and alternative fuel markets with their "green" vehicles. They hope to accelerate production and leap ahead of their American, Japanese, and European competitors with low-cost alternatives to traditional gasoline engine cars.

The largest have already begun to partner with U.S. and European auto manufacturers as the foreign firms seek to capture a share of the growing Chinese market. Automobile sales in China have been growing at an astonishing rate for several years and one of the more interesting players in the Chinese market is a relatively new and small producer called Great Wall Motors.

Great Wall Motor is located in Hebei province, about a 2 hour drive from Beijing. With 18,000 employees, the firm produces a little under 400,000 vehicles a year. Great Wall began life making farm equipment, and shifted to automobiles with the growing demand for cars in China. The firm is best known for its pickup trucks and SUVs, Great Wall manufactures four pickup truck models, four models of SUVs, one minivan, and one sedan. With so many auto manufacturers in China, Great Wall's market share is only 1.2% of the Chinese auto market. Great Wall Motor has assembly operations in China, Brazil, Iran, Egypt, Nigeria, Romania, Russia, Ukraine, and Vietnam, and exports to over 100 countries. Although export volume is tiny (30,684 units in 2008), the company hopes to greatly expand its global presence and to become a global leader in the auto industry.

Revenue for Great Wall Motor for 2008 was 4.6 billion RMB, an increase of 38% over the previous year. Net profit for 2008 was 4.2 million RMB, a decrease of 2% over the previous year. Increases in shipping, operating, and energy costs caused profits to decline, even as sales revenue increased. The firm's stock is publically traded on the Hong Kong Stock Exchange.

Some of the largest Chinese auto manufacturers had planned to enter the North American market by 2007. Dennis Reinbold, an

American famous for bringing the ill-fated Yugo to the United States, paid Chery Automobile Company $2 million to gain a distributorship in the hope of selling a Chinese branded sedan to American consumers. Selling automobiles in the United States is not easy. Consumers are very demanding and the government imposes stringent safety and environmental standards. In addition, it takes time to establish dealer networks, repair facilities, and supplier networks. With China and other emerging markets growing rapidly in auto sales, the North American market has been placed on hold for the time being.

While the United States is the largest market in the world for automobiles, some analysts predict that China will surpass the U.S. by 2020, or sooner. With automobile production slowing in recent years in the United States, Chinese production has grown rapidly. Most Chinese citizens do not yet own an automobile, yet most have a desire to one day own their own car. In the past, Chinese consumers preferred small, inexpensive cars such as Chery's popular QQ model which sells for around $4,500, but increasingly, Chinese consumers are demanding bigger and more expensive vehicles as their incomes rise. Great Wall has supplied some of that demand with its SUV models.

Chinese consumers have preferred foreign brands over domestic brands, as they have been seen as being of better quality and carrying more prestige. The larger Chinese auto manufacturers have partnered with American and European car companies in an effort to learn better production techniques, and to attach themselves to their brand identities. The Chinese government is encouraging its auto manufacturers to improve quality and to move out of the lower rungs of the quality ladder in an attempt to build an industry that can compete globally. Great Wall has yet to partner with an American or European firm for auto production, however, the company has recently signed a memorandum of understanding with Chrysler to cooperate on distribution and parts. Chrysler is hoping to import more auto parts from China, and Great Wall is hoping to affiliate with an American brand.

With a global slump in auto sales, Great Wall faces many challenges. It is a very small producer among many domestic competitors, and it faces competition from well-known international brands. Great Wall's position of producing more expensive Chinese vehicles may also present challenges as the economies of the world struggle in difficult economic times.

Discussion Questions:

1. Do you think Great Wall Motor can position itself to be a strong global competitor? Explain your answer.
2. Is the American market necessary for Great Wall's success?
3. What strategies would you recommend for Great Wall Motor Company?

Sources: Anonymous. (2008). *Chinese automakers stall North American move.* BIZCHINA, April 22; Donhardt, T. *Reinbold to sell Chinese autos in Indianapolis.* Indianapolis Business Journal, May 22; Great Wall Motors. Interim Report 2008; Kimes, M. (2008). China's drive into U.S. car market stalls. Fortune, October 30; Kelly, K. (2008). *China: Enormous threat or tremendous opportunity?* Automotive Design & Production, 120 (8), 10-11; Roberts, D. (2008). *Great Wall Motor: Gunning for glory.* Business Week, April 9; Roberts, D. (2008). *China's Geely has global auto ambitions.* Business Week, July 18; Rosynsky, P. (2008). *China ready to roll.* Journal of Commerce, January 28; Shirouzu, N. (2008). *What prosperity has to do with price of cars in China.* The Wall Street Journal, April 17; Webb, A. (2008). *U.S. companies cozy up to Great Wall.* Automotive News, April 28; Wernle, B. and L.Lan. *Great Wall becomes Chrysler's 2nd Chinese partner.* Automotive News, July 7.

Case prepared by Charles A. Rarick.

CASE 20

THE INTERNATIONAL DIAMOND INDUSTRY

Diamonds are produced in the earth's mantle when carbon is exposed to extreme pressure. Some diamonds make their way to the earth's surface and become a precious commodity. Since the 1930s the South African company, De Beers, has managed to manipulate the world price of diamonds. The long running and successful cartel began when Sir Ernest Oppenheimer, Chairman of De Beers began buying diamonds on the open market during the Great Depression; a time when diamond prices were falling. Since that time De Beers acted as the buyer of last resort for the diamond market and the firm stockpiled billions of dollars in diamonds in its London vaults. The company would buy diamonds from anyone in the world, no questions asked. The rough diamonds were taken to London where they were evaluated and sorted and ten times a year De Beers offers its diamonds to select buyers at non-negotiated prices. Since De Beers controls most of the diamond producing mines in South Africa, Botswana, and Namibia it has significant control over the world's diamond supply. This control is shrinking, however, with increasing diamond production coming out of Russia, Canada, and Australia. De Beers once controlled 80% of the world's diamonds. Now the company controls approximately 55% of global supply.

DIAMOND MINE PRODUTION (million carats)
MAJOR PRODUCERS

Botswana	30.4
Australia	31.0
Congo D.R.	25.0
Russia	19.0
South Africa	12.8
Canada	11.2

Another threat to the supremacy of De Beers is the Leviev Group of Israel. Leviev is the world's largest cutter and polisher of diamonds and was once a customer of De Beers. Dissatisfied with the lack of competition in the rough diamond market, Leviev sought out additional sources of rough diamonds and helped the Russian government develop its diamond extraction industry. The company now controls a large part of the Russian supply of rough diamonds and has begun to win favor with major producing countries in Africa by setting up shop in those countries and employing their citizens. Leviev is now both mining and finishing diamonds, and can offer host governments more employment opportunities than De Beers.

Recently concerns have been raised about diamond sourcing, with allegations made that diamonds are being used to finance rebellion in at least two African countries. It is believed that rebels in Angola and Sierra Leone, and possibly the Congo as well, have used diamond sales to finance their civil war activities. This trading of diamonds for weapons resulted in a threatened boycott of the product, not unlike the successful boycott of the fur industry that was begun earlier in protest of animal cruelty.

Fearing the "fur factor" and the threaten boycott of its product, De Beers withdrew its buyers from the African countries in question and began to promote "conflict free" diamonds. The company began to certify that its diamonds were not coming from war-torn parts of the world or used to finance rebel causes. Critics argue that "blood diamonds" will simply be funneled out of these conflict areas and through trading centers such as Mumbai (Bombay) where they could be blended with diamonds from legitimate sources.

In response to these concerns, in May 2000, representatives of diamond producing countries in Africa met in Kimberley, South Africa and drew up an agreement to certify that diamonds exported from member countries were not blood diamonds. The Kimberley Process Certification Scheme (KPSC) requires its 43 member countries to establish procedures to ensure that its diamond exports are not funding rebellion, and to package the diamonds in tamper-resistant shipping containers. Member countries are not allowed to trade diamonds with non-member countries. Any member country not in compliance with the agreement will be banned from trading with member countries. Recently, the Republic of Congo was de-listed because government officials could not account for a large discrepancy between its diamond exports and its legitimate diamond production. While the civil wars in Angola, Sierra Leone, and Congo have begun to come to an end, other concerns about diamond sourcing has arisen. The United States has passed The Clean Diamond Trade Act prohibiting the importation of any rough diamonds not certified as conflict free. The U.S., along with the European Union, (both members of the Kimberley Process) are concerned that conflict diamonds have been used to fund terrorist activities including terrorist acts by the al Qaeda network.

In addition to the concerns over conflict diamonds, the industry now faces its biggest change due to advances in diamond-making technology. The desire to make diamonds has been around for many years. In the 1950s the first man-made, or cultured diamonds were produced. The process was very expensive and diamond experts could tell if the diamond was natural or man-made. Recent advances in diamond manufacturing have produced man-made diamonds that are physically identical to natural diamonds and are almost indistinguishable. Two companies, Gemesis and Apollo are producing man-made diamonds that have the potential to change the diamond industry forever. Gemesis uses heat and pressure to turn graphite into a yellow diamond. Apollo uses a carbon vapor that attaches atom by atom to a thin wafer of diamond to make a clear diamond of any size. While the process of producing man-made diamonds is still expensive, diamonds can be made artificially and sold at prices of at least 35% lower than natural diamonds. Man-made diamonds also provide the advantage of being conflict free and not used to finance rebellions around the world.

In response to these challenges, De Beers has announced a fundamental change in company strategy. The company will shift its focus from supply management and price control to a more demand-oriented strategy. It will begin to sell off its diamond stockpile and promote its image as a quality provider of diamonds. Instead of promoting the industry as a whole, as it has done for years with its successful "a diamond is forever" ad campaign, De Beers will seek to differentiate itself from the competition and develop a strong brand loyalty. Under consideration is the possibility of branching out into other product lines such as clothing, watches, and handbags.

Discussion Questions:

1. Do you feel that a global company should change its strategy in response to threatened consumer boycotts? Explain.
2. How important do you feel it is to diamond customers that their purchases be "conflict free?" Will consumers pay more for "conflict free" diamonds?
3. How should De Beers respond to the current threats of man-made diamonds and reduced market control?

Sources: F. Guerrera and A. Parker, "De Beers to Seek Conflict Free Diamond Rules." Financial Times of London, July 11, 2000; "De Beers: All that Glitters is not Sold." The Economist, July 11, 2000; "The Diamond Business: Washed Out in Africa." The Economist, June 3, 2000; "Losing their Sparkle." The Economist, June 3, 2000; "The Cartel isn't Forever." The Economist, July 17, 2004; W. Wallis. "Africaa's Conflict Diamonds: Is the UN-Backed Certification Scheme Failing to Bring Transparency to Trade." Financial Times, October 29, 2003; M. Pressler. "Diamond Lab Produces Bling Bling for a Lot Less." Miami Herald, March 7, 2004; www.kimberleyprocess.com.

Case prepared by Charles A. Rarick

CASE 21

SAN MIGUEL CORPORATION CAN ENTREPRENEURIAL VALUES BE INSTILLED IN THE PUBLIC SERVICE INDUSTRY?

One of the most popular and well-known brands of beer in the Philippines and throughout Southeast Asia, San Miguel, has been brewing beer for well over one hundred years. The company's brewing business produces such well-known and popular brands as San Miguel Pale and Red Horse. The company also owns Ginebra San Miguel distillers, San Miguel Pure Foods, and San Miguel Packaging. The company has a vertically integrated structure in the food and agriculture industry, ranging from breeding, to canning, to retail branding. Recently shareholders approved a plan to spin off its domestic beer operations and to diversify into unrelated business areas. The spin off of the beer business (the historical core of the company) will provide capital to invest in new businesses, including the purchase of public electricity generating assets which are being considered for sale by the government of the Philippines. Questions have arisen as to whether this form of diversification is a wise strategic move for the company, and if privatization of electrical services is good for the Philippines.

San Miguel Corporation began as La Fabrica de Cerveza de San Miguel in 1890, operating in Manila under a royal charter from Spain. The company incorporated in 1913, and in the 1960s changed its name to San Miguel Corporation (SMC). Early in the company's existence it began a process of backwards vertical integration in which it acquired barley fields, and later expanded into other agricultural products. The company eventually expanded into soft drinks, spirits, and packaging operations. San Miguel has the distinction of being the first foreign bottler of Coca-Cola, acquiring the franchise in 1927. Today the company is the largest food and beverage business in the Philippines, as well as all of Southeast Asia. The company operates over 100 facilities in the Philippines, Southeast Asia, China, and Australia. San Miguel Corporation (SMC) earns most of its revenue in the Philippines, and most of its revenue is generated in its food and beverage industries.

San Miguel controls over 90% of the beer market in the Philippines, over 85% of the soft drink market, and significant shares of the processed meat and poultry markets. The core values of SMC are stated by the company as: ***Passion for Success***; ***Teamwork***; ***Respect for Our People***; ***Customer Focus***; ***Innovativeness***; ***Integrity***; and ***Social Responsibility***. The decision to move into traditional public works is innovative; however, the company's past has not been free of controversy, and there have been questions of conflict of interest, and integrity issues. The government of the Philippines owns a significant stake in the company due to seizure of assets deemed taken from the people of the Philippines during the Marcos era. One of San Miguel's owners fled the country with Ferdinand Marcos (but later returned to the Philippines) after the "people's revolution" in 1986. The company has been known as a fierce competitor, and has in the past been accused of using unethical practices to thwart its competitors.

The recent decision to rid itself of its domestic beer business has caused concern among investors. The company's share price, as traded as an American Depositary Receipt (ADR) has fallen, despite recent gains in profitability. Concerns over the ability to the company to diversify into unrelated businesses may be a contributing factor to the stock's decline. Even though SMC will maintain ownership of San Miguel brands and properties, and receive rents and royalties, spinning off the core enterprise in favor of unrelated diversification has worried some investors. Standard & Poor's and Moody's has placed San Miguel's credit rating under review, indicating the uncertainty of the strategic move. San Miguel's domestic beer sales have been showing slow, but steady growth and increased earnings.

In July 2007, shareholders approved the spin-off of the domestic brewery division and the investment of up to 35B pesos, or approximately $775M, in new business ventures. Domestic beer sales are not expected to increase significantly and the company wants to invest in more growth-oriented industries. As company chairman, Eduardo Cojuangco states, "We want to be in industries that have scale and will grow, and we are determined to build leadership positions in key areas where important trends are driving future growth, not just for San Miguel but for the Philippines too." San Miguel is partnering with a Malaysian and an American company to bid on control of the Philippines' power grid. The demand for electricity in the Philippines is expected to continue to grow, and forecasts show that current supply will soon be insufficient to meet public demand. The company also has plans to invest in mining, water, and other public sector businesses.

Managers of San Miguel feel that the company can capitalize on the proposed privatization of electrical services in the Philippines. Many of the power generating facilities in the Philippines are twenty five years old or older, and supply isn't always dependable. Some feel that the government owned service is poorly managed, and traditionally has operated as a drain on the Filipino government budget. However, recent rate increases and efficiency moves have improved the financial performance of the public utility.

The question of state ownership over private ownership has been debated by economists and others for a number of years. A more libertarian view is that all industries should be placed in private hands, with the possible exception of cases that involve market failure, where markets are not able to function effectively. Such a case is sometimes made for some utilities and public goods such as defense, public justice, and roads (with the exception of toll roads for long stretches of highways). Issues raised to support the privatization of industry generally involve efficiency, customer satisfaction, bureaucracy, corruption, accountability, and lack of market discipline.

Proponents of privatization argue that private ownership is generally more efficient than government ownership. They claim that private businesses are more competitive and must continually strive to reduce costs and insure customer satisfaction. They propose that government ownership creates bloated, bureaucratic organizational structures. Also proposed is the belief that concerns for customer satisfaction are not as strong with government enterprises. Proponents of privatization also argue that public ownership is more prone to corruption, and lacks transparency and accountability. Private companies, they argue, must account to shareholders. The basic argument is that the lack of market discipline imposed by a competitive marketplace produces underperforming organizations.

Those who feel government has a role to play in ownership point out that many of the proposed advantages of private ownership are not realized. Corruption and lack of accountability can be found in private enterprises, and the excessive salaries paid to some top managers are seldom challenged by directors or shareholders. Opponents of privatization also feel that some public goods are essential, and when placed in private hands can lead to harmful increases in market prices. Particularly in cases where private firms have a monopoly position, the ability to charge "what the market will bear" could harm the least advantaged members of a society. Proponents of public ownership also argue that politicians are accountable to voters, perhaps even to a greater degree than managers are to their shareholders. They argue that there are alternatives to complete privatization, such as partial ownership with government still maintaining some control, or localizing the public good to a lower level of government, such as a state or city, in order to reduce bureaucracy and increase customer satisfaction.

With approval of the sale of the domestic brewing division, San Miguel is looking for a buyer, and is confident that its capital and managerial skills can find better utilization in new and diverse industries. Some feel that a company that claims innovation as a core value should not cling to its past, and that seeking growth opportunities in diverse industries is a good strategic move. Others argue that such a radical change in corporate strategy is very risky, and a company with a checkered past should not be in charge of providing basic public services.

Discussion Questions:

1. What challenges does San Miguel face, in terms of corporate culture, in generating an environment that thrives on innovation and entrepreneurial thinking?
2. Do you think the strategic plan of investing in traditionally public sector   industries is a good idea for San Miguel? Explain.
3. Acting as an independent outside analyst, provide advice to both San Miguel and the government of the Philippines concerning their proposed courses of action.

Sources: Anonymous. (2007). *Energy- Powering up for privatization*. AsiaMoney, June; Bulos, H. (2005). *San Miguel's buying binge*. Business Week, April 25; Cuevas-Miel, L. (2007). *SEC clears spin-off of San Miguel beer unit*. Knight Ridder Tribune Business News, July, 30; Cuevas-Miel, L. (2007). *San Miguel profit almost doubles in first six months*. Knight Ridder Tribune Business News, August 10; Dumaual, R. (2007). *San Miguel earmarks $8M to double Vietnam plant capacity*. Business World, August 24; Landingin, R. (2007). *San Miguel investors agree to beer spin-off*. Financial Times, July 25; Lopez, T. (2006). *SMC the biggest corporation*. Manila Times, November 20; Marsh, V. (2007). *San Miguel switches its growth focus*. Financial Times, October 9; Pedrasa, J. (2006). *Big power consumers seek to purchase electricity directly from Napocor*. Business World, May 23; Sevilla, P. (2007). *San Miguel share prices being watched*. Business World, September 28; www.hoovers.com. Accessed on October 10, 2007; www.sanmiguel.com.ph. Accessed on October 11, 2007.

Case prepared by Charles A. Rarick and Inge Nickerson

CASE 22

BAHAMASAIR

The Commonwealth of the Bahamas is an independent country comprised of over 700 islands off the southeastern coast of the United States. When Columbus first arrived in the New World he landed on a small island that he named San Salvador, an island in present day Bahamas. With a thriving tourism industry, and as a center for offshore business and banking, The Bahamas has managed to develop its economy well beyond that typically found in the other island states of the region.

Although not technically located in the Caribbean, the Bahamas is viewed as a Caribbean tourist destination. The islands of The Bahamas are located in the Atlantic Ocean, close to the Florida coast and within easy reach either by sea or air. Air travel has been a popular means for tourist to travel to The Bahamas, however, increasingly tourists are arriving to the Bahamas by cruise ship. With a population of just 317,000, the Bahamas benefits greatly from this tourism. Over 5 million visitors per year, the vast majority from the United States, are attracted to the islands for shopping, beaches, water sports, and the attractions offered by the luxurious hotels such as Atlantis in Nassau. The Bahamas offers visitors parasailing, diving, snorkeling, historical tours, Caribbean dining, and much sunshine. Most tourists visit the capital, Nassau, or the other major city, Freeport. The tourism industry employs about 50%

of the Bahamian workforce and contributes approximately 40% of the country's GDP. Currently tourists spend over $2 billion a year in The Bahamas. Tourism is expected to increase in the coming years as resorts such as Atlantis expands, and new mega-resorts, such as those planned in Nassau's popular Cable Beach become operational. The government of the Bahamas is planning to develop the outer islands to attract even more tourists. The outer islands offer a slower-paced vacation and are special interest to some tourists.

The Bahamas does face stiff competition for Caribbean tourist dollars as tourists opt for sometimes more trendy destinations such as Barbados, St. Kitts, or the Turks and Caicos Islands. The Bahamas has remained a popular tourist destination despite this increasing competition. One threat facing the entire region is a new homeland security regulation. Beginning in 2007, Americans returning from the Caribbean must present a U.S. passport for reentry into the United States. Previously other forms of identification such as a birth certificate or driver's license were sufficient documentation. The effect on tourism as a result of this new regulation is uncertain.

Bahamasair, the national airline of the Bahamas, was born out of the energy crisis of the 1970s when British Airways ended its service to the Bahamas due to rising fuel costs. Fearing the effect of other carriers also ending service, the government decided to begin its own airline in 1973. The company has experienced difficulties with financial performance, labor unrest, and customer service throughout most of its existence. Currently the airline requires a government subsidy of around $10 million a year to operate. Bahamasair has been accused of being poorly managed, as represented by recent groundings due to poor maintenance record keeping, and late payments of a U.S. Customs bond.

Bahamasair flies out of four cities in the U.S. - Miami, Ft. Lauderdale, West Palm Beach, and Orlando, and has service throughout the Bahamas. Bahamasair also flies to Jamaica, the Dominican Republic, and the Turks and Caicos Islands. In 2004, Bahamasair entered into a code-sharing agreement with US Airways that allows an expansion of its market into Charlotte, Philadelphia, and New York. Code sharing allows one flight to be marketed by more than one airline and increases the market reach of cooperating airlines. Bahamasair had expanded into the U.S. market in the 1980s to include Philadelphia, Newark, and New York, but found those routes to be unprofitable at the time. The airline is a small carrier with only eleven aircraft that includes Boeing 737 jets and smaller turboprops. Bahamasair competes directly or indirectly with a number of different international airlines including US Airways, Continental, American Airlines, Jet Blue, Spirit Airlines, and Air Tran. All six American carriers fly into The Bahamas, most to Nassau or Freeport. Bahamasair would like to compete on the basis of its country identity and slogan (*We don't just fly there. We live there*), however, more often Bahamasair competes on the basis of price (see Figure 2).

FIGURE 2
Sample air fares on a round trip flight to Nassau:

	Miami	Ft. Lauderdale
American Airlines	$243	
Continental		$288
US Airways		$381
jetBlue		$218
Bahamasair	$228	$228

Source: Expedia.com. February 14, 2009

At one time Bahamasair had exclusive intra-country routes, however, a number of private airlines have now begun operating within the Bahamas, including Pineapple Air, Cat Air, Seair Airways, Western Air, and Southern Air. These domestic competitors compete with Bahamasair on some of the same intra-country routes, operating with a lower cost structure than Bahamasair. In order to offset this loss of revenue due to domestic competition, Bahamasair is considering expanding into smaller cities in the U.S. such as Cleveland and Richmond.

Faced with increased competition and a poor record of profitability, the government of the Bahamas has begun to explore the possibility of finding a foreign investor for Bahamasair. The government has requested bids from investors who would purchase a less than 50% equity interest in the airline. International investors will find in the Bahamas a favorable tax structure, close proximity of the country to the United States, an English speaking population, political stability, and a developed infrastructure. Additionally, the Bahamian dollar is pegged on par (1-1) with the U.S. dollar, reducing exchange risk volatility.

In an effort to explore the privatization issue, the Bahamian government contracted with the American consulting firm McKinsey & Co. to provide an assessment of the issue. The consultants reporting on the airline industry stated that "domestic markets are mature and saturated; Florida is over-serviced; and penetration of U.S. markets will not likely generate positive margins for Bahamasair in the short or long run." Additionally, the consultants stated that it was essential that Bahamasair improve operating efficiency, reduce costs, increase market share, and right-size the present aircraft fleet. Without improvements, finding a foreign investor would be very difficult.

While financial data are difficult to come by, it is believed that Bahamasair experienced a loss of $10 million on revenues of $76 million for the fiscal year 2005-2006 and has not yet returned to a profitable position. Bahamasair is essentially bankrupt and according to its managing director, the company has a negative equity of around $84 million. The company survives only through government subsidies that have ranged been between $10-32 million a year. Attempts at cost-cutting have resulted in labor resistance, including groundings due to sickouts by employees.

Some see Bahamasair as a typical example of the problems of government ownership of industry. They argue that governments typically do not generate the interest in efficiency and customer service found in private companies. Furthermore, government-owned industries can become vulnerable to destructive political meddling in economic decision-making.

Others argue that many countries have state-owned airlines. Some airlines are fully owned by the government, such as British Airways and Japan Airlines International. In other cases, the government has a partial equity interest in the national carrier. Government ownership of airlines varies from 100% ownership to only a token equity interest. Scandinavian Airlines (SAS) is owned 50% by the government and 50% by private investors. KLM Royal Dutch Airlines is 25% state-owned, and the German government has a small equity interest (1.6%) in Lufthansa. According to the Bahamian Ministry of Works and Utility, "The provision of reliable, efficient, low-cost airline service is essential to the social and economic development of the Bahamas and the continued growth and development of our tourism industry." Not all government officials agree with this position and a decision regarding the future of the airline must be made.

Discussion Questions:

1. Why do governments typically own airlines and not grocery stores?
2. Should the government of the Bahamas privatize Bahamasair, liquidate the airline, or continue to operate it? Explain your answer.
3. Regardless of ownership, recommend a strategy for Bahamasair to restore profitability.

Sources: Anonymous. (2005). *Search begins for Bahamasair partner.* The Bahama Journal, June 11; Anonymous. (2005). *Bahamasair sees strong summer bookings.* The Bahama Journal, August 10; Anonymous. (2006). *Chaos at Bahamasair.* The Nassau Guardian, July 20. Barlas, R. (2000). Bahamas. New York: Marshall Cavendish; Dames, C. (2005). *Bankrupt Bahamasair due for overhaul.* Bahamas News and Views, June; Henderson, J. (2003). The Caribbean and the Bahamas. London: Cadogan; Huggins, C. (2006). *Bahamasair mired in red.* The Nassau Guardian, April 5; Symonette, B. (2005). *Union not supporting Bahamasair privatization.* The Bahama Journal, May 30; Symonette, B. (2005). *Government hires consultant for Bahamasair privatization.* Jones Bahamas, June 27; www.bahamasair.com. Accessed on July 21, 2006; www.fundinguniverse.com/company-histories/bahamas-air-holdings-ltd. Accessed on July 31, 2006; www. state.gov/.r/pa/ei/bgn/1857.htm. Country background notes – Bahamas. Accessed on July 31, 2006.

An earlier version of this case was published in the Online Journal of International Case Analysis, Vol. 1 (1), 2008.

Case prepared by Charles A. Rarick and Inge Nickerson

CASE 23

CAFÉ BRITT: COSTA RICAN COFFEE

Known by various names such as mocha, java, or a cup of Joe, coffee is one of the world's most popular drinks. Coffee is also a valuable commodity and the source of income for a number of countries. Coffee is grown mainly in countries located in the equatorial region of the world, between the Tropic of Capricorn and the Tropic of Cancer. Sixty million metric tons of coffee is produced each year in this coffee belt by more than 60 countries. One of those countries is Costa Rica, a country that has traditionally relied heavily on coffee exports as a source of revenue. While coffee is a popular Costa Rican product, it did not originate in Costa Rica or anywhere in Latin America. The origins of coffee can be found in Africa.

The history of coffee can be traced to East Africa, in present day Ethiopia around the year 600AD when a local goat herder named Kaldi noticed his flock eating berries from a bush. As legend has it, the animals seemed to become energized from the berries and Kaldi himself experienced the same effect after he consumed some of the fruit. Coffee eventually made its way to the Arabian Peninsula. Beginning with the 10th Century, Arabs learned to steep coffee beans in water to produce a drink called "gahwa." It is believed that the world's first coffeehouses were established in Mecca and became places where people could play chess and argue politics. The drink grew in popularity as word of its properties spread.

Coffee beans were traded at the port of Mocha in the 13th Century, but the plant itself was prohibited from being exported out of Arabia. In the 17th century a Muslim pilgrim brought coffee seeds back to his home in India and began a coffee plantation. Dutch traders began purchasing coffee plants from India and growing them in Java. Venetian traders then introduced coffee to Europe, and a French naval officer named Captain Gabriel Mathieu de Clieu brought a single coffee plant to the Caribbean. The plant was first introduced in Martinique and from there, coffee plants made their way to Central and South America. Legend has it that from a single coffee plant comes almost all the coffee now grown in the Caribbean and Latin America. Coffee was introduced to North America in the 1660s and coffeehouses quickly sprung up in New York, Boston, and Philadelphia. The Boston Tea party was planned in one of these early coffee houses.

Coffee production began in Costa Rica in 1779. The climate of Costa Rica was ideal for growing coffee beans and the commodity soon became the leading product for export. In order to encourage coffee exports, the government of Costa Rica supplied each family with 25 plants if they agreed to grow coffee. In addition, they were given a tax exemption on all earnings from the sale of the coffee beans. This incentive resulted in most families being engaged to some extent in coffee production. In order to insure that Costa Rican coffee maintained a quality image in the world marketplace, the Costa Rican government passed a law banning the growing of any coffee other than Arabica in the country.

Coffee is from an evergreen that produces a blossom that hardens and turns from green to bright red in color. The coffee plant belongs to the botanical family called Rubiaceae and the average coffee tree produces about a pound of coffee a year for 25-30 years. The fruit of the coffee tree, referred to as cherries, contains two-sided beans from which coffee is produced. There are two basic species of coffee in the world: Arabica and Robusta. Arabica beans are considered to be the higher quality coffee beans and are grown in higher altitudes. The higher altitude causes the beans to grow more slowly and to develop what is called a "hard bean." Robusta coffee beans can grow in lower altitudes and mature more quickly. The bean is less expensive to produce but gives a less desirable taste. Robusta coffee is often sold in cans in supermarkets and is often the bean found in instant coffee. Arabica coffee plants, while considered superior in taste, are more difficult to grow and yield fewer beans per plant. Robusta are easier to grow, yield more beans per plant, and are disease resistant. The Robusta bean produces a harsher taste and is generally not considered appropriate for a premium coffee product. Arabica coffee is grown primarily in Latin America and India. Robusta beans are primarily grown in Africa and South-East Asia.

Coffee beans are usually harvested by hand and dried either by placing them in the sun, called patio drying, or using a mechanical tumbling dryer. After the beans have been dried, they are milled, which removes the outer skin of the bean and give the bean a shine. The beans are sorted and graded before being sent to market. To turn coffee beans into a desirable drink, the beans must be roasted. The roasting process heats the beans to between 320F and 480F degrees in a steel drums.

Coffee beans are turned into a liquid drink in a variety of ways. All methods have in common the use of hot water to extract the essential oils and caffeol from the ground coffee beans. Coffee can be made using a filter method or a percolator, both traditionally popular in the United States, or consumers can use an espresso machine and force hot water through finely ground and compacted coffee. This method has become increasingly popular in the U.S. and has been popular in Europe for some time. Turkish coffee is made using a cooper pot in which the ground coffee is boiled in the pot, usually three times, producing a very strong coffee.

The coffee industry is very susceptible to commodity price changes. Coffee retailers profit from falling prices and coffee producers benefit when prices are rising. The coffee producing industry has experienced some difficult years as the price of coffee reached record lows in recent years. Coffee prices were held constant during the 1960s, 1970s, and 1980s as the coffee cartel was able to control supply and maintain price stability. In 1989 the cartel collapsed, causing prices to begin a long and significant drop. Although prices spiked during poor harvesting seasons, the long-run trend was downward from about 1990 to 2004. Increased volume coming from Vietnam and Brazil fueled the price decreases. Vietnam was able to increase coffee production during the 1990s, becoming the second largest coffee producing country behind Brazil. Coffee is traded on the New York Coffee Sugar and Cocoa Exchange and the price is volatile.

In addition to increased supply, technological breakthroughs in the processing industry allowed roasters to use more Robusta beans without getting the harsh taste. This change in processing allowed for a greater supply of Robusta beans to be processed. Vietnam and Brazil produce most of the Robusta coffee in the world market. The Big Four coffee sellers in the world, Nestle, Procter and Gamble, Sara Lee, and Kraft had previously blended only a small amount of Robusta beans into the blend of Arabica beans, but now are able to significantly increase the Robusta content.

Worldwide coffee prices continued to fall during the 1990s and in 2001 reached a record low. Sometimes price levels were below production costs. The worldwide coffee glut appears to have now ended with prices rising in 2007/8. Prices at the supermarket and at coffeehouses, such as Starbucks, have been rising as commodity prices increase.

Coffee plantations require a labor-intensive work force of seasonal workers to hand pick berries and wash and dry them. Vietnam has a competitive advantage in coffee production over most of the rest of the world. It is estimated that production costs are three times higher in Central America than in Vietnam, for example. The world's largest coffee producing countries can be seen in Figure 1.

Figure 1
Major Coffee Producing Countries
(60 kilo bags Oct. 08-Jan 09)

Brazil	11,467,000
Vietnam	5,755,000
Colombia	3,610,000
Peru	1,607,000
Indonesia	1,515,000
Uganda	1,078,000
India	713,000
Mexico	573,000

Guatemala	544,000
Ethiopia	418,000
Honduras	419,000
Cote d' Ivoire	306,000
Costa Rica	294,000

Source: International Coffee Organization (www.ico.org)

Per capita consumption of coffee has been declining in the developing world but growing in developed countries. Premium coffee sales, using only high quality Arabica beans, has grown approximately 40% in the United States. When the world price of coffee was declining, specialty retailers such as Starbucks reaped greater profits. As the price of coffee is now increasing, the additional costs are being passed on to consumers. Coffee demand is relatively constant, however, coffee supply is often unpredictable due to weather conditions.

Some coffee has a worldwide reputation for high quality, including Blue Mountain coffee from Jamaica and Kona coffee from Hawaii. A number of niche coffee products exist including the world's most expensive coffee called Civet. Civet coffee comes from the undigested discharge of the fruit eating civet. The civet is a cousin of the mongoose and lives in South-East Asia. The civet eats coffee beans, the beans pass through the animal undigested, and are then collected by processors. The coffee is very scarce and highly prized for its unique flavor and aroma. Other less exotic specialty coffee includes estate, shade grown, and organic coffee. Estate coffee is coffee from only one plantation. Estate coffee is not blended with beans from other producers and maintains its pure or consistent flavor. Shade grown coffee is grown under shade trees and appeals to consumers who feel this practice is more environmentally responsible in that the practice avoids soil erosion and is also beneficial to wildlife. Some coffee is also certified as "fair trade coffee" meaning that a price baseline is maintained by buyers who insure against falling prices paid to growers. This coffee appeals to consumers who feel that a market based pricing system can at times cause farmers to suffer extreme and unexpected drops in income. Fair trade coffee accounts for only about three percent of the coffee market. Organic coffee is grown without chemicals and fertilizers and appeals to a limited segment of the coffee industry as well. Organic coffee prices generally are fifteen cents a pound higher than non-organic coffee.

The Costa Rican coffee industry consists mainly of small farms or fincas. While Costa Rican coffee has traditionally been considered to be a quality product, the country was not well known as a producer of gourmet coffee. Café Britt was founded in 1985, being the first gourmet coffee roaster in Costa Rica. Café Britt was founded by its current president and chairman, Steven Aronson. Aronson, who was an American permanently living in Costa Rica, had studied agricultural economics at the University of Michigan and had been involved in several coffee processing companies in Latin America. The current CEO and general manager is Pablo Vargas, a Costa Rican who holds graduate degree in agricultural economics and business from Michigan State University. Vargas, who has worked for Café Britt for the past thirteen years, was responsible for implementing the quality assurance program, establishing the Internet sales concept, and promoting the retail store concept. The company is headquartered in Heredia, a town near the capital, San José. The privately held company sells the Café Britt brand through the Internet, in its 50 retail stores, and through hotel chains and restaurants. Café Britt operates retail stores in airports of Costa Rica, Peru, Curacao, St. Thomas, Chile, and Miami, Florida. The company also sells unprocessed coffee (green coffee) to processors. Café Britt Corporation was incorporated in Curaçao and consists of the following subsidiaries: Grupo Café Britt, S.A. and Finca Tropico, S.A. incorporated in Costa Rica; Café Britt Arabica Marketing, NV incorporated in Curaçao. The company operates a successful Internet site (www.cafebritt.com) where customers can purchase coffee, sweets and nuts, music, and Costa Rican crafts. The Internet site has been highly rated by BizRate for its level of customer satisfaction. Customers can also call a toll free number to order Café Britt products. Shipping costs for orders of 1-5 items are $8.95. If customers order more than five items, shipping is free.

Figure 2
Sales Distribution

Retail Stores	59%
Supermarkets, Restaurants, Hotels	17%

Internet	10%
Green Coffee	10%
Coffee Tour	4%

Café Britt sells 12 ounce coffee bags that retail for $8.95. The coffee is offered in the following varities: Dark Roast, Light Roast, Espresso, Decaffeinated, Shade Grown Organic, Tarrazu Montecielo, and Tres Rios Valdivia. The Company also sells a variety of candies and nuts such as Creamy Coffee Cheros, Chocolate Covered Coffee Beans, and Chocolate Covered Macadamia Nuts. Café Britt promotes Costa Rican artists through the sale of local music and crafts.

Café Britt considers its quality product to have a strong advantage in this highly competitive market. The Company seeks to be a leader in customer service and to provide an exceptional product at a competitive price. Café Britt is ISO-9000:2000 certified and promotes a quality mission statement.

Café Britt maintains a 100% customer satisfaction policy and will replace any product or give a refund if the product does not meet customer's expectations. The coffee is grown in Costa Rica by over 4,000 smaller growers, milled and patio dried, roasted and packed all by Café Britt. Café Britt seeks to capture the higher end of the coffee market and to be identified with Costa Rica. Café Britt is as much about Costa Rican tourism as it is about coffee production. As current CEO Pablo Vargas likes to state "Costa Rica sells Café Britt and Café Britt sells Costa Rica."

Costa Rica is well known as a desirable tourist destination. Each year tourists flock to the country to see its many natural attractions including volcanoes, rain forests, and wildlife. With one-fourth of the country devoted to national parks and protected areas, Costa Rica has become a popular eco-tourist destination. Tourism growth was strong until 2001 when the terrorism attack in the United States reduced travel to many parts of the world including Costa Rica. Tourism had grown from 435,000 visitors in 1990 to 1,131,000 in 2001. Most visitors to Costa Rica are from the United States, however, significant numbers of visitors come also from Canada and Europe. Increased airline flights, more hotels, and a strong Euro have helped tourism rebound in Costa Rica. Capitalizing on this aspect of the Costa Rican economy, Café Britt conducts a very popular multimedia coffee tour of its facilities. The tour is one of Costa Rica's more popular tourist activities and attracts over 40,000 visitors a year to the plantation.   For about $30US, tourists are taken from their hotels by bus to the plantation and are provided with a highly entertaining introduction to coffee growing and processing. Through this professionally conducted tour, visitors learn about the history of coffee, how coffee is grown and roasted, and what it takes to produce a premium coffee product. Many visitors are introduced to the Café Britt brand through this tour. The tours are heavily promoted and arranged through local hotels in the capital city. Following the tour, visitors can stroll through the Café Britt shop at the plantation and purchase products, or use the Internet Café and send electronic Café Britt greeting cards to their friends back home.

Café Britt competes with a number of Costa Rican brands including Bardu Coffee, Café Delagro, Café Rey, Café Volio, Doka Estate Coffee, Dota Coffee, and Kiry Coffee. Another Costa Rican coffee producer, Américo, has established an exhibit in the San José airport and touts itself as the "genuine Costa Rican coffee." In addition, Café Britt must compete with other gourmet brands, each with a particular niche in the market.

With significant gains in sales and profitability since 2002, Café Britt looks towards the future with a desire for further expansion. The company has increased its production capacity through its expansion into Peru. Café Britt hopes to duplicate its successful business model in Peru. Although not generally known for quality coffee, Peru does have some exceptional quality production and Café Britt hopes to duplicate its business model there using the same tourism link. With sales expansion into airports in Curacao, St. Thomas, Chile, and Miami, Café Britt is growing its global retail presence. The company is concerned about its dependency on Costa Rican tourism, and tourism in its other markets. Based on its current success, Café Britt looks optimistically towards the future.

Discussion Questions:

1. What are the strengths, weaknesses, opportunities, and threats for Cafe Britt?

2. What could Café Britt do to establish itself in retail stores in the United States? Is this important to Café Britt's continued success? Explain.
3. What advice would you offer Café Britt as it seeks further global expansion?

Sources: Batsell, J. (2004). *Cup by cup, coffee fuels world market from Costa Rican origins.* Knight Ridder Tribune Business News. September 19; Brackey, H. (2005). *Java lover's jolt: Prices going up.* Miami Herald. March 4; Katona, C. and T. Katona. (1992). The coffee book. San Leandro, CA: Bristol Publishing; Mackenzie, C. (2005). *Fair trade price certification spurs debate.* Miami Herald. March 28; Personal interview with Pablo Vargas in Heredia, Costa Rica on April 8, 2005; Stein, N. (2002). *Crisis in the coffee cup.* Fortune. December 9; Teves, O. (2004). *Undigested coffee beans: Good to the last drop.* Miami Herald. December 26; Telephone interview with Steven Aronson. March 28, 2005. www.cafebritt.com. Accessed on February 15, 2005; www.cnn.com. Accessed on October 18, 2002. www.hoovers.com. Accessed on February 15, 2005; www. ico.org. Accessed on February 15, 2005. www.lind-waldock.com. Accessed on February 15, 2005; www.ncausa.org . Accessed on March 25, 2005; www.wto. org - Costa Rica Tourism numbers. Accessed on April 12, 2005; www.cafebritt. com. Accessed on March 2, 2009.

Case prepared by Charles A. Rarick, Martine Duchatelet, and Anne Fiedler.

EXERCISE 8

COMPETITIVE ADVANTAGES OF NATIONS

Purpose: To gain a better understanding of the *Competitive Advantage of Nations* theory, and to use critical thinking skills to assess strategic choices facing countries and firms.

Procedure: Read the background material below and then select a country of your choice. Research that country in terms of the factors cited in the theory, and provide an assessment of the competitive position of your chosen country. Also investigate one industry in your chosen country and assess its competitive position as well.

Background: Michael Porter, of the Harvard School of Business conducted an extensive study into the competitiveness of countries. Porter's findings emphasize the importance of a country's industries and their   competitiveness to He argued that a country's competitiveness, and ultimately its wealth, is created through four conditions.

Factor Conditions: The basis for a country's output, including natural resources, labor, and capital. The lack of natural resources, in some cases, may actually help a country become competitive. Such countries are forced to make better use of limited resources and to develop "homegrown" resources such as human capital.

127

<u>Demand Conditions</u>: Countries which possess a strong domestic demand produce strong domestic competitors. Sophisticated and demanding consumers at home make companies and industries stronger and more competitive internationally.

<u>Related and Supporting Industries</u>: Competitive countries and industries can be found in clusters. Clusters include related industries and supplier networks. Long term sustainable competitiveness is usually not gained by a single resource or industry.

Strategy, Structure, Rivalry: Competitive industries are well managed industries with appropriate strategies, structures, and intensive competition. Good management makes a difference and competition makes firms stronger.

Exercise is based on *Competitive Advantage of Nations*. Michael E. Porter. New York: The Free Press, 1990.

PART FIVE

INTERNATIONAL MARKETING

Cases:

Exercise:

WAL-MART JAPAN: WORLD'S LARGEST RETAILER CAN'T MAKE A YEN

"The best part is if we work together, we'll lower the cost of living for everyone, not just in America, but we'll give the world an opportunity to see what it's like to save and have a better life."

Sam Walton, Founder of Wal-Mart

Wal-Mart entered the Japanese market in 2002 with a minority stake in the Japanese retailer, Seiyu, hoping to duplicate its success that started in the United States in the world's second largest economy. Japan has a population of 127 million, and a very high disposable income level. Wal-Mart has demonstrated strong a commitment to the Japanese market by investing an additional $1 billion in order to acquire a 51% stake in Seiyu. In 2007, Wal-Mart increased its ownership through an additional investment of approximately another $1 billion to acquire 95.1% ownership of Seiyu. The company also has a plan for control of the remaining shares. Wal-Mart felt that additional ownership would allow for greater flexibility and more rapid decision making, independent of its Japanese partners. Wal-Mart's investment in Japan represents a significant part of the company's overall international presence strategy. While Wal-Mart has been very successful in other international markets, including Mexico and China, it has not been very successful in Japan. Wal-Mart has yet to earn a profit from its 393 Japanese stores.

Wal-Mart sees great potential in transplanting its operating model, characterized by lean ordering and processing costs, across the globe, and thus far has been mostly successful. With a few setbacks, notably in Germany and South Korea, the international unit is performing well and represents a sizable share of the company's revenue. Wal-Mart opened its first international operation as a Sam's Club in Mexico in 1991. Foreign revenues have rapidly risen over the years. International sales for fiscal year ended January 31, 2007 were $90.6 billion, which represented a 17.5% increase over the previous year's sales. International sales account for over 20% of the company's revenue, and represent the fasting growing component of the company. With 95% of the world's population living outside the United States and with retailing in many countries lacking the efficiencies of Wal-Mart, many see the future growth prospects for the company as being primarily international in nature. In October 2007, Wal-Mart announced that it would begin to slow its domestic store growth in favor of international growth. While Wal-Mart looks to the international market for increased growth, in Japan, the company faces a strong local competitor, Aeon, and has had difficulties adapting to Japanese consumers and distribution methods.

Due to a declining birth rate, in 2006 Japan's population actually began to shrink. If the present trend continues, Japan will lose a quarter of its population within the next 25 years. With a declining population, and in recent years, cautious consumer sentiment, it isn't surprising that retail sales in Japan have been falling (Japan Chain Stores Association). Globally, consumer confidence has been shaken by the recent problems in the financial markets. Some argue that tougher economic times could be good for a company that has an ability to deliver low priced goods to consumers. While such predictions may be true, Wal-Mart has struggled in many ways in the Japanese market.

In 2007 Wal-Mart announced that it intended to cut 450 management jobs at Seiyu and take a one-time loss of $39 million due to the need to pay for buy-out offers and early retirement. Wal-Mart had earlier encouraged its partners in Japan to reduce employment in order to gain efficiencies. These workforce reductions were met with negative reactions from both employees and customers. The employment reductions have been viewed even less favorably due to the fact that Wal-Mart is a foreign company. Japanese society is influenced by its strong orientation towards "soto" and "uchi." The Japanese now view the company as *soto*, or outside, due to its American ownership and control. Prior to the Wal-Mart investment, Seiyu was seen as a Japanese company and *uchi*, or inside. Japanese culture segments things and people into these inside/outside frameworks. Cumulative levels of foreign direct investment in Japan only represent approximately three percent of GDP, as compared to twenty two percent in the United States. In additional to perceptual problems of *soto*, foreign companies also complain about the cost of business regulation and the demanding nature of Japanese consumers. Carrefour, the French supermarket chain known for adapting well to foreign markets abandoned its Japanese operations after four years of struggling to be accepted.

In the case of Wal-Mart, the Japanese market did not respond well to the low price concept, which is the core of the company's strategy. Japanese consumers are more inclined to equate price with quality. The initial perception of Japanese consumers to the low prices found at Seiyu was to assume the goods were inferior. This perception was enhanced by the fact that Wal-Mart continued to source many of its products from China, ignoring local suppliers who were viewed as too small and inefficient. In addition, Japanese consumers were more accustomed to selective deep discounting on products, instead of Wal-Mart's "every day low price" approach. In addition, Japan's distribution system is unique in many ways from the distribution systems found throughout the world. In Japan, the distribution system is very fragmented, and channels tend to be much longer. High retail density tends to better serve customers who make smaller and more frequent purchases at local shops. Japan also has placed legal restrictions on large store development. While the restrictions are changing, there is a lingering effect in terms of consumer usage and preferences.

In addition to being a foreign company and being perceived as a low quality source of goods, some have questioned the managerial ability of the top staff, including the selection of Edward Kolodzieski as CEO. Kolodzieski, an American, is assisted by other Americans, Canadians, and Britons. Many successful foreign companies in Japan have placed Japanese natives in the top positions in the company. Seiyu's former top manager, Masao Kiuchi, resigned in 2005 citing his lack of ability to make the company profitable. Kolodzieski, who started his retailing career as a store manager of a Kash n'Karry Food Store in Florida has had little experience and understanding of the Japanese market and culture. Other critics feel that Seiyu's organizational problems are the result of too much decision-making about Japan being made from the Wal-Mart headquarters in Bentonville, Arkansas. Kolodzieski dismisses many of the critics, insisting that the management model is working. He states: "If you look at our financials, we're starting to increase in sales. We're starting to improve in profitability. But we really have an opportunity to improve quite a bit." Wal-Mart's Seiyu posted a loss of Y20.9 billion ($193 million) in fiscal year 2007 and announced the closing of 20 of the most unprofitable stores to improve operating results. Investors did not interpret the financial results in the same fashion, nor do they appear to share Kolodzieski's optimistic view. Seiyu's share price continued to weaken until Wal-Mart purchased almost all of the outstanding shares of Seiyu. Chief financial officer, Tom Schoewe feels that Wal-Mart will be able to see a turnaround of its Japanese operations in the next three to five years. According to Wal-Mart's international head of operations, Mike Duke, Seiyu is performing much like the early Wal-Mart stores in Mexico, which also struggled with profitability.

Wal-Mart has instituted a number of changes in order to improve its financial performance, including remodeling stores and making them larger, and operating some stores on a 24-hour basis. In the remodeled stores, sales increased by an average of six percent. In addition to store operations, Wal-Mart improved its supply chain management in Japan with the development of a large distribution center. When stores place an order, the distribution center can have the goods delivered in the 24-48 hours. In addition, Wal-Mart is working more closely with its suppliers to reduce inefficiencies and to develop a more collaborative approach to supply management. The stores now stock more expensive merchandise to appeal to the quality conscious Japanese consumers.

Wal-Mart hopes to avoid a repeat of its experiences in Germany. In 2006 the company sold its 85 stores to a German competitor and exited the country. Wal-Mart had difficulties adapting to German culture and regulations. Standard Wal-Mart customer service and employee relations did not blend well with the German culture, and Wal-Mart fought German laws concerning store hours and price lowering. As company spokesperson, Amy Wyatt stated: "Looking at the international business around the world and where we would have the greatest impact on growth and investor return, it became increasingly clear that given the German business environment, we could never obtain the scale and results we desired." Some feel that the same situation could be true of the Japanese market for Wal-Mart. In 2006, Wal-Mart also sold the 16 stores it operated in South Korea. In Korea Wal-Mart's one-stop shopping concept ran counter to the Korean way of buying from a variety of local stores that specialize in different product categories. Wal-Mart's no frills décor also turned off Korean consumers who were accustomed to a more upscale shopping experience.

As Wal-Mart's top management team in Japan looks forward, it must make a decision on how it will turn the company around. Wal-Mart has clearly indicated that it intends to remain in Japan and the company has further expansion plans in Asia. Wal-Mart recently established an Asian headquarters in Hong Kong to better serve its store operations in China and Japan, and plans to enter the Indian market in 2009 with the help of a local partner. Further plans are underway for entry into the Russian market. With over 620,000 employees in 3,242 foreign stores in 13 countries, Wal-Mart is truly becoming a global organization. What remains to be seen is how well its globalization effort will work in Japan.

Discussion Questions:

1. Do you think Japan is a good market for Wal-Mart? Explain.
2. What were the most significant mistakes Wal-Mart made in Japan?
3. What suggestions do you have for increasing the financial performance of Seiyu?

Sources: Anonymous. (2008). *Seiyu loss more than double its forecast.* Financial Times, February 13; Anonymous. (2008). *Wal-Mart abroad.* Financial Times, February 16; Anonymous. (2008). *Wal-Mart to build headquarters in Hong Kong.* SinoCast China Business Daily News, September 4; Birchall, J. (2007). *Wal-Mart plans big expansion outside US.* Financial Times, October 24; Birchall. J. (2008). *Wal-Mart resets its global focus.* Financial Times, June 18; Cateora, P. (2007). International marketing. New York: McGraw-Hill/Irwin; Fackler, M. (2005). *Chief quits Wal-Mart's Japan unit.* International Herald Tribune, July 21; Holstein, W. (2007). *Why Wal-Mart can't find happiness in Japan.* Fortune, August 6; Lander, M. and M. Barbaro. (2006). *Wal-Mart finds that its formula doesn't fit every culture.* The New York Times, August 2; Pilling, D. (2007). *A tough nut to crack for foreign investors: While some businesses have arrived and done well in the country, many have suffered serious setbacks.* Financial Times, March 13;

Rousek, L., D. Michaels, E. Taylor, A. Osborn, and S. Canaves. (2008). *Wary consumers pinch firms in Asia, Europe.* Wall Street Journal, October, 9; Rowley, I. (2005). *Japan isn't buying the Wal-Mart idea.* Asian Business, February 28; Seiyu Annual Report 2007; Soble, J. and J. Birchall. (2007). *Wal-Mart to cut Seiyu management jobs.* Financial Times, September 19; Wal-Mart Annual Report 2007; www.rand.org/pubs/research_briefs/RB5044. Accessed on September 19, 2007; www.walmart.com. Accessed on October 22, 2008; Zimmerman, A. and E. Nelson. (2006). *With profits elusive, Wal-Mart to Exit German; local hard discounters undercut retailer's prices; "basket-splitting" problems.* Wall Street Journal, July 29.

Case prepared by Kasia Firlej, Charles A. Rarick, and Lori Feldman.

CASE 25

FRITO-LAY ADAPTS TO THE CHINESE MARKET

In the 1930s, two men in different parts of the United States began businesses that would eventually come to dominate the global snack food market. In 1932, Elmer Doolin, an ice cream salesman, stopped for lunch at a local San Antonio café. He noticed a package of corn chips at the café and purchased it for five cents. This small purchase would come to change his career and his life. The chips Doolin purchased were made from corn dough used for centuries by Mexicans to bake bread. Impressed with the product, Doolin sold his ice cream business and purchased the corn chip producer's business for one hundred dollars. The brand, Frito, was created in the kitchen of his mother, along with the early production of the corn chips. Doolin would bake the chips at night and sell them during the day. Early sales were in the range of $8-10 a day. As business expanded, the company was moved from San Antonio to Dallas. Frito became a major chip producer in the Southwestern United States.

Around the same time, an entrepreneur in Tennessee named Herman W. Lay was selling potato chips produced by an Atlanta company. Lay sold the chips from his personal automobile until 1938 when the chip manufacturer fell on hard times. Lay managed to buy the business and changed its name to H.W. Lay and Company. The company's products became popular with consumers due to their good taste and convenience making Lay and Company the dominant producer of snack foods in the Southeastern United States.

After World War II, the two companies began to cooperate in the area of product distribution. At this time they were still limited to their respective geographic markets, with Frito in the Southwest and Lay in the Southeast. In 1961, the two companies merged to form Frito-Lay, Inc., and in 1965 the company was merged again, this time with the Pepsi-Cola Company. The Pepsi-Cola Company became PepsiCo and consisted of the Pepsi-Cola Company, the Frito-Lay Company, and Tropicana Products. The company now also markets the popular brands Quaker Oats and Gatorade.

Although the U.S. market is the largest market in the world for snack foods, due to its saturation, Frito-Lay has expanded significantly into international markets. The company tries to capitalize on its economies of scale and global brand image to compete with local brands. The typical entry strategy is to first learn which company is the leading snack company in the foreign market, and then attempt to purchase that company. If that fails, Frito-Lay aggressively competes against that local company. Frito-Lay's international operations add $9 billion to PepsiCo's $25 billion revenue. International markets have in many cases been more profitable for PepsiCo than the domestic market of the United States.

Pepsi entered China in 1981 to sell soft drinks, and since that time has invested more than $1 billion. In 1994 Frito-Lay entered the Chinese market with its popular Cheetos brand snack. Potato chips were not introduced into the Chinese market until 1997, due to the Chinese ban on potato imports. Frito-Lay had to establish its own farms in order to grow potatoes acceptable to company standards. Early adaptation to local markets required Frito-Lay to make significant changes. For example, Frito-Lay's Cheetos sold in China do not contain any cheese due to the propensity of the Chinese to be lactose intolerant. Instead of cheese flavoring, Cheetos is offered with barbecue or seafood flavoring. In addition, the packaging was made smaller so that the price would be more acceptable. Other international adaptations had previously been made in other markets by Frito-Lay, including the popular Thai product, Nori Seaweed Chips.

Frito-Lay found that the Chinese market was not a single entity. Regional tastes and preferences had to be considered and products altered accordingly. Chinese living in Shanghai, for example, prefer sweeter foods, and Chinese living in the Northern region prefer a meaty taste. Frito-Lay also has found that having a good understanding of culture helps sell products. The Chinese belief in the Great Unity, or yin and yang, have marketing and product development implications. Yin and yang are the opposing forces in the universe and seek balance. The Chinese also seek balance, including balance in their foods. Fried food is seen as hot and not appropriate in the summer months so Frito-Lay developed a new product, cool lemon potato chips. This product consists of chips dotted with lime specks and mint and packaged with cool climate images to connote winter months.

Promotion in China has required other adaptations, including advertisements showing the peeling of potatoes to indicate the product's basic ingredient. Promotion in China has successfully related collectivist tendencies of the Chinese people and the desire of the Chinese to try new products outdoors, in a conspicuous fashion. Early adopters in China want others to see their consumption of Western products. As with many Western products, young consumers are the first to try the product, and in the case of Frito-Lay, the focus has been on young women. As Jackson Chiu, sales director for Frito-Lay states: "We market to girls and the boys follow." Frito-Lay has been very creative in its promotion efforts in China, however, one advertisement resulted in a small problem. Using the picture of Mao Zedong's cook in its promotion resulted in the company being ordered to offer an apology and to pay the cook 10,000 yuan (1,200USD) for violating a Chinese law that requires getting permission before using someone's picture.

Frito-Lay's entry into the Chinese market has also caused some controversy. Some critics charge that companies like Frito-Lay have caused the Chinese diet to become unhealthy. Many Chinese can remember when food was rationed, long food lines existed, and consumers were offered little choice. Today the Chinese have a large variety of food options, and snack foods are a popular choice. As a result of their dietary changes, the Chinese have become more overweight. In the past ten years, the percentage of the Chinese population considered overweight has risen from almost none to a little under one third of the population. A common way of greeting someone in Chinese is the English equivalent of "Have you eaten yet?" The Chinese are now able to answer yes more often to that question, and many are selecting foods that are considered by some to be unhealthy.

Concerned with the health effects of its products, not only in China, but also in health-conscious markets such as the United States, PepsiCo has begun to change its product offerings. Based on medical advice, PepsiCo has divided its products into three groups: 1) "Good for you" foods such as Gatorade and oatmeal; 2) "Better for you" foods such as Nacho Cheesier Baked Doritos; 3) "Fun for you" foods such as Pepsi Cola. The good for you foods are naturally healthy or engineered to be healthy. The better for you foods contain more wholesome ingredients or have reduced fat and sugar. The fun food isn't considered to be especially healthy. PepsiCo is moving product development towards the "good for you" and "better for you" groups. According to nutrition expert, Professor Marion Nestle of New York University, "Frito-Lay products are still high in calories, salt, and rapidly absorbed carbohydrates." For now the Chinese do not seem too concerned and Frito-Lay continues to develop this rapidly expanding market.

Discussion Questions:

1. Evaluate the approach Frito-Lay used as it entered the Chinese market. Would you consider the approach to be ethnocentric, polycentric, or geocentric? Explain your answer.
2. Is the company being socially responsible in your opinion by selling products that may be considered unhealthy?
3. What lessons can be learned by examining the experiences of Frito-Lay in China?

Sources: Author unknown. (2004). *Frito-Lay Sees Crunchy Business for Chips Here.* The Economic Times, June 3; Author unknown. (2004). *Chairman Mao's*

Cook Wins Lawsuit vs Pepsi. China Economic Net, July 23; Flannery, R. (2004). *China is a Big Prize.* <u>Forbes</u>, May 10; Kurtenbach, E. (2004). *Urban Chinese Struggle with Battle of the Budge.* <u>LaTimes.Com,</u> July 18; Parker-Pope, T. (1996). *Custom-Made: The Most Successful Companies Have to Realize a Simple Truth – All Consumers Aren't Alike.* <u>Wall Street Journal</u>, September 26; Sellers, P. (2004). *The Brand King Challenge.* <u>Fortune</u>, March 21; <u>www.abcnews.com</u> *Using Potato Chips to Spread the Spirit of Free Enterprise,* September 9. 2004; <u>www.fritolay.com</u>. **Accessed on July 12, 2004.**
<u>www.pepsico.com</u>; Accessed on July 12, 2004.

Case prepared by Charles A. Rarick

BRADFORD LTD LEARNS ABOUT COUNTERTRADE

Bradford Ltd. manufacturers cement, the gray talc-like powder that is used to make concrete when water, sand, and aggregate (stones) are added. Cement is treated as a commodity type product and Bradford is looking to expand its markets by exporting cement to Russia.

Mark Miller, Bradford's CEO is directing his team in establishing a trading relationship with Hydzik's Development, a major building contracting company located several miles from St. Petersburg. Myron Sczurek is Hydzik's CEO and is working with Mr. Miller to "cement" a deal. All of the specifics related to the transaction have been agreed upon and they are now at the final stage and trying to reach agreement as to form of payment.

<u>Hydzik's Perspective</u>:
1. Desire to pay in rubles (the Russian currency)
2. Desires to take title of cement shipment upon arrival in their facility near St. Petersburg
3. Desires to keep transaction as simple as possible; a handshake would be nice

Expresses a strong belief in a growing and stable Russian government and economy

Bradford's Perspective:
1. Mr. Miller fears the dollar/ruble exchange rate is unstable and that it will deteriorate
2. Wants Hydzik's to take title of the cement when it leaves U.S. port
3. Fears a handshake may not be sufficient
4. Doesn't share Mr. Sczurek's optimism regarding the stability of the Russian government or economy

The Proposed Solution:

After several days of discussion, Mr. Miller and Mr. Sczurek both feel that the trade is in both parties best interests; a win-win situation. They both agree that a possible solution includes the use of "countertrade" as a form of payment, and that Hydzik's will take title at the U.S. port. Mr. Sczurek offers to pay for the cement by shipping an equal value of vodka for the cement. The first shipment of cement is to have a market value of $1,000,000 to which Hydzik's will ship $1,000,000 worth of vodka to Bradford. Mr. Miller left the meetings to discuss the offer with his staff to draw-up a counteroffer and is to get back to Mr. Sczurek by the end of the week.

Discussion Questions:

1. Which party do you believe benefits most from the proposed solution and why?
2. If the quantity of vodka is determined by fair market value in U.S. dollars ($1,000,000) at the time of the trade, is the $1,000,000 in cement protected from fluctuations in the currency exchange rate in this proposal?
3. If you were Mr. Miller, where would the favorable F.O.B. (U.S. port or Russian port) and why?

4. You work for Bradford and are charged with writing the counterproposal for the amount and value of the vodka needed to "cement" the deal. How would you approach reaching this value and how would you justify it to Hydzik's Development?

Case prepared by Jack Kleban

CASE 27

HONG KONG DISNEYLAND: MISSING THE MAGIC

Disney's fifth theme park opened in Hong Kong in 2005 with great expectations, but the venture has yet to come close to meeting those expectations. By 2009 there was even talk that Hong Kong Disneyland would not be able to survive. Disney had hoped to gain a foothold in the potentially lucrative Chinese market through Hong Kong and to promote its other products, such as movies and toys, to the Chinese. Those expectations have instead resulted in disappointing results.

Hong Kong Disneyland is a joint venture between the Walt Disney Company and the government of Hong Kong. The Hong Kong government supplied about 80% of the cost of the facility ($2.9B) and received a 57% ownership stake in the joint venture. Hong Kong seemed like a good location to enter the Chinese market. Hong Kong, a long time colony of Great Britain, has a population of 7 million and a per capita GDP of over $30,000. Hong Kong is a Special Administrative Region (SAR) of China with its own constitution and operates with a more Western legal system of protection for foreign companies. While China has a much larger population (1.3B), it has a much lower per capita GDP of only $2,500. China's legal system is still developing and many foreign companies complain about contract enforcement and property protection in the People's Republic.

The Disney theme park in Hong Kong is the smallest of Disney's operations. Disney operates theme parks in California, Florida, Paris, and Tokyo. Hong Kong Disneyland covers only 126 hectares of land and contains only four segments: Main Street USA, Tomorrowland, Fantasyland, and Adventureland. The park has only 16 main attractions, compared to 52 in Paris. Many park visitors complain that is facility is simply too small to justify the ticket cost of 350 Hong Kong dollars or that there is no reason for a repeat visit. Hong Kong Disneyland draws about 4 million visitors a year in equal proportions from Hong Kong, China, and the rest of the world. Expectations for park attendance were over 5 million visitors a year.

When Disney opened its park in Paris, it received much criticism for not adapting to French culture. In order not to repeat the same mistake in Hong Kong, Disney hired a feng shui expert who advised the company on proper balance in its design. Hong Kong Disneyland carefully balanced earthly elements of water, earth, wood, and fire to create the proper environment. The main gate at the park is positioned in a north/south direction as a sign of good fortune.

Disney faced some difficulties in entering the Chinese market. Hong Kong has competing attractions such as Ocean Park which consists of not only adventure rides, but also a panda habitat, hot air balloon rides, and an undersea voyage experience. Ocean Park has a more natural environmental setting and is less costly to visit. Disney also had the disadvantage of not having a strong brand image, in the sense that many Chinese children did not grow up with the same love and familiarity of the Disney brand and its characters.

In an effort to improve the performance of the park, Disney has been negotiating with the government of Hong Kong to expand the size of the facility. Those plans have been placed on hold as disagreement arose as to who would pay for the expansion. In the mean time, Disney has been planning to open another park in China by 2014. A Disney theme park is being planned for Shanghai that would be approximately 800 hectares in size, located in a city of over 13 million, and be able to more easily draw visitors from other parts of China. The effect on Hong

Kong Disneyland of an additional theme park in China is unclear. Some feel that it could be a drain of the approximately one-third of the current Chinese visitors to the park, or it could enhance the overall popularity of the Disney brand and increase attendance in Hong Kong.

Discussion Questions:

1.   Was the choice of Hong Kong as an entry point a good decision for Disney? Explain.
2   Research Chinese culture, geography, and demographics and make recommendations to Disney concerning its plans to open an additional park in China.

Sources: F. Balfour and B. Einhorn (2009). *Hong Kong Disneyland's Future is in Danger.* Business Week, March 17; J. Lau (2009). *Cuts Cloud Hong Kong Disneyland Expansion.* Financial Times, March 18; M. Schuman (2006). *Disney's Hong Kong Headache.* Time, May 8; www.disneylandreport.com. Accessed on March 25, 2009; www.state.gov. Country Background Notes on Hong Kong and China.

Case prepared by Charles A. Rarick

CASE 28

INTERNATIONAL BRAND PIRACY: A CASE OF NEW BALANCE IN CHINA

China is the product piracy capital of the world. Once confined to less expensive consumer goods such as cigarettes, clothing, and soap products, China has increased its brand theft into markets such as pharmaceuticals, aircraft parts, and entire cars. In 2005, U.S. Commerce Secretary Donald Evans provided evidence that the Chinese auto producer, Chery Automobile Company, had stolen an entire car design from General Motors. Chery produces a model called QQ, that is essentially identical to GM's model produced in Korea called the Spark. While engaged in black market, or counterfeit goods activity for some time, China has recently become a major source of authentic products sold outside the legitimate channel of distribution. Additional countries known for their brand theft include Taiwan, Pakistan, Korea, and Indonesia. The development of the Internet has facilitated the practice of brand theft, allowing product pirates to gain product information and to sell pirated goods through on-line channels.

As American and European companies have increased their outsourcing to lower labor cost countries they have increasingly faced the threat of counterfeit products developing. These companies have given proprietary information and technology such as trade secrets, mathematical formulas, and product designs to their foreign suppliers. The outsourcing trend has occurred at the same time as international brand values have risen. With much of a product's value being composed of its brand, and with increasing outsourcing of manufacturing occurring in less developed countries, the stage has been set for increased difficulties with brand theft. Increasingly, manufacturers are seeing their goods being copied by foreign companies, and in some cases, foreign suppliers are selling the real product through unauthorized channels.

Sometimes called the "midnight shift" or "third shift," foreign suppliers have begun to sell authentic or real products, for which they are licensed to produce, without the consent or knowledge of the brand owner. Essentially, additional production runs are "sold out the back door" by the foreign supplier who pockets the proceeds from the unauthorized sales. A variation of the midnight shift involves the stealing of product information and technology by managers or employees of the foreign supplier who then establish their own illegal operations. In some cases a foreign supplier is told to stop producing a product and continues to make the product on his/her own. This was the case with the American shoemaker, New Balance, who experienced great difficulty with one of its Chinese suppliers.

Founded in 1906 by William Riley as a manufacturer of arch supports and orthopedic shoes, New Balance of Boston now produces a valuable brand of athletic shoes. The company has long maintained a strong commitment to domestic production, however, with rising production costs in the U.S., New Balance shifted a large percentage of its manufacturing to China. While New Balance still operates five plants in the U.S., the company has shifted 70% of its manufacturing to China.

New Balance sought to maintain control over its foreign suppliers with a strong code of supplier conduct which contained provisions concerning issues such as child labor, health and safety, discrimination, and environmental concerns. While the company has not had much difficulty with its suppliers in those areas, the company has experienced much difficulty with brand theft.

The problems began for New Balance when one of its Chinese suppliers asked to be licensed to sell some of the shoes it produced for New Balance in the Chinese market. Soon these low priced shoes were being exported to Japan, causing strained relations with Japanese distributors and potentially harming the premium image of the brand in Japan. In 1999, New Balance terminated its contract with this Chinese supplier, but the supplier continued to produce the shoes on his own using the proprietary information and technology supplied by New Balance. Under the terms of the contract, the Chinese supplier was required to return technical information, shoe molds, and packaging to New Balance but the supplier refused to comply with the requirement. New Balance was able to get the Chinese government to confiscate about 100,000 pairs of the supplier's shoes, but the supplier then began to manufacture its own brand which appeared almost identical to New Balance. The shoes, the shoeboxes, and stores of the pirate were essentially identical to those of New Balance.

New balance had an arbitration clause in its contract with the Chinese supplier in order to avoid dealing with the Chinese legal system, however, the arbitrator could only render a decision and could not enforce the judgment or issue an injunction. Unhappy with this situation, New Balance took the case to a Chinese court in 2000, and in 2002 the court ruled (reportedly against most legal reasoning) in favor of the Chinese supplier. Lawyers for New Balance suspected court corruption, not an uncommon situation in China.

New Balance appealed the decision to the regional High Court but received no response for months. Finally word came through an intermediary that a decision could be given for a payment of $300,000. New Balance refused to pay this bribe and refused repeated attempts, including from the leading judge himself, and a lower offer of $50,000 to rule on the case. In 2005 the High Court finally made a decision and ruled against New Balance.

According to the U.S. Trade Representative, over 90% of intellectual property in China is copied. This figure includes music, books, movies, and computer software, all important exports of the United States. Many U.S. manufacturers have pleaded with the Bush Administration to take action to force China to conform to international laws and agreements. Since its entry into the World Trade Organization (WTO) in 2001, China has been obligated to protect the intellectual property rights of WTO member states through the TRIPS (Trade Related Aspects of Intellectual Property Rights) program. This program establishes minimum levels of protection of intellectual property and provides for dispute settlement.

China has begun to get tougher with its enforcement of intellectual property rights by passing more laws and increasing its enforcement activity. The Chinese government has also begun a campaign of public awareness against the practice of brand theft. While the government has stepped up enforcement on a national level, local public officials have been slow to act, fearing increased unemployment if they crack down on counterfeiters. Some have argued that it is essentially impossible to stop Chinese piracy due to the cultural acceptance of copying the work of others. Yet others have pointed out that China was very successful in prohibiting the counterfeiting of its 2008 Olympics mascots due to fear of prosecution.

A case could be made that it is in the best interests of China to enforce intellectual property rights. As China seeks to become more integrated with the global community it will be necessary to follow international rules and regulations. It can also be argued that product piracy hurt a country by holding back the potential innovators of the country. The incentive to create new brands and product concepts is reduced when others can easily steal these ideas.

According to Bill Thompson of Pinkertons–Shanghai, the solution to ending product piracy is working on what he calls the "Four E's." Focusing on enforcement, education, external pressure, and economic growth can reduce brand theft. In order for intellectual property rights to be meaningful, it must have sufficient enforcement by local governmental bodies. The incentive to copy product ideas is too great when there are no negative consequences to the action. In many cases, a public education campaign can be effective in informing potential pirates of the dangers of copying product ideas, particularly in cases where the practice has been considered acceptable. External pressure by other governmental bodies and organizations can also be effective in forcing compliance. If history can be used to predict the future, economic growth can reduce the extent of piracy as economic opportunities provide legitimate business activities for members of less developed economies. Unfortunately for international marketers, the slow progress made on these dimensions continues to erode market share and potential profit potential.

Discussion Questions:

1. Research the intellectual property protection offered through the World Trade Organization (WTO) and summarize your findings.
2. Would you buy a pirated good such as a DVD or software if offered to you at a fraction of the normal cost? Explain your answer.
3. What should firms do in order to protect their brands from international piracy?

SOURCES: Anonymous. (2003). *Imitating Property is Theft*. Economist, May 15; Evans, D. (2005). *U.S. Steps Up Public Campaign Against China's Pirated Products*. Wall Street Journal, January 14; Hu, P. and B. Gomez. (2005). *Chinese Counterfeits Hurting Industry in China, Experts Say*. www.usinfo.state.gov/eap/archive/2005/may/19-596040.html; Nussbaum, B. (2006). *China's President Hu Jintao Visits Microsoft's Bill Gates – Who is More Innovative?* Business Week, April 19; Parloff, R. (2006). *Not Exactly Counterfeit*. Fortune, May 1; Yoon, E. (2005). U.S. Shoemaker Faces Chinese "Gall Factor". CNN International.Com, May 19; www.newbalance. com. Accessed on April 24, 2006; www.wto.org - Intellectual Property: Protection and Enforcement. Accessed on April 24, 2006.

Case prepared by Charles A. Rarick

INSULTING GOD, ONE STEP AT A TIME

Pegasus Footwear was an international manufacturer, well known throughout the world for its product design and marketing savvy. Products were designed at company headquarters in the United States and Pegasus used an extensive system of contract manufacturing to produce a variety of mostly athletic shoes sold throughout the world.

Charles Clark, or C.C., was the regional manager in charge of Pegasus operations in Southeast Asia. Clark, a British citizen, was responsible for manufacturing and marketing in the entire region. C.C. had been with Pegasus for 10 years and was recently promoted to his present position. The position was seen as a very important one, since most of the contract manufacturing for Pegasus occurred in this region of the world. C.C. was a graduate of Oxford University and began work at corporate headquarters in Los Angeles shortly after receiving his M.B.A. from Stanford. His management style was often described as visionary; however, some of the local managers felt that C.C. possessed a somewhat condescending attitude toward employees from less-developed countries.

C.C. and his team in Southeast Asia were considered very successful by top management back at corporate headquarters. As a result, C.C. earned an unusual degree of autonomy for his group. C.C. oversaw the manufacturing operations in the region (which employed over 1,000 people) and was primarily responsible for the marketing of products that were manufactured in the region. Most of the products, however, were sold in the United States and Europe, and responsibility for marketing in these regions was held by the respective regional managers. All product design was created in the Los Angeles office.

When C.C. arrived in his office on Tuesday morning, he received word of a problem. Storeowners in Indonesia were reporting problems with a particular shoe that had recently been designed by Pegasus. The shoe called AirBurner was upsetting Muslim consumers who objected to the design found on the outer heel of the shoe. The design, which spelled "air," was written to resemble fire, but some consumers felt that the design spelled "Allah" in Arabic. Since the shoe is considered by many to be the dirtiest part of clothing, it was considered a major insult to find the word for Allah, or God written there. Storeowners tried to explain that the word was not "Allah" but rather "air," written in flaming letters. Most consumers were not satisfied with the explanation.

C.C. asked for an accounting of the number of shoes produced with the design and was told that 100,000 pairs had already been produced, and that more were being made. One-fourth were to be sold in his region and the rest were on sale in other parts of the world. Although each shoe had a direct cost of production to Pegasus of $6.75 and a recall of all 25,000 pairs in his region would not significantly affect profitability, CC decided not to recall the controversial shoes. He stated: "Pegasus is proud of the fact that we have never had a product recall and we don't intend to start one with this silly design issue. The design clearly spells the word air and it should not be an insult to anyone." C.C. felt that the whole issue would "blow over" in a few days and that a recall would just tarnish the image of Pegasus Footwear.

The problem did not go away and on Thursday C.C. received an urgent call from an employee in Indonesia who informed him that angry crowds were damaging stores that carried the shoe. Newspapers in the country had reported the story and implied that the product was part of an America plot to discredit and insult Muslims. An international

Muslim organization was now calling for a worldwide boycott of all Pegasus products and there was fear that the problem would spread to other countries with significant Muslim populations. C.C. had just been told that the CEO of Pegasus Footwear was waiting on the telephone to speak with him and that she was quite upset about the whole affair.

Discussion Questions:

1. What went wrong in this situation?
2. Do you think that an early recall of the product would have headed off the problem?
3. What would you recommend to C.C. and Pegasus?

Note: This case is based in part on an actual situation; however, it is a fictionalized account and not intended to represent the facts of the real case.

Case prepared by Charles A. Rarick

Case 30

POTTERS FOR PEACE: THROWING CLAY IN NICARAGUA FOR PEACE AND PROFIT

In 1986 a group of a potters in Washington, DC held a benefit sale to support fellow potters from Nicaragua, and to oppose U.S. military aid to the Nicaraguan contras. One of the organizers of the event created a banner that read: "Potters for Peace," and a nonprofit organization by the same name was soon developed. Potters for Peace (PFP) was created due to the political and economic difficulties of Nicaragua in the 1980s and a desire to see change in a troubled country.

During much of its recent past, Nicaragua has been known for dictators, revolutions, earthquakes, and hurricanes. The second poorest country in the Americas has seen more than its share of difficulties. While the country is now a democracy, and has been since 1990, per capita GDP amounts to only $1,023 and unemployment remains stubbornly high. By some estimates, 50% of the Nicaraguan workforce is unemployed or underemployed. Many Nicaraguans have had to leave their homes in the rural parts of the country to seek work in the larger cities. Many of the rural citizens are experienced artists, with craft skills that have been developed from generation to generation.

Nicaragua gets its name from the Native American tribe name, Nicarao. The tribe name was combined with the Spanish word for water and the name Nicaragua was born. Spanish explorers claimed Nicaragua for Spain, but Spanish rulers had little interest in the territory due to its lack of significant gold and silver deposits. Nicaragua gained its independence from Spain in 1881 and briefly joined the other newly freed Central America countries in a federation. Nicaragua declared its independence in 1883 and has experienced political instability during much of its early existence. American involvement in the internal affairs of the country eventually led to the Somoza family ruling the country. The Somoza's accumulated vast wealth while the people remained extremely poor. An earthquake in 1972 led to the end of Somoza rule in Nicaragua as international funds intended for relief ended up in Somoza family bank accounts. Opposition against the Somoza regime grew and the communist Sandinistas gained power in 1979. The Sandinistas nationalized many industries, and the United States suspended aid to the country in 1980. The U.S. began to fund a counter-revolutionary group, the contras, as the economy of Nicaragua remained in ruins. It was against this backdrop of economic desperation and political instability that a group of altruistic potters from the United States formed an organization to promote the pottery industry of Nicaragua.

Located about an hour's drive from Managua is the town of San Juan de Oriente, the pottery capital of Nicaragua. The town is close to another town well known for its artistry, Masaya. Visitors to San Juan de Oriente pass Masaya and a large figure of Sandino, the inspirational figure of the Sandinistas, as they make their way to the many pottery shops of the town. San Juan de Oriente is the location where Potters for Peace first began its helping operations.

The Nicaraguan potters of San Juan de Oriente have also benefited from another nonprofit group dedicated to advancing the economic welfare of the less fortunate. Pro Mujer is a women's development organization that operates in Latin America and provides micro-loans to female entrepreneurs and women who wish to start a business. Pro Mujer also provides educational activities devoted to entrepreneurial education. The organization has a branch in Nicaragua and has provided over 13,000 micro-loans to women in Nicaragua. A typical example is Elsa del Carmen Mercado Nicoya, a mother of five who used a micro-loan to purchase a potter's wheel and begin her pottery business in San Juan de Oriente.

Another typical potter, Dina Gutierrez owns a pottery store in San Juan de Oriente where she and her mother sell pottery made by the family at home. Dina has an outdoor oven, a room for pottery painting, and several rooms filled with inventory. Not only does Dina sell the family's pottery in her store, but she has also developed an exporting component to her business. Potters for Peace has helped Dina and other women of San Juan de Oriente develop a business that employs the entire family. With few employment opportunities in the area, the family businesses allow a measure of financial independence. Unlike some of its neighbors, Nicaragua does not have a thriving tourism industry. Without a tourist infrastructure in place, Nicaragua is bypassed as other Central American countries such as Costa Rica and Belize attract wealthy visitors from Europe, Asia, and the United States. Many Nicaraguans are forced to work in the country's many free zones, earning a meager living in the many forms of light manufacturing found in those zones.

The women of San Juan de Oriente make pottery basically the same way previously generations before them made their pottery. Clay arrives, sometimes via oxcart to the pottery area from nearby farms and it placed in water to make it more plyable. Sand is added to the clay and the clay is worked to remove any air bubbles. The clay is then shaped into the desired form, and a black liquid form of clay is painted on the object. After drying, the piece is painted again, this time with a white oxide and then dried again. The object is then decorated and placed in a wood-fired kiln and baked. The piece is removed from the kiln and polished, and is then ready for sale. Nicaraguan pottery has increased in popularity in recent years, however, the production process lacks efficiency and is not always considered healthy. The United Nations Industrial Development Organization warns that smoke from the rudimentary ovens of such home-based businesses generate an unhealthy home environment, and that chemicals used, such as oxides, produce an additional hazard to the potters' families. The pottery designs are a mixture of Native American and Spanish influences. San Juan de Oriente pottery is now sold in local retail outlets, to wholesalers in the United States and Central America, through the Internet, and is promoted by Potters for Peace.

Headquartered in Bisbee, Arizona, Potters for Peace seeks to fulfill its dual mission of promoting peace and advancing the economic well being of Nicaraguan pottery makers and other less fortunate artists. The organization's mission statement follows:

POTTERS FOR PEACE MISSION

Our goals are to offer support, solidarity and friendship to developing world potters; assist with appropriate technologies sustained using local skills and material; help preserve cultural traditions; and assist in marketing locally, regionally and internationally.

Potters for Peace refers to itself as a "U.S. based nonprofit network of potters, educators, technicians, supporters, and volunteers interested in peace and social justice issues." The organization does most of its work in Nicaragua, however, recently PFP has branched out into Central America, Asia, and in Africa. Potters for Peace is a registered nonprofit organization and donations made by U.S. citizens are tax deductible.

The organization conducts regional sales of Nicaraguan pottery in Denver, San Francisco, and in Yellow Springs, Ohio. PFP also maintains a booth at the annual National Council for Education in Ceramic Art (NCECA) meeting where they educate the industry about Nicaraguan pottery and their role in its development. PFP conducts educational tours to Nicaragua, with visits to San Juan de Oriente, and supports cultural exchanges among Central American potters. PFP also publishes a newsletter twice a year to inform members of events and to report on the organization's progress.

Potters for Peace maintains a website (www.pottersforpeace.org) through which they solicit donations which can be made through PayPal. Potters for Peace also advertises T-shirts, bumper stickers, coloring books, and clay jewelry through the website. All purchases require the printing of a form, and mailing it to the organization's address in Arizona. The website does not allow for on-line purchases. PFP does not sell pottery directly through its website but lists places where the pottery can be purchased. Currently only eight retailers in the United States are listed on the website as selling Nicaraguan pottery.

When PFP first began to provide assistance to the potters of Nicaragua it was discovered that the potters didn't need help making pottery, they needed funds to buy supplies and equipment. The potters of Nicaragua were skilled in their craft but lacked the ability to effectively market their products. They needed help in promoting their works and exporting them to the United States and Europe. Potters for Peace developed a brochure and organized tours of the area. Potters for Peace also organized informational visits by retailers from the United States such as Pier 1 Imports, which placed a one-time order for 18,000 ceramic pieces.

One of the newer projects PFP promotes is a ceramic water purification system. The portable unit is a low-cost alternative to more expensive systems, and is aimed at residents of less developed countries and victims of natural disasters. The system costs about $10 and requires no electricity to operate. Replacement clay filters cost around $4 and are replaced once a year. The units consist of a porous clay filter that uses colloidal silver as a germicide and disinfectant. Potters for Peace does not sell the filters but promotes their use and teaches potters how to make the filters in order to increase their income opportunities. Although PFP had a significant role in developing the filters, the organization decided not to patent the process in order to ensure widespread usage.

Potters for Peace now seeks to help the poorer and more remote regions of Nicaragua where access to the international market is almost impossible. Potters for Peace found that the transportation costs of moving pottery from these remote locations was prohibitive, and so the organization encouraged the potters of the remote area to develop ceramic jewelry. The jewelry is sold through PFP and other NGOs and church groups. Potters for Peace seeks to generate employment, and give the poor people of Nicaragua dignity. It is hoped that this will promote peace in a country not known for a peaceful existence.

Discussion Questions:

1. Evaluate the mission, activities, and success of Potters for Peace.
2. Can entrepreneurs in less developed countries such as Nicaragua gain access to the global marketplace without the assistance of organizations such as Potters for Peace? Explain.
3. Suggest a marketing strategy that would increase the success of Potters for Peace.

Sources: Barbaformosa. (1998). The potter's wheel. Barcelona, Spain: Parramón Ediciones; Morrison, M. (2002). Nicaragua. New York: Scholastic; Shields, C. (2003). Central America: Facts and figures. Broomall, PA: Mason Crest Publications; Yetter, L. (1999). *Potters for Peace: Throwing clay in Central America*. Living Buddhism, October; Internal documents provided by Peter Chartrand, U.S. Coordinator of Potters for Peace, May, 2005; Personal visit to San Juan de Oriente, Nicaragua on June 24-25, 2005; Telephone interview with Ron Rivera. May 23, 2005; www.adifferentapproach.com. Accessed on May 19, 2005.www.pottersforpeace.org. Accessed on March 3, 2009; www.state.gov –Country Background Notes Nicaragua. Accessed on March 1, 2009; www.promujer.org. Accessed on May 19, 2005; www.seattleedu/asbe/studytour/nicargua/papers/pottery.html. Accessed on May 19, 2005; www.unido.org/doc/5222. Accessed on May 19, 2005.

Case prepared by Charles A. Rarick and Martine Duchatelet

EXERCISE 9

MARKETING TO THE MEXICANS

Purpose: To determine the suitability of a promotional campaign developed in one country for use in another. The exercise is designed to highlight potential differences that should be considered when developing a multinational advertising campaign.

Procedure: Read the short incident below and in small groups discuss why the recommended promotional strategy may not be effective. Also provide suggestions for changing the advertising campaign to be more successful in Mexico.

Incident: The CEO of a successful online investment brokerage firm has decided to enter the Mexican market. He discusses his views with you concerning the firm's promotion in this new market. The CEO feels that the same advertising copy can be utilized, except that Spanish will be substituted for English. The advertisements typically emphasize the firm's low commission structure and operating efficiency. Many of the ads feature a young American couple outsmarting older couples who use traditional brokerage services. The promotional material uses irreverent humor to show that investing wisely leads to long-term financial gain.

PART SIX

IMPORT/ EXPORT, LOCATION DECISIONS, GLOBAL MANUFACTURING

Cases:

Ozark Electronics
A New Dawn for Vietnamese FDI?
Rocko Handbags
Samuel Bonnie: International Entrepreneur
Better Factories Cambodia

Exercise:

Overseas Private Investment Corporation (OPIC)

CASE 31

OZARK ELECTRONICS: PROFITING FROM A FOREIGN TRADE ZONE

Located in Southwest Missouri, Ozark Electronics is a manufacturer of small electrical appliances, such as toasters, toaster ovens, can openers, mixers, and blenders. Ozark assembles these products in its Springfield, Missouri facility using a number of foreign suppliers for component parts. Virtually all products are assembled from parts from Japan, Taiwan, Korea, and China.

All of Ozark's production occurs in the Springfield facility and the company employs over 400 people. Although labor costs might be lower in Mexico or Asia, Ozark has never considered moving its production operations out of the country. Wages and benefit costs are moderate and the work force is productive. Ozark exports approximately 25% of its production output to Latin America, Europe, and Asia. The company hopes to increase its export potential with some product design changes and increased international marketing efforts.

Jim Harrison, vice president of logistics for Ozark, has been communicating with an old college friend who recently took a job at the Toyota production facility in Kentucky. Jim's friend told him that Toyota utilizes a foreign trade zone (FTZ) and that Ozark could benefit from one as well. After further discussions on the telephone, Jim decided to fly to Kentucky to see the Toyota facility and learn more about the FTZ concept.

Jim learned that Toyota imports from Japan component parts for its automobile manufacturing and that by utilizing a FTZ, the company avoids paying any customs duties on the component parts until the cars leave the FTZ. If the autos are exported out of the United States, then Toyota pays no tax on the component parts at all. It was explained to Jim that an FTZ is an area in the United States, that is considered to be international territory, and, therefore, U.S. customs duties do not apply.

Jim has further learned that there are two types of foreign trade zones, a general-purpose trade zone and a subzone. The general-purpose trade zone operates for the benefit of several different companies and the subzone is established for one company's use exclusively. Toyota has a subzone for its production operations in Kentucky. From his visit Jim has decided that there are three benefits to operating in an FTZ: (1) delay of payment of custom duties, (2) possible elimination of custom duties, and (3) the bypassing of U.S. Customs regulations. He is confident that Ozark can realize all three benefits, but he wants to further investigate this idea before he formally presents a proposal for adoption to senior management.

Discussion Questions:

1. Research foreign trade zones and determine if Jim is correct in his assertions concerning the potential benefits.
2. Specifically, how might Ozark benefit from the establishment of an FTZ? Are there any disadvantages?
3. Would you recommend that Ozark establish a subzone? Explain.

Sources: G. Hanks and L. Van "Foreign Trade Zone", <u>Management Accounting</u>, January 1, 1999; J. Daniels and L. Radebaugh, <u>International Business</u>, Upper Saddle River, NJ: Prentice Hall, 2001.

Case prepared by Charles A. Rarick

CASE 32

A NEW DAWN FOR VIETNAMESE FDI?

On February 28th, 2006, Intel Corporation announced its decision to invest $300 million to create a semiconductor assembly and testing facility in Vietnam. Intel Chairman Craig Barrett while in Ho Chi Minh City (formerly known as Saigon) stated, "We applaud the progress the country has made in building up their technology infrastructure and support of education programs to advance the capabilities of the local workforce."

The Intel investment represents the largest U.S. non-oil investment in Vietnam. Prior U.S. investment had mainly been in low-tech manufacturing such as shoes, food processing, and textiles. Vietnam has experienced a sizable, ongoing increase in FDI in recent years, and political leaders hope to expand an economy and improve living standards shattered by wars and poor prior economic performance. While Vietnam has a number of features attractive to foreign investors, some analysts question the desirability of investing in a country that has only recently experienced political stability and economic freedom.

Vietnam has attracted the attention of Western governments since at least the 19th Century. In 1858 the French colonized Vietnam. After internal fighting in an eight-year war, the French signed the

Geneva Agreement in 1954 which led to their withdrawal from the country and the division of Vietnam into the communist north and noncommunist south. The Geneva Agreement required elections to be held for unification, however, the government in the south refused to participate and proclaimed itself the Republic of Vietnam. Armed conflict between the communist north and noncommunist south started shortly thereafter and intensified as the decade progressed.

U.S. involvement commenced in 1961 as President Kennedy sent U.S. military advisors to Vietnam. In 1965 President Johnson sent military combat forces to Vietnam. The war in Vietnam escalated, and without a clear sign of victory the American public grew increasingly tired of the conflict. In 1973 a peace agreement was reached and the U.S. withdrew its military forces. Within two years the communist government from the north invaded the south and unified the country into the Socialist Republic of Vietnam. Many Americans felt the United States had lost the war in Vietnam and still harbor negative views and sentiments about the country.

With its population and economy suffering under the strains of a socialist economic system, the Communist Party of Vietnam - the only political party permitted in the country - instituted a program of economic liberalizations and structural reforms in 1986. The program, referred to as doi moi (renovation) signaled the country was ready to move towards a market economy.

The cornerstone of the doi moi was an export-led economic growth strategy, a strategy that had already been pursued with reasonable success by the so-called "Asian Tigers." Vietnam sought to position itself as a lower cost location than countries such as Taiwan, Hong Kong, and Singapore for targeted manufacturing and assembly operations. Under the doi moi economic sectors and industries with potential for significant export growth were targeted and given preferential treatment in the forms of tax breaks and subsidies. Foreign investment was steered to the preferred sectors to provide the capital necessary to support expansion. Finally, Vietnam instituted a controlled, fixed exchange rate policy designed to maintain an undervalued currency in order to promote exports. While the country has moved towards a market economy, Vietnam still remains a communist country. The Propaganda and Training Department still controls newspapers, books, and even tourism companies to insure that the political ideology of the communist party is maintained. Government bureaucracy and corruption are seen as impediments to further economic growth.

In the late 1980s foreign investment began to flow into Vietnam as economic liberalization began to take shape. Lured by the prospects of cheap labor and untapped markets for consumer and industrial goods, foreign investors made their way to Vietnam in hopes of finding a new "Asian Tiger." The initial inflow of foreign capital was motivated by economic reform (doi moi) and the prospects of an underdeveloped market. Vietnam also benefited from a trend in FDI being directed towards emerging markets and increased intra-regional investment and trade in Southeast Asia. The enthusiasm for FDI in Vietnam, however, didn't last long, as communist bureaucracy and corruption began to make the country a less attractive market. Many early investors retreated from Vietnam and FDI peaked in 1996. The Asian financial crisis of 1997 further dampened foreign investor interest. Subsequent to the liberalization of the economy, Vietnam began to experience significant inflows of foreign direct investment and rapid economic growth. Real GDP expanded at a robust 9.00 percent annual rate from 1993 to 1997. Per capita income more than doubled, rising from about $810 in 1987 to roughly $1750 in 1997. Many Western companies raced into Vietnam during this period due to its low labor costs, the preferential treatment provided by the government and the view that Vietnam was an untapped market for industrial and consumer goods. With the sudden drop in foreign investment in 1997, Vietnamese leaders knew a different direction in policy was needed.

Vietnam responded to the problems experienced by foreign investors and made some necessary changes. These changes re-affirmed its commitment to economic liberalization and international integration, and allowed it to become a member of the ASEAN Free Trade Area. In December 2001, Vietnam signed a bilateral trade agreement with the United States and started the process of applying for membership in the World Trade Organization. Once again, FDI has begun to make its way back into Vietnam. With rising labor costs in China, increased trade agreements with the United States and the EU, and the expected entry into the World Trade Organization (WTO), Vietnam attracted foreign investment at record rates. By the end of 2004, Vietnam had over 5,000

FDI projects worth more than $46 billion. Vietnam attracted a record $1.3 billion in FDI in the first two months of 2006. Vietnam in 2005 attracted more FDI, as a percent of GDP, than China.

Economic growth has also accelerated in Vietnam. After slowing to an annual growth rate of less than 7.00 percent from 1998 to 2004, real GDP advanced by about 8.00 percent in 2005. Per capita income reached $3,000. Moreover, there are a number of reasons to expect economic growth, per capita income, and FDI to continue to expand in coming years. Factory workers in Vietnam earn on average $55 a month and are considered to be hardworking and dedicated employees. Vietnam has a young population, with two-thirds of its 84 million inhabitants in the prime working ages of 16 to 64. It has a literacy rate of 96% and a growing middle class. English is favored as a second language providing an advantage to global commerce. Vietnam also offers lower production costs, not only due to low labor rates, but also because of additional lower operating costs including land, rents, and shipping expenses.

International investors consider Vietnam's political environment to be an increasingly stable one. Although Vietnam has a communist form of government, it has provided stability, unlike its neighbor Thailand which experienced a bloodless coup in September 2006. Vietnam has not suffered from the internal Islamic terrorist attacks which have occurred in Thailand and the Philippines. Vietnam also offers an attractive alternative to firms who seek to diversify their supply sources in the region. These and other factors have prompted A.T. Kearney, the international consulting firm, to rank Vietnam twentieth of the top twenty-five countries in its 2004 Offshore Location Attractiveness Index. Kearney's index ranked Vietnam the second highest, trailing only India, in categories such as compensation costs, infrastructure costs, and tax and regulatory costs. However, Kearney's index placed Vietnam at the low range of the rankings in categories related to people skills and availability, and business environment. According to the Kearney Index Vietnam's attractiveness ranked it ahead of countries such as Russia, Spain and Ireland but behind countries such as Malaysia, Thailand and the Philippines.

The decision by Intel to invest in Vietnam is seen by some as confirmation that Vietnam has arrived as a major international player in the global sourcing game. Intel chose Vietnam over Thailand, the Philippines, Malaysia, and China mainly due to its low production costs. As Chairman Barrett stated, when responding to why Intel chose Vietnam, "Cost is always a driving force." Intel continues to operate manufacturing facilities in China, Malaysia, the Philippines, and Costa Rica. It appears likely that Intel will continue to invest in Vietnam. According to Barrett, "We consider this to be a small step in a long journey of involvement in Vietnam."

Intel is not the only large, multi-national technology company showing interest in Vietnam. Canon is building a manufacturing plant in Vietnam to produce ink jet printers and Fujitsu is already producing circuit boards for personal computers and telephones in the country. Nidec plans to build two plants to manufacture electronic components, and Sparton of Michigan, from the United States, makes chemical diagnostic equipment in Vietnam. Intel's facility will be located in the Saigon High Tech Park in Ho Chi Minh City, where a number of foreign software firms are currently operating.

While it appears that Vietnam may have a new day dawning for foreign investment, the country still has a number of difficulties that may make the future less certain. Vietnam remains a one-party communist country, and some of the problems that early investors experienced still are present. Although the country has become more capitalistic the government maintains significant control over the economy and operates many state-owned enterprises. Corruption and government bureaucracy continue to be problems, as well as a poor infrastructure, and restrictive laws concerning business operations. The region is also perhaps more vulnerable to an outbreak of the deadly H5N1 (bird flu) virus which is expected to cause economic turmoil, especially in countries ill-prepared for its arrival.

Vietnam imposes export taxes on some products and maintains high import tariffs on products that the government desires to be produced locally. Both export and import taxes have been reduced or eliminated in recent years, however, the government has a history of making policy changes quickly in order to achieve its objectives in international trade. The government maintains tight control over FDI, and this regulation is fragmented and sometimes ambiguous. Vietnam still is a developing country and its rule of law is considered weak by many observers. Vietnam ranks 99th out of 155 countries tracked by the World Bank in terms of the ease of doing business. Particular concerns include restrictions on hiring and firing employees, protection of foreign assets, and contract enforcement. The Fraser Institute, in its Economic Freedom of the World 2003 report ranked Vietnam 103rd of 127 countries – the lowest of all evaluated Southeast Asian nations except Myanmar. The Fraser Institute scored Vietnam low in areas related to the size of government, security of property rights, and access to sound money but considerably higher in categories dealing with freedom to trade internationally and regulation of credit, labor and business. Vietnam must continue to compete with other countries in the region in order to attract foreign investment. Compared to Thailand, for example, Vietnam is considered to be more corrupt, maintains more restrictions on foreign investment, and has a weaker rule of law and contract enforcement, a weaker currency, and a less desirable quality of life for expatriate managers.

Discussion Questions:

1. Do some types of FDI make more sense than others for international investors? Explain.
2. What role, if any, does the political system of a country play in its attractiveness as a host for FDI?
3. Do research comparing the attractiveness of Vietnam (as a host country for FDI) with other Southeast Asian nations. What factors make it more and less attractive compared to other Southeast Asian nations?

Sources: Anonymous. (2006). Merrill Lynch Upbeat on Investing in Vietnam. *Vietnam Business Forum, February 9; Anonymous. (2005).* Vietnam: Investment Regulations. *EIU News Wire, May 9; Balfour, F. (2006).* Good Morning Vietnam: Intel's Deal to Build a Factory is Likely to Spur More Western Investment. *Business Week, March 13; Buchel, B. and T. Lai Xuan. (2001).* Measures of Joint Venture Performance from Multiple Perspectives: An Evaluation of Local and Foreign Managers in Vietnam. *Asian Pacific Journal of Management, 18(1), 101-111; Freeman, N. (2002).* Foreign Direct Investment in Vietnam: An Overview. *DfID Workshop on Globalization and Poverty in Vietnam, September 13-14; Johnson, K. (2006).* Vietnam Trades Up: By Joining the WTO, Asia's Second Fastest Growing Economy is Poised to Kick its Exports into High Gear. *Time Asia, November 13; Kazmin, A. (2006).* Intel to Spend $300M on Chip Plant in Vietnam. *Financial Times, February 28; Minh, A. (2006).* It's High Time for FDI. *Vietnam Economic News, 49 (6); A.T. Kearney (2005).* Making Offshore Decisions: A.T. Kearney's 2004 Offshore Location Attractiveness Index; *Prasso, S. (1999).* Vietnam: Welcome Back? *Business Week. August, 16; Stone, M. (2006).* Battle for the History of the Vietnam War. *Vietnam. June; Venard, B. (1998).* Vietnam in Mutation: Will it be the Next Tiger or a Future Jaguar? *Asian pacific Journal of Management, 15(1), 77-95; Webster, L. (1999).* The New Breed. *Vietnam Business Journal, 8(4), 1-8.*
www.business-in-china.com/investment.comparison.html Accessed on March 15, 2006.
www.cia.gov/publications/factbook/geos/vm.html. Accessed on May 22, 2006.
www.china-asean.net/asean_biz/vietnam/investment. Accessed on March 15, 2006.
www.fraserinstitute.ca/admin/books/chapterfiles/EFW2005ch1. Accessed on May 22, 2006; www.intel.com Accessed on March 14, 2006; www.state.gov/backgroundnotes/Vietnam. Accessed on June 8, 2002.

Case prepared by Charles A. Rarick and Stephen O. Morrell

ROCKO HANDBAGS, LTD: PROFITING FROM SELLING BELOW COST?

Rocko Handbags manufactures and sells a variety of upscale purses, totes, and other handbags under its popular label. An enterprising young woman named Natalia Martinez, who developed a popular purse, invented the name Rocko, and developed a European flavor for the brand. She formed the company five years ago and it has done well, commanding a premium price for its products, which are especially popular among teenagers and young women.

At present, the brand is only sold in the United States and Canada. All products are manufactured in the company's Georgia plant, but Rocko has created the illusion that the products are really Italian designer bags. Natalia's promotion message emphasizes European style and quality even though each bag carries a label identifying that the product is "Made in the U.S.A." Savvy promotion has kept the European image alive and it has served the company well.

Natalia wants to develop this image and strong brand loyalty internationally. She hopes to duplicate her domestic success by first entering the Latin American market and later Asia. Through personal contacts, she has been introduced to the senior buyer for a major retail chain in Brazil who expressed interest in carrying the popular Pippi bag. This bag is especially popular among American teens and the Brazilian buyer feels that it probably would be equally popular among young women in Brazil.

Natalia has just received an offer from the Brazilian retailer to supply 20,000 Pippi bags at a price of $18 per unit. Natalia is surprised and disappointed by the offer, since the Pippi bag is sold to retailers in the United States at $42 per unit. After consultation with Rocko's accountants, Natalia learns that the $18 offer is below the cost of production. The total production cost per unit for the Pippi is $20, and in addition, the accountants worry that not only will Rocko lose $2 for each of the 20,000 units, but also the premium image may be jeopardized if the offer is accepted. There is concern that the product would be sold in Brazil at a price considerably lower than the average U.S. retail price of $55 to $65.

Natalia does not see how she can accept the offer; however, she does want to enter the South American market as soon as possible. Her accountants advise against the move at this time based on their financial analysis (shown below). Although the Georgia plant (operating at 70% capacity) could produce the additional units at this time, Natalia is concerned with the potential loss of profits and prestige.

Pippi Product Line
Cost Analysis

Total Fixed Cost (salaries, depreciation, utilities): $500,000

Variable Cost per Unit:

Direct Labor	$13.00
Direct Materials	2.00
Total per Unit	$15.00

Average Volume - Units per Year:	100,000
Average Fixed Cost (500,000/100,000)	$5.00
Variable Cost	$15.00
Cost per Unit to Produce	$20.00

Discussion Questions:

1. Will Natalia lose money if she accepts the Brazilian offer? Explain.
2. What factors other than costs and revenue should be considered in this case?
3. What would you recommend to Natalia?

Case prepared by Charles A. Rarick

CASE 34

SAMUEL P. BONNIE: INTERNATIONAL ENTREPRENEUR

Emily Devine could not stop staring at the customer sitting at table five. She knew it was wrong to stare, but she could not help herself. Ever since the man walked into the café on South Beach, where Emily works to pay for her MBA classes, she could not shake the feeling that she knew this man's face. He was very handsome, perhaps he was a model, or better yet, an actor or musician. It was not unusual to see rich and famous people in the café on Miami Beach. The man was reading some papers that looked very much like a business plan, and Emily nearly dropped the food in his lap as she read over his shoulder while placing his order on the table. All she managed to see was the letterhead SPB International. Again Emily could not help but feel like she knew that name. "Oh well" sighed Emily, "I better forget about him and get back to my work or I will be looking for a new job."

It was not until that night when Emily was researching a paper her economics class that it dawned on her who this man was. "Where did I put that magazine?" she wondered as she searched the piles of books and journals cluttering here desktop. Finally she found it, last month's issue of *Young Entrepreneur*, and there he was on the cover.

She recalled reading the article last month and thinking how he was so good-looking, charming and smart. Emily decided that this is whom she would write her report about and sat down to reread the story of SPB International founder, Samuel P. Bonnie.

Samuel P. Bonnie, Sam to his friends, was just an ordinary guy. He liked to hang out with friends, fish, surf, and when he had a little extra time on his hands, he dabbled with molecular chemistry. It was on one of those rainy afternoons in South Florida that Sam made what turned out to be the greatest mistake of his life. It seems that he was fooling around with the properties of foam rubber in order to come up with a better beer coolie to keep his beer cold when he went out fishing. (You know those foam rubber things that people stick beer cans in; they usually have advertising on them.) Sam was trying to develop a liquid that could be put on the foam rubber that would increase its insulation qualities. Sam told the story this way:

> "I was working in my garage lab, and had just put the foam rubber into a tub of the chemical compound when I heard Jack at the door. You all know Jack, Jack Hughes the "American Dream Boy" who won the Gold Medal in cycling at the Olympics in Sydney. I met him when he was in Florida training for the Olympics. Anyway, Jack, who had stopped his training ride because of the rain, and I started talking and watching TV. I think the Wimbledon tournament was on, and I forgot about the experiment in the garage. About an hour later I remembered and ran out to the garage to take the foam rubber out of the solution. The strangest thing had happened. The foam rubber had become hard and what was more peculiar, it had somehow lost over ½ of its weight. About that time the rain had stopped and Jack decide he was going to head home before it started up again. He was putting his bike helmet on when I got a crazy idea..."

The article recalled how Sam spent the next few weeks fashioning a bicycle helmet out of foam rubber and treating it in the same solution. Jack tried the helmet and liked it so much that he wore it to train, and eventually in the Olympics where he won the Gold. There was a great deal of talk in the cycling world (where events can be won by fractions of a second) about "Mr. Hughes' New Helmet." The article went on to quote Sam on his strong beliefs about social welfare. Emily read this with fascination.

"It has always bothered me to see companies become rich off the blood and sweat of the third world people. Now do not get me wrong I am not saying that companies should not do business in the third world, I just believe that if they do they should be ethical. Pay the workers a wage that will house and feed a family and do not hire children to work when they should be going to school. I mean this is not rocket science, just treat people with basic respect."

Young Entrepreneur told of how SPB International's plant was one of the first to receive SA 8000 certification for socially responsible manufacturing. SA 8000 certification indicates to the world that the manufacturer who possesses this certification has passed an independent audit of employment practices in areas such as health and safety, discrimination, free association, child labor, working conditions, compensation, and management systems. Employers who are SA 8000 certified agree to pay a living wage, refrain from engaging in forced or child labor, allow employees to join labor unions if they desire, and provide fair and humane working conditions and supervision. The article described how SPB International had recently built a school and a medical clinic at the plant. These facilities were free to workers and their families, as well as other local people.

Jessica Francis and Bryan Saba, the senior partners of Francis & Saba Consulting, had advised SPB International as it was starting out. They both were greatly impressed by Sam's business savvy. "Sam brought us in to advise on several aspects of the business, but in actuality we just confirmed most of his decisions" Saba said when interviewed for the article. "It was amazing," gushed Francis, "I have never seen a new comer to an industry make all the right decisions." Francis and Saba had analyzed the bicycle helmet industry. They had discovered that the global market was $230 million and that there were seven firms in the industry with the top 4 firms claiming $195 million or 85% of the market. Francis and Saba had considered advising Sam not to enter such a concentrated market. "We had prepared our report advising Sam to sell his patent to one of the big boys in the market and to live well on the proceeds until Congress changed everything", Francis remembered.

Jessica Francis was referring to the Bicycle Helmet Act of 2000. In an attempt to lower the staggeringly high number of deaths caused by head trauma resulting from bicycle accidents, and under extreme pressure from the insurance lobby, the United States Congress passed a two-pronged law. The law provided that any state that failed to pass legislation requiring every cyclist to wear a helmet would lose 85% of all federal highway funds it currently received. The bill also allows for tax incentives for companies that produce helmets.

Most of the states were quick to respond, passing laws that fined un-helmeted cyclists from $500 to $5,000. Many of the states offered subsidies to low-income cyclists that would pay up to half the price of a helmet. Sam recalled what happened next.

> "The American market was going to explode, and here I was sitting on a new formula that could produce better lighter helmets at a fraction of the cost. I had to get into the market. But you cannot wade into a market like that a little at a time, you have to jump in, and jump in big. You know like a cannonball. I knew that the current firms in the industry were not going to make it easy for me. But I was the man who designed the helmet that won the Gold Medal and I think maybe I was just too dumb to be scared. I took all of my savings and got a loan from a buddy of mine who had gotten rich during the dot com boom. (He was one of the few who knew when to get out.) I found a place where we could get the helmets produced and then with the help of Jack as a spokesman I started getting these things on the market."

"Boy" Emily thought, "I can't believe this guy. He is so smart and socially minded, yet he is so humble too." Emily read the conclusion of the article, which outlined the success of SPB International. SPB International has already claimed ten percent of the American market and according to Sam they are now looking at new markets.

> "We may have gotten lucky with the timing on this thing but the truth is we have the best product on the market. If it weren't for Congress, we might not have gotten this big this fast, but I think we would have gotten here eventually. We are now moving into the European market. Jack has done a good job as spokesman here in the US for us but in Europe

he is very well known, so we are talking to the better known champions of last year's *Tour de France* about endorsement deals. I expect our sales to become huge in Europe. Besides expanding geographically, we are now looking at branching out into the production of motorcycle helmet industry and construction hardhats.

And you know, I still need to work on that beer coolie..."

Emily decided that she would use this company as the subject of a paper she needed to write for her economics class. As SPB International expanded, Sam was looking for additional locations in which to establish manufacturing operations. Emily knew from the article that SPB was considering three countries: Indonesia, Cote d'Ivoire (Ivory Coast), and Moldova. An initial investigation into the backgrounds of these countries produced the following information:

	INDONESIA	COTE D'IVOIRE	MOLDOVA
Population	238M	19M	4.2M
Population Growth Rate	1.2%	3.8%	-.3%
Main Religion(s)	Islam	Islam, Christian, Indigenous	Orthodox
Government	Republic	Republic	Republic
GDP	$433B	$33B	$4.5B
Per Capita GDP	$3700 US	$1740 US	$1259 US
Life Expectancy	62 years	46 years	67 years

As Emily looked over these data it became clear to her that there were perhaps more things to consider in a location decision.

Discussion Questions

1. Is Sam's attitude about social welfare and corporate responsibility typical of an entrepreneur? Is it desirable? Explain.
2. What additional information should Emily consider in her analysis for country selection?

3. Which country should SPB International chose for its next manufacturing facility?

Sources: Baye Michael, (2000) <u>Managerial Economics & Business Strategy</u>. Boston, MA: McGraw-Hill Higher Education; Pfeffer Jeffrey, (1998) <u>The Human Equation</u>. Boston, MA: Harvard Business School Press; Social Accountability International's website: <u>http://www.cepaa.org</u>; State Department Country Background Notes: <u>http://www.state.gov</u>.; Van Horn, James, (2002) <u>Financial Management & Policy</u>. Upper Saddle River, NJ: Prentice Hall; <u>World Facts and Maps</u>, Rand McNally 2000 Millennium Edition.

Case prepared by Michael Wilcox, Martine Duchatelet, and Charles A. Rarick

CASE 35

BETTER FACTORIES CAMBODIA: HOPING TO BUILD A COUNTRY VOID OF SWEATSHOPS

Many of the employees who work in Cambodian factories do not earn enough money to afford the goods they produce. The young women in Cambodia who work in the garment industry sewing Disney characters onto pajamas cannot afford the products they are making. Many do not even know much about Mickey Mouse, Cinderella, or the other treasured Disney characters. Working long hours for low pay, under less than ideal working conditions, is common in Cambodia. Even though government imposed minimum wage levels, and working conditions are very low by Western standards, getting employers to honor those standards has been difficult. International companies that contract with manufacturers in developing countries have increasingly come under scrutiny by consumer groups because of the poor working conditions and employment practices of those local manufacturers. One country which is trying to improve the working conditions of its citizens and improve its image is Cambodia.

Cambodia is located in Southeast Asia and borders Vietnam to the east, Thailand to the west, and Laos to the north. Cambodia's 14 million inhabitants are some of the poorest people in the region, and have suffered some of the worst experiences in recent human history. Cambodia gained its independence from France in 1953 and experienced war and major political upheaval until free elections were conducted in 1993. Cambodia was an unwilling participant in the military conflict between Vietnam and the United States, and for a time, was occupied by Vietnamese forces. Under the regime of the Khmer Rouge and its leader Pol Pot, Cambodia experienced the horrors of genocide and the starvation of its people. Cities were evacuated and educated people were considered enemies of the state. Mass executions and starvation resulted in the deaths of an estimated 1.7 million to 3 million people. With a peace accord signed in 1991, and elections held in 1993, Cambodia began the long process of rebuilding itself. The garment industry of Cambodia is a major export for the country and employs hundreds of thousands of Cambodians. Cambodia, with a per capita GDP of only $450, seeks to become a competitive location for low wage manufacturing. One of the areas in which Cambodian leaders see promise for improved economic conditions in their country is in low-skilled manufacturing. Wage levels are very low in Cambodia (minimum wage of $45 per month for a 48 hour work week) and government leaders feel this advantage can attract foreign contract manufacturing opportunities. One concern, however, is the perception that Cambodian factories are little more than sweatshop operations in which workers are exploited due to their desperate economic situation.

Better Factories Cambodia was established as a result of a trade agreement between the United States and Cambodia. Under the agreement, the United States agreed to increased market access for Cambodian goods if these goods would be produced under better working conditions. Better Factories Cambodia became a project of the International Labour Organization (ILO), a specialized agency of the United Nations (UN) which seeks to promote social justice, human rights, and better working conditions. The ILO, headquartered in Geneva, sets minimum standards for employment such as freedom of association and the right to unionize, equal employment opportunity, and humane working conditions and pay. One of the core beliefs of the ILO is that "poverty anywhere constitutes a danger to prosperity everywhere." The ILO has been working to improve the living conditions of workers in developing countries, and partners with other organizations to implement and enforce generally agreed upon employment standards. While wage levels in Cambodia are low, the country is in a less competitive position overall in terms of being a desirable manufacturing environment. Cambodia, with its recent political past, has a poor image in the minds of many foreign companies. The country's infrastructure is less than ideal and worker productivity, while reasonable by developing country standards, is lower than China and Vietnam. Better Factories Cambodia seeks to increase the competitiveness of the country by focusing on the issue of image and making the country competitive with its neighbors through good employment standards.

Better Factories Cambodia is managed by the ILO and supported by the government of Cambodia. The organization monitors the employment practices of manufacturing firms in the country and has certified over 200 companies, meaning that they meet the basic international standards for humane employment practices. An incentive for company participation is the requirement of certification in order to gain an export license from the government. Participating companies sign a memorandum of understanding in which they agree to abide by certain employment standards and open their factories to inspection. Better Factories Cambodia conducts unannounced factory inspections and uses a 500 item checklist in its inspections. The audit covers issues such as wages, hours, child labor, and worker safety. Auditors, who have been trained in Cambodian and international employment standards, inspect the factories and conduct interviews with employees both on and away from the worksite. The results of the audits are available for public inspection through the website of Better Factories Cambodia. The estimated cost of the program is less than $3 per employee per year and the program is supported by the government of Cambodia and a number of international companies such as Disney, Nike, Adidas, and Levi Strauss. Better Factories Cambodia competes with other auditing agencies such as Social Accountability International (SAI) which certifies companies with its SA 8000 designation, and with the auditing processes of separate international companies such as Wal-Mart who conduct their own audits of companies that make the products they sell.

One area of <u>concern</u> is the <u>reliability and credibility</u> of the auditing <u>process</u>. In China, where more attention has been directed recently to labor conditions and social auditing, a number of cases of <u>corruption</u> in the auditing process have been <u>uncovered</u>. It appears that manufacturers keep <u>separate records</u> concerning <u>wages</u> and <u>working conditions</u> and regularly <u>instruct</u> their <u>employees</u> on how <u>to respond</u> to the questions posed by the auditors. In <u>some cases</u>, much of the work is subcontracted to other firms that are <u>hidden from</u> the <u>auditing process</u>. Such practices are not unique to China and can be found throughout Southeast Asia as well, especially in the poorer countries of the region, including Cambodia. Few workers in developing countries are inclined to speak honestly to outsiders if they feel that such action will result in possible job loss. Many of the workers have little opportunity for other employment. In many developing countries factory workers come from rural parts of the country and are willing to endure long work hours with low pay due to the lack of better opportunities. Take the case of Deth Chrib, who survived the death squads of the Khmer Rouge only to find herself and her two children back in Phnom Penh working as a prostitute in order to support her family. Her current job at June Textiles, where she sews for 16 hours a day, makes her very happy. She is, however, in danger of losing that job due to Western media reports of child labor being used by June Textiles and the threatened cancellation of contracts by Nike and the Gap. While Deth would prefer to work fewer hours and to receive better compensation, her present job is much better than the other opportunities available to her.

Some producers complain that the standards increase their costs which they are not able to pass on to their international buyers. One such contractor, Ron Chang of Shoetown Footwear states, "We can't ask Nike to increase our price. How can we afford to pay the higher salary?" Some critics of the system argue that companies such as <u>Wal-Mart</u> and <u>Nike</u> continue to <u>demand lower prices</u> from their <u>suppliers</u> and <u>this increases</u> the <u>likelihood</u> that <u>manufacturers</u> will <u>find ways of cheating</u> the <u>auditing system</u>. Factories <u>owned</u> and <u>directly controlled</u> by <u>international companies</u> operating in developing countries seem to experience fewer problems with unethical and illegal employment practices.

Better Factories Cambodia is on a mission - to rid Cambodia of sweatshops and to be the model country in terms of socially responsible manufacturing. The organization hopes that by creating an image of a sweatshop free country, Cambodia will be able to effectively compete for international manufacturing contracts.

Discussion Questions:

1. Do consumers care how the goods they purchase were produced? Should they care?

2. Rank the following participants in terms of responsibility for insuring humane working conditions in foreign manufacturing operations: consumers, local manufacturing management, multinational firms who contract the production, local governments.

3. Do you think Better Factories Cambodia will be successful? What can the organization do to insure the completion of its mission?

Sources: Better Factories Cambodia Newsletter. February, 2007; Chon, G. (2000). *Inside story: Cambodia: Dropped stitches*. Asia Week, December 22; ILO Report: Better Factories Cambodia and the World Bank: Justice for the poor program. (2006). New York: International Labor Organization; Kazmin, A. (2005). *The rag trade patches up its image*. Financial Times. September 13; Roberts, D., P. Engardio, A. Bernstein, and S. Homes. (2006). *Secrets, lies, and sweatshops*. Business Week. November 27; www.betterfactories.org. Accessed on April 10, 2007; www.ilo.org. Accessed on April 10, 2007; www.sa-intl.org. Accessed on April 10, 2007; www.state. gov. Accessed on April 10, 2007.

Case prepared by Charles A. Rarick and Kasia Firlej.

EXERCISE 10

WEB-BASED EXERCISE:
EXPORT ASSISTANCE

Web Address: www.export.gov

Purpose: To gain an understanding of the assistance which is provided to American companies seeking to export their products.

Procedure: Visit the Webpage list above and explore the various methods by which the government of the United States helps companies seeking to export. Write a one page essay on those methods.

EXERCISE 11

WEB-BASED EXERCISE:
OVERSEAS PRIVATE INVESTMENT CORPORATION (OPIC)

Web Address: www.opic.gov

Purpose: To gain a better understanding of the functions of this private, international agency and its role in global financing.

Procedure: Visit the web page of the Overseas Private Investment Corporation (OPIC) and answer the four questions below.

Questions:

1. When was OPIC started, where does it get its funding, and what services does it provide?
2. What types of funding are available from OPIC?
3. What protection does OPIC political risk insurance provide?
4. Select a recent OPIC project and briefly explain what it seeks to accomplish.

PART SEVEN

INTERNATIONAL HUMAN RESOURCE MANAGEMENT AND CULTURE

Cases:

A Gringo Manager in Mexico
Kidnapped in Colombia
Good Career Move?
AmeriTech in the Philippines
Bindi Auto Parts - India
An Expat in Paris

Exercise:
Hofstede's Cultural Classification Model

CASE 36

A GRINGO MANAGER IN MEXICO

Ted Dorman was looking forward to his new assignment as plant manager at a newly formed American-Mexican joint venture in Guadalajara, Mexico. The American company, Sterling Metal, produced hardware and decorative fixtures for furniture manufacturers in the United States and Mexico. The new joint venture was an attempt to lower labor costs by operating in Mexico.

Ted had worked at Sterling Metal since graduating from college with a degree in accounting. He had worked his way up in the company through accounting, and eventually shifted his career focus to production. Ted found the challenges of managing the production function very interesting, and he was successful in this area. His position at the new company, SterMexicana, would be a promotion for him, and he looked forward to the opportunity of building a new company.

Although Ted had not worked outside the United States before, he felt confident that his managerial abilities would transfer "south of the border." He and his wife enjoyed vacationing in Cancun and they both liked Mexican food, so the idea of spending a few years building a new company in Mexico appealed to him. Ted's wife, Kim was not as excited about the move, since she and their two small children would have to leave family and friends. Kim would also probably not be working in Mexico, as she had done in the United States.

Before the move, both Ted and Kim read travel books on Mexico and visited Guadalajara to select suitable housing. While Kim had reservations about the move, she felt that it would be a good opportunity for Ted and that she and the children would learn to adapt to their new surroundings. After all, she reasoned, they were only planning on living in Mexico for two years; just long enough for Ted to get the plant up and running and profitable. None of the Dorman's spoke Spanish fluently; however, Kim thought that she could get by, since she had taken three years of Spanish in high school. She had heard that Guadalajara was home to a large expatriate community, and that she could isolate herself and the children from Mexican culture if she felt the need. Ted would be working with English speakers mostly, and many people at the plant could translate for him. A number of SterMexicana managers had been to the United States and were familiar with its culture. Ted and Kim concluded that cultural adaptation would not be difficult, and no matter how hard the assignment, its short duration was manageable.

When the family arrived in Guadalajara, Manuel Angel Menendez Mata met them at the airport. Manuel would be Ted's Mexican counterpart, acting in the official capacity of assistant plant manager, and unofficially as a cultural mentor. Ted and Kim were surprised by the warmth and friendliness of Manuel and his wife Adriana, and they felt very welcomed by their new Mexican friends. Over the next few days Manuel and Adriana helped the new expatriates get settled in and familiar with their new home. Ted appreciated the personal attention Manuel was giving him and his family; however, Ted was anxious to begin discussing the needs of the new business. It sometimes seemed to Ted that Manuel didn't care to discuss the business or that he was very excited about the new opportunity. Manuel seemed more interested in showing Ted and his family the city and discussing its history, politics, and culture.

Once the Dorman family had settled in, Ted was able to turn his attention toward the business. He had many matters to attend to, including a review of the preliminary work Manuel had done in securing the facility, hiring a work force, and establishing an organizational structure. Manuel explained what he had done and how it would work well. He predicted that the new plant would be fully functional in less than two weeks. Ted was very impressed with Manuel's work and looked forward to the opening of the plant.

During their many conversations, Ted felt that Manuel was very friendly and polite, but that he was a bit too formal and not very relaxed. Manuel wore a suit and tie, even when Ted told him that a more casual form of dress would be appropriate. Ted stated that he had no intention of ever wearing a tie the whole time he would be in Mexico. Manuel sometimes referred to Ted as "Mr. Dorman," even though Ted had instructed him to call him by his first name. During their meetings with outside business associates, Ted noticed that Manuel was even more formal. Manuel, who had visited the United States many times and spoke English very well, understood that Americans were more relaxed when it came to such matters, but he was not happy when Ted began to call him "Manny." Manuel was also unhappy with Ted's refusal to recognize his title, "Licenciado" (licensed one), and that he sometimes referred to him as Senor Mata.

Although things seemed to be progressing toward the opening of the plant, Ted began to worry that Manuel's estimate of when the plant would be functional was too optimistic. Manuel insisted that everything was on schedule and that there would be no problems. It did, however, become obvious as the days went by that the plant was not going to be ready, as Manuel had promised. Ted felt that he had been misled by Manny and that he would have to explain to his superiors back in the U.S. why the plant was not going to open on schedule. Manuel finally admitted that some problems had developed with work permits, but he assured Ted that the plant would be operational in an additional week's time. The plant finally opened, five weeks past the scheduled date.

This delay caused tension between Manuel and Ted, and Ted felt that he could not trust Manuel. Manuel felt that Ted was too impatient, and that he was not sensitive enough to the problems sometimes found in conducting business in Mexico. Manuel complained to a friend that Ted was trying to do business in Mexico, "gringo style." He offered as an example the failed attempt Ted had made to establish a business relationship with a new supplier. Manuel had arranged for a business lunch between Ted, himself, and representatives from a well-respected metals supplier. Manuel explained how Ted offended the Mexican businessmen by attempting to get down to business quickly. The supplier's representatives felt that Ted was too concerned about business matters, especially price, and that he was rushing to close a deal. They were also offended when Manuel offered to take the visiting businessmen on a tour of the city and show them some important cultural sites and Ted refused to come along. Ted later told Manuel that he felt that the suppliers were not really serious about getting SterMexicana's business, and that, if they wanted to do business with the company, they would have to send only one representative to his office with samples and a price list. Ted told Manuel that he would no longer spend hours discussing politics, sports, and history without any consideration given to the actual business deal.

The plant had been functioning for about six months without any serious problems when Ted received word from corporate headquarters that the plant needed to improve its efficiency. The quality of the product was considered acceptable, however, the American managers were disappointed with the productivity of the plant. Sterling's main incentive for investing in Mexico was the desire to reduce its labor costs and improve its overall operational efficiency. Ted worried that his career mobility was in serious jeopardy if he did not make major improvements. With this in mind, Ted began to look more carefully at Manuel's work.

From the beginning Ted had turned over to Manuel the day-to-day responsibility for running the plant, but he now felt that he would have to intervene and make some significant changes. After analyzing the situation Ted concluded that three major changes should be made. He proposed to Manuel that an incentive pay system be introduced, that a more participative approach to decision making be implemented, and that a number of workers be fired.

The productivity level of the plant was considered low by American standards and Ted felt that there was simply no incentive for workers to do more than the minimum level of work. He proposed a pay-for-performance plan in which workers would essentially be paid on a piece-rate basis. The workers would also be given more responsibility for planning and organizing their work, and, in some cases, even planning their own schedules. Ted felt that a more flexible scheduling system would eliminate the excessive time off requested by many workers to handle family matters. Ted also created a list of the lowest-performing workers and instructed Manuel to fire all of them immediately. Since the unemployment rate was much higher in Mexico than in the United States, Ted reasoned that he would have no problem replacing the workers.

Manuel was stunned by what he was hearing from Ted. Manuel was upset, first, that Ted had chosen to invade his areas of responsibility, and he was further upset by Ted's recommendations. Manuel felt that Ted was being too aggressive and insensitive in labor relations matters, and that his recommendations would not be successful in Mexico. He told Ted that there would be problems with these proposed changes; however, Ted did not seem to want to listen.

Although Manuel did not agree with the recommendations, he did as Ted had instructed and began by firing some of the employees Ted had targeted as low performers. He then implemented the pay-for-performance plan and attempted to explain how it would work. Most workers felt confused by the complex, flexible working-hours plan, which involved basic quotas, a two-tiered pay system, and a time borrowing option, which could be used for personal time off, such as doctor's appointments. Manuel simplified the plan so that workers could go home when they had met their quota, or they could continue to work for additional compensation at a slightly lower per-unit rate. Ted felt that workers would be willing to work longer hours even at a reduced rate if their total compensation would rise. After all, he reasoned, "Mexico is a dirt-poor country and people really need money." Finally, Manuel told the plant supervisors about the plan to empower factory workers and allow them some of the decision-making authority that the supervisors had exercised in the past.

Ted had high hopes that his recommendations for change would produce significant improvements at SterMexicana. He was aware that Mexican culture was different from his; however, he felt that business activities were for the most part universal and that efficiency was not a cultural issue. Ted felt that the proposed changes would result in an immediate improvement in overall operating efficiency.

Slowly, however, Ted began to realize that problems were developing with his recommendations. The first problem he confronted was notification that severance pay would have to be paid to the employees he had recently fired. Ted was unaware, and Manuel did not mention, that Mexican law does not operate the same way as U.S. law, in which workers are considered to be hired at will and subject to at-will termination. Ted was also surprised to learn that not all the employees he had targeted for termination had, in fact, been fired. After investigating the situation further, he discovered that five of the employees whom he had instructed to be fired were still working for the company. Ted was shocked to learn that the five employees were close relatives of Manuel. When confronted with this fact, Manuel just shrugged his shoulders and told Ted that he could not bring himself to fire them.

Although Ted was upset with Manuel's insubordination, he was far more concerned with the lack of any productivity gains at the plant. He was told that most workers did complete their tasks more quickly under the incentive plan; however, they elected to go home rather than work additional hours for more money. Ted was confused by this behavior so he asked some of the supervisors to explain it. They didn't provide satisfactory answers so Ted decided that he should conduct interviews with the employees themselves. Working through an interpreter, Ted asked workers about their jobs and what he could do to make them more productive. He was frustrated by the lack of responses he was getting from the employees. When Ted probed more deeply he discovered that the supervisors had not implemented the participative management practices he had ordered.

Faced with poor operating results during the first year of operation, Ted wondered if the decision to take the job in Mexico had been a mistake. To make matters worse, Ted's family was very unhappy about living in Mexico. Ted had been working long hours at the plant and had basically discounted the complaints he had heard from his wife and children. At this point he began to feel that perhaps they were right in their frequent criticisms of Mexican culture. With over a year left in his assignment in Mexico Ted felt frustrated and wondered what he should do next.

Discussion Questions:

1. What mistakes did Ted make in his management of SterMexicana?
2. Is Manuel responsible for any of the difficulties presented in the case?
3. What should Ted do now to correct the situation?

Sources: R. Malat, <u>Passport Mexico</u>. San Rafael, CA: World Trade Press, 1996; P. Beamish, A. Morrison, and P. Rosenweig, <u>International Management</u>. Chicago: Irwin, 1997; R Sanyal, <u>International Management: A Strategic Perspective</u>. Upper Saddle River, NJ: Prentice Hall, 2001; J. Scarborough, <u>The Origins of Cultural Differences and Their Impact on Management</u>. Westport, CT: Quorum, 2001.

Case prepared by Charles A. Rarick

KIDNAPPED IN COLOMBIA

Although Melissa Woodruff still felt compassion for the people of Colombia, she now realized that she made the biggest mistake of her life when she encouraged her husband to accept a temporary assignment in Medellin. As she reflected on that decision, she felt as if she would never recover from the Colombian experience.

Melissa and Dan Woodruff met in college and married as soon as Dan graduated. Although the couple wanted to start a family, they decided that it would be best to wait until Dan became more established in his career as a marketing manager with Carolina Textiles. The couple settled into a nice home in South Carolina and Melissa was able to complete her undergraduate degree in fashion merchandising. Melissa wanted to design women's clothing, but she had difficulty securing a position with an established company. She instead began to design and manufacturer her own line and sold the garments on eBay. Although she didn't make much money, she greatly enjoyed the challenge of designing a piece of clothing and seeing its actual completion. Dan did well in his career at Carolina Textiles and the couple thought that they might spend their entire lives in the tranquil surroundings of the small South Carolina town where Carolina Textiles was headquartered. However, that vision was not to be.

After working for Carolina Textiles for only five years, Dan was offered an opportunity which he never envisioned. The firm offered Dan the opportunity to manage a large manufacturing arrangement, which the firm had recently established in Colombia. In an effort to reduce labor costs, Carolina Textiles had contracted with a local textile manufacturer in Medellin, and the company needed someone to manage the day-to-day operations, and to protect Carolina Textiles interests in Colombia. Colombia was seen as one of the desirable locations for foreign manufacturing in that Colombia, along with Bolivia, Peru, and Ecuador were part of the Andean Trade Preferences Act. The Act was amended in 2003, which provided for textiles to be brought into the United States, duty-free, provided that the products were manufactured with U.S. cloth. The city of Medellin seemed like a good choice in that the city had a long history in textile manufacturing. Many of the local manufacturing facilities in Medellin operate in free trade zones, or "Plan Vallejo," and they export much of their output to the United States. The industry was well developed and accustomed to exporting.

Dan, and especially Melissa, were at first hesitant about spending two to three years in Colombia. Not only would they miss their friends in South Carolina, but they were aware of the political violence in Colombia. After a visit to Medellin, and after much discussion, the couple decided to give it a try. Melissa reasoned that the experience would be good for Dan's career, and he would be getting a promotion along with the assignment. The couple was still young and could start a family after the assignment. The fact that the couple could easily afford to have a maid who would also cook for them was appealing. Melissa also felt that she could continue her design business, and perhaps, even expand it with the abundant manufacturing facilities in Medellin. The couple sold their home in South Carolina, said good-bye to friends, and headed for the challenges which awaited them in Colombia.

Dan and Melissa settled into a rented three-bedroom home in the suburbs of Medellin. For the most part, the couple enjoyed living in the "City of Eternal Spring," however, life in Medellin was also stressful. Without much international travel experience, and only a very basic proficiency in Spanish, the couple experienced a significant degree of culture shock. Melissa would email friends about how different it was living in Colombia; from seeing all the armed guards at the mall, to the ability to purchase medicine at a pharmacy without a prescription. Every day presented its own set of challenges for Dan and Melissa but the couple adjusted fairly well. Dan was busy with work and Melissa was scouting out new ways to establish her design business.

Dan and Melissa had been warned about the political troubles and violence in Colombia. Before leaving the United States they read much on the history of Colombia. They were especially interested in the revolutionary groups that operated against the government. Dan and Melissa learned that Colombia was still a divided country with the smaller, but dominate population of European descent often in conflict with the larger population of mixed ethnicity. The two rival political groups which developed in Colombia, the Conservatives and Liberals, had fought in a bloody civil war called "La Violencia" which began in 1948. The main revolutionary group, the Revolutionary Armed Forces of Colombia or FARC developed out of the frustration of some members of the Liberal party. In the 1980's FARC began to fund its revolutionary cause by taxing the illegal drug industry of Colombia. The group continued to control an increasingly larger share of the country and now claims over 40% of Colombia. FARC also began to diversify its source of funding through the kidnapping of prominent Colombians and expatriates. While the kidnapping threat worried Dan and Melissa, they reasoned that neither one of them was a likely target for kidnapping since they were "just average people." They did not limit their outings and generally tried to blend into Colombian society including frequent attendance at the bullfighting events in the city.

The couple felt acclimated to the culture, for the most part, after about six months. Melissa enjoyed getting dressed up and shopping. She enjoyed buying gifts to send back home to friends. The couple developed a daily routine in which Dan would leave for work every weekday morning at 8:30 A.M. driving himself, and Melissa would begin her day on the Internet, answering emails and developing business ideas. Although the couple did not have the opportunity to make many American friends, they did enjoy the company of a few Colombian couples from Dan's work. Melissa truly enjoyed these friendships and developed a degree of sympathy for the less fortunate members of Medellin society. Sometimes she would open her wallet and drop a large cash roll (large by Colombian standards) into the hat or canister of street beggars. This made her feel as if she was making a big difference in someone's life, something she felt she could not do in the United States.

The compassion she felt towards the Colombian people was not tempered even when her purse was snatched in the local market. While she had the equilivant of about $200 U.S. in the purse, she was more concerned about replacing her credit cards and identification. This made shopping difficult in that she would have to carry cash for all transactions, including larger transactions. The purse snatching worried Dan, but he reassured himself that petty crime was a problem in Colombia and that the couple would just have to be more careful. The event passed quickly, and was almost forgotten when a very impressive article was written in the local newspaper profiling Dan and Carolina Textiles. The article was clipped and mailed back to a number of friends in the United States. The couple felt as if they were making new friends in Colombia and that Dan's career was heading in a very positive direction.

All of this, however, was about to change. On a particularly spring-like day, as Dan left for work he had much on his mind. There were a number of improvements he hoped to suggest to the contract manufacturer, including the addition of a more efficient computerized layout pattern for cutting cloth. As he drove the usual route to his office he was reviewing the different supplier options for the new software, and he kept thinking about the recent article about himself in the newspaper. Suddenly his thoughts were interrupted as the vehicle in front of him came to a stop and the driver opened the hood of the car. A second vehicle moved very and very closely behind Dan's new 700 series BMW, so close in fact that Dan was concerned that the two vehicles would crash. Dan motioned to the driver of the van behind him to move back. Instead four armed men wearing handkerchiefs over their noses and mouths got out of the van, grabbed Dan, and placed a cloth sack over his head. They pushed him into the back of the van and quickly took off. Dan, unable to see what was happening, and unable to understand much of what was being said was confused and scared. Surely he thought to himself, "I'm not being kidnapped. They must have made a mistake." Unable to see, and having some difficulty breathing Dan tried to speak to his captors in English, but he got no response. Dan kept asking them "what's going on" and trying to assure them that they must be making a mistake. After a few hours of riding in the back of the hot van and having no water, Dan was hopeful when the van stopped and the door opened. He hoped the ordeal was coming to an end. Unfortunately for Dan, the ordeal was just beginning. He was placed inside another vehicle and it was the beginning of a very long drive into the remote areas of Colombia - an area Dan and Melissa had planned on visiting some day, although under very different circumstances.

Back at home, Melissa was very busy planning her day when someone knocked at the door. Adriana, the housekeeper answered the door as usual and came very quickly calling for Senora Woodruff. She said a man had left this note for her and she seemed very upset. Melissa was confused as she opened the paper she had been given. The note, written in broken English, stated that her husband had been kidnapped and that she should get a short-wave radio. The note indicated a frequency to use with the radio and the times to use it. It was signed "Gabino." Melissa asked Adriana what this all meant and she told her that Senor Woodruff had been taken by FARC and that he was in great danger. Melissa was beginning to become very upset, however, she retained her composure and called Dan's office, hoping it wasn't true. When Dan's assistant told her that he had not yet arrived, she immediately called his mobile phone. There was no answer. Melissa was now frantic. She called Dan's assistant again and explained what had happened. The assistant, Manuel Chacon told her to stay calm and that he would immediately come to the house. Melissa asked Adriana if she should call the police and Adriana told her that it would not be advisable.

When Manuel arrived he told Melissa to remain calm. He had already contacted Carolina Textiles and told them what had happened. Manuel told Melissa that, unfortunately, kidnapping of foreigners was common in Colombia, but that Dan would be released as soon as Carolina Textiles paid the ransom that would be demanded by FARC. Manuel assured Melissa that no harm would come to Dan and that he would be released very soon. Manuel told Melissa that there was nothing that they could do at this time but purchase the short-wave radio and wait for the designated time to contact the kidnappers. He also advised her to pray for a safe and quick return of her husband. Melissa decided to call her parents with whom she had little contact since moving against their wishes to Colombia. It would be a difficult call but she needed their support.

Quickly Manuel purchased the short-wave radio and set it up in the Woodruff's home. He was in constant contact with Carolina Textiles and he relayed their concern to Melissa. Manuel also had to report to Melissa that Carolina Textiles did not have ransom insurance and that this made the situation more difficult. He reassured Melissa that once the kidnappers learned of this fact they would release Dan, maybe with a "token ransom payment." Melissa, after contacting her parents got their pledge to help pay the ransom.

Three very long days passed before Melissa and Manuel were able to make contact with Gabino, the FARC negotiator. Manuel explained how Dan was not a wealthy man and that the company he worked for did not carry ransom insurance. Gabino told Manuel that unless a $2,000,000 U.S. ransom was paid for Dan they would never see him alive again. Manuel again insisted that this was not possible, however, Gabino was unsympathetic. The first contact ended without any hope of agreement. Manuel was instructed to try again, once he had arranged for the money transfer. Manuel assured Melissa that the demands were just typical bargaining and that if she could raise about $50,000 USD the matter could be settled. Melissa knew that she could raise that much with their savings and the help of her parents. Dan's parents were deceased. Manuel told Melissa that he would seek the help of Carolina Textiles.

With the help of Manuel, Carolina Textiles decided that they should contact a kidnapping and ransom expert to help with the negotiations. Since they did not carry kidnapping and ransom insurance, they would have to pay the costs of the negotiator but it was felt that this was a small price to pay for their employee's safety. The external negotiator would not arrive in Medellin for three days, enough time for Manuel to try again with Gabino. On the second attempt at negotiation the same situation arose. Manuel told the kidnappers that they should release Dan since he was not able to pay the ransom and Gabino continued to make threats. Manuel offered the $50,000 with an expectation that the negotiators would agree to a quick resolution. Gabino told Manuel, with Melissa listening, that for $50,000 he would cut off a certain body part from Dan and mail it to Dan's wife. Melissa became frantic and the second session ended very badly.

During all this time, Dan was still traveling with his captors deeper into the Colombian jungle. The first few days he was riding in several vehicles but afterwards he was on foot, always chained to his captors. Dan tried repeatedly to explain that he was not an important person and that no sizable ransom could be paid. He truly believed that the captors would release him, even if in the middle of a jungle, once they believed their effort would not result in a ransom. Although Dan was optimistic that he would be released, he felt very helpless and vulnerable. He worried how Melissa would be handling the news of his abduction. Although exhausted and poorly fed, Dan continued to insist that he be released. Each day brought increasing frustration for Dan, and Melissa.

Melissa began searching the Internet for information about kidnapping. She learned that on an average day 10 people are kidnapped in Colombia. She also learned that in most cases the kidnappers would eventually settle for 10-20% of the original demands. The prospects for a safe return of the hostage were not very good if the negotiation was not conducted properly. Further searching revealed that many companies, which operate in countries with a high probability of kidnapping, carry kidnapping and ransom (K&R) insurance. The policies typically cover the ransom payment, consultant fees, and transportation needed to deliver the ransom and return of the hostage. It appeared that many companies which carry K&R insurance do not advertise the fact for fear that their employees will more likely become targets of kidnapping. Melissa began to wonder if Carolina Textiles did in fact have K&R insurance but it was not being disclosed at this time.

Melissa heard a knock at the door and a man entered. It was Charles Griffith, a security consultant hired by Carolina Textile to help negotiate the release of Dan. Charles introduced himself and appeared to have great confidence in his abilities. He told Melissa not to worry, and that he had successfully handled the negotiations for two other expatriates, one in Mexico and one in Venezuela. He did state that because Carolina Textiles had no K&R insurance it would make the negotiations more difficult. Melissa told Charles that she had read on the Internet that the typical settlement was between 10-20% of the initial demand and that she could probably raise that amount with the help of the company. Charles just responded by saying "we will see."

Charles began the negotiation process with Gabino and the first session did not go well. Gabino at first refused to talk to him and asked to speak with Manuel. Charles informed him that he, Charles, would be handling the negotiations from now on. The communication ended when Charles asked for proof that the rebels did in fact have Dan and that he was alive. Melissa began to worry that Charles was not the right choice for the negotiation sessions and confided this to Manuel.

Days went by and there was no response from Gabino. Feeling frustrated, Melissa asked Manuel to once again attempt to contact Gabino. He agreed and they decided that they would tell Charles that he should defer to Manuel, at least for a while. Charles strongly opposed this suggestion but agreed to let Manuel do the next session due to the strong insistence of Melissa. He encouraged Manuel to explain that a new negotiator was working for the family.

For Dan, boredom was becoming a major issue. He spent his days at a rebel camp, chained either to a tree or to his bed. Dan would often think of Melissa and the various trips they took together back in the United States. He sometimes replayed movies he had seen in his head to relieve the boredom. The heat, lack of food and water, and constant boredom were beginning to fray his nerves. His frequent outburst caused some guerrillas to threaten him with death. All the rebels carried assault rifles and machetes, and some of them appeared to enjoy the possibility of doing harm to Dan. On a couple of occasions Dan attempted to befriend some of the younger rebels by explaining, in broken Spanish, that he and his company were trying to help the Colombian people by creating jobs. It didn't seem that this mattered to the rebels.

Back in Medellin, with Manuel again doing the negotiations it appeared that progress was being made. Gabino told Manuel that it might be possible to release Dan if $1,500,000 could be paid quickly. While it was impossible for Melissa to raise that much money, even with the offer of $100,000 from Carolina Textiles, at least the kidnapper's demands were being reduced. Manuel also was able to have proof delivered, via a photo of Dan holding a copy of El Tiempo (a daily Colombian newspaper) and he seemed to be developing some rapport with Gabino. Charles, while listening to the negotiations offered suggestions to Manuel, but he was becoming increasingly dissatisfied with the role he was playing.

Charles reported back to Carolina Textiles and expressed his concerns with the fact that Melissa was insisting on having Manuel do the negotiating. Charles expressed his doubts that Manuel could ever reach a settlement. The CEO of Carolina Textiles, Ben Goodin called Melissa to persuade her to allow Charles to take over the negotiations. Melissa insisted that Manuel was better suited for the negotiations and that the life of her husband was at stake. Mr. Goodin was not about to press the issue further, and so he wished Melissa luck and asked that he be kept informed. When news got back to Charles that he was not going to be doing the negotiations he decided to leave Colombia. He did offer suggestions to Manuel and told both Manuel and Melissa that the process could take some time.

Every third day Manuel attempted to contact Gabino. Most of the time there was only static over the airways. The process continued for five long months and it was clear that Melissa was feeling the strain. While Carolina Textiles continued to pay Dan's salary, Melissa felt as if they could do more. Not much progress was being made, however, Gabino did agree to reduce the ransom to $1,000,000. This amount was still much more than Melissa could raise. It appeared to her that time was running out and that there was little hope of rescuing Dan.

It was during one of the darkest periods when a bright spot developed for Melissa. A reporter from the BBC was doing a story on Colombian kidnappings and he interviewed her for the story. Once the article was published, Carolina Textiles developed an increased interest in Dan's safety. Mr. Goodin told Melissa that the company was prepared to help with the ransom to the tune of $250,000 and that he would be sending yet another security expert down to Colombia to help in the negotiations. Melissa felt that the $250,000 may be enough for the rebels, and she could even add more from their savings and the contributions from her parents, if needed. Mr. Goodin insisted that the new security expert would be making the new offers and that he would be more successful than Manuel had been.

Upon hearing the good news, Manuel and Melissa contacted Gabino and told him that the company was prepared to make a final offer of $250,000 and that a new negotiator would be contacting him to arrange for the transfer of funds and delivery of the hostage. Gabino did not share the excitement of Manuel and Melissa and all he said to them was that the amount was "not sufficient." Although somewhat surprised by the reaction, Melissa and Manuel maintained their optimism and awaited the arrival of the new negotiator.

Melissa and Manuel met the new security expert at the airport. Frederick Hervitz was a very experienced hostage negotiator and he wasted no time in telling Manuel and Melissa what they would be doing. Frederick insisted that he, and he alone, would be talking to Gabino. Melissa felt confident in Frederick's abilities and was optimistic that the ordeal would soon be over. Manuel agreed that Frederick should take over the negotiations. He was impressed with Frederick and besides; the whole process was becoming a strain on him personally. Manuel and Melissa told Frederick what they had done and what they had accomplished. He told them that they had made many mistakes.

Frederick attempted many times to reach Gabino, but each time all he heard was static. Frederick at first assumed that Gabino was just making it difficult on him in order to raise the ransom, and lower the expectations of Melissa and the company; however, the long silence did begin to worry Frederick. Weeks went by and there was no communication with Gabino. Mr. Goodin telephoned Melissa and told her not to worry, that Frederick would be bringing Dan home soon.

The words of Mr. Goodin were all too true. After six months of enduring the ordeal, Melissa received a call from the American embassy in Bogotá. It was bad news. Melissa was informed that a body, that appeared to be that of her husband had been discovered in a remote northern province of Colombia. Melissa was devastated. She couldn't speak. She thought, surely it is a mistake, but deep down she feared it was true. Frederick arranged a flight to Bogotá for Melissa, Manuel, and himself. Melissa positively identified the body, although Dan looked much different to her than the last time she saw him. He was dirty, had a long beard, and he looked much older. The cause of death was not readily apparent. It deeply saddened Melissa that the last days of Dan's life were spent in such dire conditions.

As Melissa prepared to take the body of her dead husband back to the United States for burial, she couldn't help wonder what went wrong and why the negotiations were unsuccessful. She loved the Colombian people she had met, and she hated the country. Melissa deeply regretted the decision to become an expatriate in Colombia.

Discussion Questions:

1. Were Dan and Melissa foolish in accepting the assignment in Medellin given the current state of danger?
2. What mistakes, if any, did Dan and Melissa make concerning their safety in Colombia?
3. What mistakes, if any, did Dan make during the hostage ordeal?
4. Were there any mistakes made during hostage negotiations?
5. Do you think the situation would have ended differently if Carolina Textiles had K&R insurance?

SOURCES: DuBois, J. (1994). <u>Cultures of the World: Colombia</u>. New York: Marshall Cavendish; McDermott, J. (2002). *Colombia's Most Powerful Rebels*. <u>BBC News</u>. January 7; McDermott, J. (2002). *Analysis: Colombia's Security Crisis*. <u>BBC News</u>. May 4; www.countrywatch.com/colombia. Accessed on July 22, 2003.

Case prepared by Charles A. Rarick

CASE 38

GOOD CAREER MOVE?

As his plane lands at the Santa Maria International Airport in San Jose, Costa Rica, Ed Moore reassures himself that he made the right decision in accepting his first international assignment in this Central American country. The new job will be a promotion, the first time Ed will be entirely responsible for an entire plant, and it will give him international experience, which he hopes to use to continue his advancement in the company.

Ed Moore has worked for his present employer, Jestin Apparel, for 16 years. Ed is viewed as a loyal employee and he prides himself on the fact that he has worked for Jestin longer than he has been married to his wife, Susan. Susan and their two children (Eddie, age 10, and Jessie, age 13) are not as enthusiastic about the idea of living in Turrialba, a rather isolated town about a two-hour drive from San Jose. Although Turrialba is in a beautiful area of the country and offers abundant hunting and fishing opportunities for Ed, Susan worries about the ability of the children to adapt to the isolation. In fact, since the children do not speak Spanish, it will be necessary for Eddie and Jessie to attend school in San Jose, which requires a long bus ride daily. Both Ed and Susan want their children to become "citizens of the world" and they both feel this opportunity may be good for personal development. Although the family vacationed in Europe once before, their international experience was very limited and none of the Moore family members speak another language.

Ed will be the new plant manager for the Costa Rican manufacturing facility of Jestin. This plant sews together pre-manufactured garments and exports the finished product back to the United States. The previous plant manager relocated to San Salvador to open a new, larger facility for Jestin. Most of the 230 employees are young females, although a number of young men and older women are also employed at the plant. The workers receive an hourly wage which is considerably higher than the average wage in Costa Rica. By most reports the workers are happy with their jobs at Jestin. Turnover at the plant is mainly due to young women getting married and starting a family, or young men moving to the capital for better wages.

Although the quality and efficiency of the plant are considered acceptable by management, Ed has been instructed to try and improve both areas. Ed is known as a rather tough manager, who feels that the best way to motivate employees is through a combined program of threats and incentives. Corporate management felt that Ed's somewhat autocratic style of management would be effective in Costa Rica.

Susan was employed in the United States as an assistant human resources manager, even though she had no formal training in that area. She enjoyed her job and she was hoping that she would be able to work in Costa Rica in a similar capacity. The Turrialba plant already had a bilingual HR manager who was familiar with Costa Rican labor laws and regulations; however, it was felt that perhaps Susan could first learn Spanish and then assist the HR manager. Ed's salary as plant manager will be more than their combined incomes in the United States, and the family will be provided with free housing, a maid, and company-provided transportation. The family will live in extreme luxury by local standards.

As the plane touches down in San Jose, Ed remembers the trip the family made to Costa Rica three months earlier. The company had sent the family to Costa Rica to preview the country and to acquaint them with Costa Rican culture. The Moore's enjoyed the cultural tours and the whitewater rafting experiences, however; the children still protested against the move. Leaving friends in the United States is not easy, and they know that they will be giving up the comforts they have become accustomed to in the United States. Ed hopes the assignment will only be for a couple of years, although no plans have been made for his repatriation back to the United States.

As the plane comes to a halt at the gate, Susan looks at Ed and the worry in her face tells him that not all the Moore's are confident that the decision was a good one.

Discussion Questions:

language barrier

1.   What stress factors will Ed and his family likely encounter in this new assignment?
2.   How significant a factor will family happiness be when it comes to Ed's success in this new job?
3.   How do you think the Costa Rican employees will respond to Ed's management style?
4.   Was Ed the best choice for the position? What criteria should be used in selecting expatriates?
5.   What could Jestin do to increase the probability that this international assignment will be successful?

Case prepared by Charles A. Rarick.

Case 39

AMERITECH IN THE PHILIPPINES
FAILURE TO ADJUST TO FILIPINO CULTURAL NORMS?

AmeriTech was started in Lexington, Kentucky by a small group of former IBM employees who accepted a buyout package offered by the company when the Lexington division was reorganized in 1991. Originally, AmeriTech produced computer supplies such as ink cartages, cables, and other small computer supplies in a facility in North Carolina. The operation proved successful as the demand for such products rose globally, however, over time AmeriTech found itself less competitive in terms of cost over rivals from a number of Asian countries. In an effort to reduce labor costs, the founders moved their operations to Mactan Island near the city of Cebu in the Philippines. Instead of starting a Greenfield operation, AmeriTech was able to purchase an underperforming Korean firm that was operating in the economic zone of the island. AmeriTech purchased the facility and retained the entire workforce of the former Korean owned business. AmeriTech had hoped to continue its efficient and quality-oriented production techniques from North Carolina in the low wage environment of the Philippines.

The Republic of the Philippines is a country in Southeast Asia consisting of over 7,000 islands. The capital is Manila, located on the island of Luzon. The Philippines was "discovered" by Ferdinand Magellan in 1521, who claimed the islands for Spain. The country was named after the Spanish King Philip (Felipe) and missionaries converted most of the population to Catholicism. The Philippines is unique in being the only Christian country in Asia. While Magellan met his death soon after arriving in the Philippines, the country was under Spanish control for a number of years. The Philippines came under the rule of the United States in 1898, when Admiral Dewey defeated the Spanish, and Spain ceded the islands under the Treaty of Paris. While Tagalog, or Filipino, is the official language of the Philippines, English is widely spoken, especially among educated Filipinos.

In 1935 the Philippines became a self-governing commonwealth, and there continued to be a strong push by the Filipinos for complete independence. This independence movement was interrupted by World War II when the Japanese invaded the country. With the help of the American forces, the Filipinos defeated the Japanese and gained their independence in 1946. After a number of different administrations, strongman Ferdinand Marcos ruled the country for a number of years and maintained strong ties with the United States. With increasing discontentment of the Filipino people, a "people's revolution" occurred and Marcos was forced to leave the country. Political instability resulted for a time, however, democracy quickly retook a firm hold in the Philippines. Fidel Ramos became president of the Philippines in 1992, and he opened the economy to market forces and encouraged foreign investment, including the establishment of export processing zones (EPZ) and incentives for foreign firms to establish a presence in the Philippines.

With an increasing wage rate in North Carolina and the incentives offered by the Philippines, AmeriTech made the decision to close its American facility and begin operating in the Mactan Economic Zone of the Philippines. The area is in the part of the Philippines called the Visayas. With a compatible operating facility being offered for sale, AmeriTech relocated with the hope of gaining a competitive advantage with lower labor costs and access to the emerging markets of Asia. The only employee from North Carolina that would be making the move to the Philippines was William "Bill" Dawson. Dawson was the son of a tobacco farmer in North Carolina, who while deemed by his teachers and peers to be highly intelligent, never attended college. He worked in a number of manufacturing jobs after high school, and through hard work and ability, gained a number of supervisory positions. He was hired by AmeriTech when the firm first began operating in North Carolina as a first line supervisor. Through an unusual series of personnel turnover and one death, he was promoted to plant manager in a few years after first being hired. Dawson instituted a number of quality improvement and inventory management techniques and gained the respect of his superiors. While Bill could be intimidating to some (he was a large, and somewhat heavy man, with a loud voice), he was generally well liked and respected by the employees at AmeriTech. Bill was known for being "firm, but fair." He was very informal with his employees and dressed in a casual, or some would say "sloppy" fashion. The employees appreciated the fact that he was just a "regular guy." Bill was looking forward to his new assignment, however, he feared he would miss watching his beloved North Carolina Tar Heels play basketball on television. While he had never been to the Philippines, he did have a favorable impression of the country from the stories his uncle, who served in World War II, had told him about the Philippines, and the courage of the Filipino fighters. Bill also learned that basketball is a favored sport in the Philippines and so "maybe the place wouldn't be so bad after all."

With an unusually easy transition, AmeriTech took control of the former Korean facility. While adjustments had to be made in the production process, and many of the workers could not be used during this time, AmeriTech generated goodwill by paying the employees their normal salaries during this startup period. The employees that were needed to work were paid their normal salaries plus a 50% bonus during this time. AmeriTech realized that there were going to be additional costs during the startup, including increased training in the "AmeriTech way." In general the employees welcomed the new owners, and many commented that they much preferred working for an American company than a Korean one. One new hire was Miguel Santos, a 26 year old MBA graduate of De la Salle University in Manila. Miguel was hired as an assistant to Bill, and someone to help Bill with any cultural difficulties he might experience in his assignment.

Miguel was born and raised in Manila and did not consider himself to be a Cebuano (someone from Cebu or the surrounding area). The employees in the plant were mostly Cebuanos and were at time untrusting of people from Metro Manila. They felt that they were too urban, too serious, and too self-centered for their tastes. Miguel was very deferential to Bill Dawson, refusing to call him by his first name and always referring to him as "Mr. Dawson," and sometimes, "Plant Manager Dawson." Miguel was not as cordial with the lower level employees at the plant, however, and at times had strained relations with employees. Miguel also was not very happy with the fact that he had to leave his family in Manila, and, because of the distance, only see them every few months.

The productivity level of the plant remained low for a number of months and Bill had decided that it was time for a change. While he had expected that it might take some time for productivity to reach the levels achieved in North Carolina, he was beginning to feel as if without some intervention, things would not improve. Of particular concern to Bill was the amount of "wasted time" he observed in the plant. Employees would often take extended breaks, chat endlessly among themselves, and often engage in non-work activities while on company time, such as celebrating an employee's birthday. Miguel explained to Bill that it represented "pakikisama" and was quite common in Filipino culture. Bill seemed unconvinced, but proceeded with caution and allowed this to situation to continue, as he was in a phase of "employee relations building" with the employees. After a few more months productivity still had not improved, and Bill decided it was time to take action.

In North Carolina, Bill had learned that when employees were "schooled" in the ways of productivity, they improved their performance. The North Carolina plant also had an individual incentive plan which acted as a strong motivator. Bill reasoned that he should now begin to change the corporate culture of the plant. With the help of Miguel, he organized after-work training sessions and stressed the importance of reducing "wasted time" on the job. Most of the employees were females and many had not worked previously in a manufacturing environment. The training sessions were a bit frustrating to Bill as he could not get the employees to participate nor contribute their thoughts. He felt that if he allowed for employee input, he could win over the employees to his ideas for productivity improvement. The only employee who spoke frequently was a middle aged woman named Millet, who often joked and teased Bill during the training sessions. Bill had gotten the impression that Millet was romantically interested in him, and he was unhappy with the situation. After yet another training session in which little was achieved, so Bill thought, except the asking of personal questions from Millet, Bill decided to have her fired. He instructed Miguel to terminate her employment immediately. Miguel warned Bill that Millet was a productive employee who had worked for the previous company for many years, and that she was very well liked by her peers. Bill responded that he was tired of her teasing and personal questions and that "it was nobody's damn business if he is married or not." Miguel did as he was told and informed Millet she would not be returning to work tomorrow.

The mood of the employees, especially those in Millet's department, changed almost immediately. While it was common to hear cheery voices and laughter in the plant, in the days and weeks that followed, the plant was void of much humor. Employees seemed to be more formal and less warm to Bill, however, there was a slight improvement in productivity. This made Bill happy. He thought that, just maybe, he needed to use a firmer hand in dealing with the workers. He was a bit concerned that employee turnover had increased, but he reasoned that it was probably just employees who did not want to really work. Bill turned his thoughts to ways to introduce a monetary incentive program and to start a quality improvement program.

While Bill pondered such issues, Miguel informed him that another industrial plant was opening in Mactan and that he feared that AmeriTech might lose more employees. Bill was unconcerned, but finally agreed with Miguel that he would call a meeting and announce the incentive program he had been developing. The meeting was scheduled after work hours, and a number of employees did not attend. This angered Bill and he expressed his displeasure by calling out the names of the employees who were not present. He suggested to the gathered employees that maybe those missing employees would not be returning to work next week. The meeting went on, with the rather complex incentive program being explained. The basic idea was that employees would no longer be "entitled" to a salary, but that they could, if properly motivated, earn more money. Within a week, close to 20% of the workforce resigned.

With turnover becoming a problem, and the resulting disruption to production, Bill was under fire from his superiors to turn the situation around. Bill decided to have yet another meeting with his employees, but this time to pay them for attending. Bill expected 100% turnout for the meeting but instead, roughly half the employees attended. Bill was outraged and proceeded to lecture the employees present that the work culture of the company must change. After a very tense 10 minutes of hearing this, Miguel politely interrupted Bill with the suggestion that a break be taken and food delivered to the plant for the employees. This suggestion was not well received by Bill, who then proceeded to criticize Miguel for not understanding the importance of profitability. The meeting ended with a somber mood, as it had begun, and employees quietly left for home. Miguel was one of the first employees to leave the building.

The following day Miguel called in sick, complaining of stomach troubles. Bill decided that maybe he had been too hard on Miguel and the other employees. As he sat at his desk wondering how to proceed, the assistant director of human resources called him to tell him that the director of HR had resigned, for "medical reasons." The department had been busy attempting to fill the vacancies created by the turnover and Bill worried that he was losing the respect of his employees. Bill decided to host an event for all employees in nearby Cebu City, honoring the most dedicated and outstanding employees. When Miguel returned to work the following day, Bill informed him of his decision. Miguel seemed less than excited about the idea. When pressed for an explanation, Miguel admitted that a party was maybe a good idea, but that he, Bill, should not take a very active role in the event. Surprised by this recommendation, Bill pressed Miguel for answers. After much pressuring Miguel blurted out that the employees had a nickname for him – "baboy." Bill was told it meant pig in Tagalog. With this revelation Bill decided to cancel any plans for a party and to resume his normal style of management. He instructed Miguel to begin looking for a new HR director and to ramp up the recruitment of employee replacements.

Charles A. Rarick

Discussion Questions:

1. What mistakes, if any, did Bill make in his management of the   plant?
2. Was it necessary for Bill to change, in any way, in his new assignment in the Philippines? Explain.
3. What is the significance of the nickname the employees gave to   Bill?
4. If you were advising Bill, what would you suggest?

Sources: L. Francia. *Passport Philippines*, 1997, San Rafael, CA: World Trade Press; U.S. Department of State, *Background Notes: Philippines*, 2008; T. Gochenour. *Considering Filipinos*, 1990, Yarmouth, ME: Intercultural Press. Personal experiences of the author interacting with the Filipino business community and American Chamber of Commerce of the Philippines in 2007.

Case prepared by Charles A. Rarick, Inge Nickerson, and Arifan Angiawan

CASE 40

BINDI AUTO PARTS - INDIA

It was the opportunity of a lifetime, or so Brian Moseley thought, as he accepted a managing director position for Aspen Automotive's new acquisition in India. Aspen Automotive was a supplier to American automobile manufacturers. The company supplied various component parts for the American automakers, and the recent acquisition of an Indian brake-pad company was seen as a keen strategic move for the company. The Bindi Auto Parts Company was an established manufacturer of automotive brake pads that supplied a few European car companies with a high-quality product. Competition in this market is fierce, and Bindi experienced difficulty in recent years competing with American and Japanese firms. Aspen thought it could capitalize on the experience and low costs of production found in the New Delhi operation, and it sent Brian Moseley, an experienced automotive engineer, to India in order to "make the Indians efficient."

Brian and his family quickly adapted to India. Although many expatriates from developed countries experience overwhelming culture shock, the Moseleys' assimilated well into the expatriate community of New Delhi. With the help of personal assistants and with the children in private schools, the Moseleys' could separate themselves from most of the challenges of everyday life in urban India. Although they sometimes missed some of the luxuries they had taken for granted back in the

United States, they enjoyed the standard of living they were experiencing as privileged expatriates in India. Brian knew that his job responsibilities were to turn around the newly acquired Indian operation, and that if he did this within two years, he would be promoted and moved back to U.S. He felt that this assignment could greatly advance his career.

Managers at Aspen's corporate headquarters felt that the introduction of certain Western managerial practices would be beneficial to Bindi and improve overall efficiency and profitability. Brian was selected to direct the organizational change effort because of his past record of accomplishments in the U.S. and abroad. He had been successful in the turnaround of troubled parts-manufacturing plants in Louisville, Kentucky, and Toledo, Ohio. Additionally, he had worked internationally in Canada, Mexico, and Brazil. Aspen felt that his M.B.A. in management from Michigan State, coupled with his previous domestic and international experience, made him a suitable person to direct the Indian productivity improvement strategy.

Although Bindi produced reasonably high-quality brake components, and labor costs were exceptionally low, the overall efficiency of the operation was considerably below that of other Aspen plants. Top management felt that if the Indian operation could match the level of efficiency of even the least efficient American plant, the acquisition would be a success. After an initial plant visit, top management concluded that the plant was crippled with bureaucracy and that there was no incentive for exceptional performance. Aspen managers observed what they felt were too many Bindi employees drinking tea and socializing instead of working at a brisk pace. They were also shocked to find that no Bindi employee ever received a performance review and that pay for performance was never even considered by past management. Bindi employees were seldom discharged, even when they were clearly not well suited to their jobs and performed poorly. Pay increases and other rewards were administered on the basis of seniority. Employees were often hired, not based on their abilities or potential, but because they were related to a current employee of Bindi. The number of sick days and personal days requested was well above the average of the other Aspen plants.

Brian was directed to make the India subsidiary more like the rest of the Aspen corporate family. For the first three months, Brian did little more than observe and learn about Bindi's current managerial practices. He spoke with managers and employees alike, and made mental notes of the conversations. Brian identified employees whom he felt should be replaced and employees whom he felt had the greatest potential for advancement. After this initial three-month investigation, Brian met with his senior managers at Bindi and proposed that they collectively formulate a turnaround strategy. All of Bindi's managers were Indians and most had been educated in Indian universities. One manager, Rajan Patel, had studied in London and received a postgraduate diploma from the University of London in economics. Brian felt that Rajan was one of the most promising candidates for advancement, and he hoped that Rajan would take the lead in structuring the change management program.

Although Brian had hoped that the Indian managers would formulate a plan for change among themselves, he increasingly became frustrated after a month when no one came forth to recommend a plan. Brian suggested to the group that they consider changes such as pay-for-performance programs, annual performance reviews, management by objectives, and perhaps a 360-degree performance appraisal program. In his view, if the group emphasized performance appraisal, many of Bindi's efficiencies would disappear. Brian believed that most of the employees had the potential for great improvement, and that all they needed was a better system of management. A more scientific and objective approach to management, coupled with a more participative approach, would succeed in increasing the efficiencies and ultimate success of Bindi.

Over the next several months, Brian became increasingly dissatisfied with the progress of the Indian managers in coming up with any constructive plan for changing Bindi's managerial practices. Highly frustrated, he sometimes angrily criticized members of his managerial team in front of their subordinates. The relationship between Brian and the managers became increasingly strained; he was being referred to behind his back as "sahab" or "big boss." A throwback to the British colonial days, this term was used in some instances to refer to a manager who had little understanding of Indian culture.

One of Brian's biggest critics was Rajan Patel. Rajan often criticized Brian's managerial style as being too direct and forceful. On at least one occasion, Rajan referred to Brian's tactics as "culturally imperialistic," asserting that Brian was too immature to be the managing director. He was concerned that Brian was trying to change India's culture to fit an American model of management. Although educated in the West, Rajan did not feel that Indian employees were receptive to many Western managerial practices, which ran counter to basic Indian cultural values. He openly questioned Brian and Aspen's approach to changing the corporate culture of the Bindi Auto Parts Company.

After seven months in India, Brian decided that if change were to occur, he would have to be the one to initiate that change. He called his senior managers into his office one morning and told them of the following changes that were to be effective immediately. First, Brian announced that C.P. Rao would replace Prakash Nur, the assistant plant director and the most senior manager. Rao was a young engineer, educated at an American university, and a person who Brian felt would be best able to implement his vision of change at Bindi. Second, Brian announced that performance appraisals would begin immediately and that at least two employees in each work group would be eliminated in the interest of organizational efficiency. Third, a new plan of 360-degree feedback would be implemented: Subordinates would evaluate their superiors, and annual compensation increases would be contingent on these reviews. No annual increases in compensation would be automatic, and all raises would now be based on merit. Finally, all personal assistants (chaprasi) would be fired and their responsibilities assumed by the managers themselves. Even though the salary expense of the personal assistants was small, Brian felt that it created an unnecessary level of administration, and no other Aspen unit allowed such positions.

At first, the Indian managers seemed stunned by Brian's mandates. No one spoke, and a dead silence filled the room. When Brian asked for feedback on his "recommendations," the managers looked down at the table in front of them and said nothing. Prakash, who got up and left the room, broke the silence. Later, a few of the managers politely told Brian that the ideas were too bold and too sudden a change for Bindi. Brian angrily responded that the change was long overdue and that anyone who would not go along with the new plan should leave the company.

Much grumbling was heard at Bindi over the next few days, as the managers announced the changes. Brian learned that Prakash had resigned and that Rajan was telling everyone about his dissatisfaction with Brian's managerial style. Brian decided to talk individually with all the managers, starting with Rajan. The meeting was less than cordial, and ended with Brian's warning Rajan that he'd "better come on board soon" or he too would be replaced. During subsequent meetings with all the Indian managers, Brian tried to convince them of the urgency and necessity of these proposed changes. At times, it seemed as if they agreed with him and he felt that change would finally occur. After all, when asked directly, no one actually refused to implement the changes.

After a week in which no changes were taking place, Brian reasoned that it might take a little longer than he thought due to cultural constraints. However, he worried that Rajan might be trying to sabotage the change effort. Brian kept a close eye on Rajan, and one morning he was told that Rajan would not be in the office for a week because his brother was getting married in Bombay. Brian was suspicious, checked the personnel records, and discovered that Rajan did not have any brothers. He waited for Rajan to return and then asked him where he had been. Rajan replied that he had attended the wedding of his brother in Bombay. Brian, outraged by the lie, immediately fired him on the spot. Rajan left without a word to Brian.

Although things seemed to be a bit tense at Bindi, Brian told himself that change is difficult and that the long-term consequences would be good for Aspen, Bindi, and India. He continued to quiz the managers on their progress in carrying out the change efforts, and was told that all changes were being implemented, as he had instructed. But further investigation revealed that no changes were being made. Brian called for another meeting of his managers and was shocked to learn that a number of them had decided to quit rather than attend the meeting. Included in the group who resigned were C.P. Rao, whom Brian was convinced would be a leader in making his vision of change a reality at Bindi. Brian sat alone in his office, wondering if change would ever come to the Bindi Auto Parts Company.

Discussion Questions:

1. Evaluate the managerial style of Brian Moseley and explain how it fits with Indian culture. Be specific in identifying any mistakes Brian made in managing Indian workers.
2. Rank the following principals and justify the ranking in terms of responsibility for the lack of change at the Bindi Auto Parts Company: Brian, Rajan, Aspen, the Indian manager.
3. What could each of the above-named principals have done differently to avoid this situation?
4. What should Brian do now?

Case prepared by Charles A. Rarick

CASE 41

AN EXPAT IN PARIS

Margaret Williamson, age 50, has just returned to London from Paris, where she worked for the past six months as a marketing specialist for a British and French joint venture called EUROi. British computer manufacturer RoyalPC formed the joint venture with a French ISP called Internet du France (IDF). The two companies hope to capitalize on their particular strengths and grow a Pan-European Internet service. EUROi competes in Europe on the basis of price, and has positioned itself as an alternative ISP in an already crowded market. EUROi targets the 16 to 24 year-old market by offering programming that appeals to a more youthful market. The company also offers subscribers sizable discounts on Royal personal computers.

Margaret began her career at Royal fifteen years ago as a secretary. As a recently divorced mother of two, Margaret entered the work force for the first time and displayed a strong work ethic. Although she did not attend college, Margaret is a very intelligent individual and a quick learner. These traits did not go unnoticed at Royal, and she was promoted out of the secretary pool and placed into the Marketing Department. Margaret advanced in the department, gaining a reputation for handling difficult assignments. With a strong devotion to her children and her work, she chose not to remarry. With her children now grown she became interested in an international assignment.

Her colleagues viewed Margaret as an effective manager. She was seen as fair to all, conscientious, a good decision maker, and very loyal to the company. Because of her abilities, she was selected to act as marketing liaison between her company and the French partner in the newly formed joint venture.

Mrs. Williamson, as she prefers to be called, is a refined British lady. She possesses excellent manners and prides herself on her personal composure. Her ability to remain calm and level-headed in tense situations would be challenged when she moved to Paris for her new assignment.

Georges DuPont, age 35, is director of marketing for EUROi. DuPont, a graduate of the prestigious Ecole Nationale d' Administration, comes from an elite French family. Somewhat of a renegade, Georges refused to work in the family business after college. He instead, found employment in a number of computer-related businesses. DuPont became fascinated with the creative side of the computer and Internet business. He had been at IDF for four years, and was highly regarded as an effective manager and creative promoter. As marketing director of the joint venture, DuPont was given the responsibility of working with Williamson to find a way to increase revenue for EUROi. DuPont prides himself on his literary and artistic skills and enjoys engaging others in verbal debate.

From the start of their working relationship, problems surfaced between Margaret and Georges. At first, small personal habits of the two seemed to cause friction. Margaret often remarked that Georges never smiled at her, and Georges called Margaret's personality as "interesting as a bottle of cheap California wine." Over the early weeks of the relationship, the situation deteriorated further. Margaret was convinced that Georges was an incompetent and lazy manager. She felt that Georges was too autocratic and did not delegate enough responsibility to lower levels in the organization.

Margaret further complained to her superiors back in London that Georges frequently broke company policy, canceled meetings with little notice, took two-hour lunch breaks, and never admitted his mistakes. She felt that he did not respect her as an equal partner; in fact, she felt that he actually resented her help in promoting the joint venture.

To add more tension to the already strained relationship, Margaret learned that Georges (a married man) was having an affair with his secretary, Giselle. This fact came to light when Margaret found out that the two of them were going to a resort in the south of France for three weeks of vacation. Margaret was offended by Georges's lack of morality, which included his affair with Giselle as well as his advances to other women in the company.

Georges was equally unimpressed with Margaret. He felt that she was uneducated, insensitive, and too concerned with money and company regulations. Georges frequently joked to others about the way in which Margaret dressed. He felt that she had no taste in fashion, and that this alone made her abilities in the company suspect. Georges was unhappy that Margaret forced everyone to communicate with her in English. Although she spoke little French and Georges and most others spoke fluent English, he resented this, nevertheless. When Margaret requested that she be referred to as "Mrs. Williamson," Georges just rolled his eyes and muttered something in French that Margaret did not understand. He seldom used either her first or last name in conversations with her.

The workplace tensions continued for some time, with Georges and Margaret frequently disagreeing and complaining about each other. It was known throughout EUROi that the two did not get along, and their strained interactions were often the butt of jokes around the company. Georges tried to avoid Margaret as much as possible, which put her in the awkward position of having to go through Giselle to communicate with him. Margaret did not like to deal with Giselle because of her "illicit" behavior with her boss.

The situation finally came to a head when a creative team was to be assembled to design a large advertising campaign for EUROi. Margaret had already developed a plan to assemble the team and empower them with the responsibility of creating a more youth-oriented advertising theme. Margaret had identified five people whom she felt would be best suited for the project. Her plan was to allow these people to work independent of management in creating a new series of advertisements. Margaret felt that a more creative approach to promotion was needed, and she wanted this team to develop a breakthrough design for the promotional strategy.

When Margaret approached Georges with her idea, he refused to accept it. He told Margaret that he felt the current campaign was effective, but admitted that he could see a need for some improvement. Georges recommended that he solicit the advice of a few key people and that he create the new ad design. After all, he was the director of marketing for the new company. Margaret tried to explain to Georges why her plan was better, and that a similar approach had been successful with RoyalPC. Georges just stared at the ceiling, smoking his cigarette. Margaret wasn't even sure if he was listening to her.

After a few weeks of attempting to convince Georges that her plan was better, Margaret decided that she needed help from London. She arranged for a video conference call to be held between London and Paris, in which she and some senior managers at Royal would discuss the issue further with Georges. Margaret sent an e-mail message to Georges, informing him of the conference but received no response. After two days, she asked Giselle if her boss knew of the proposed meeting and if he could attend. Giselle just smiled and responded that he could attend the meeting, if he desired to do so. Margaret sent a memo to Georges indicating the date and time of the conference call and emphasizing the importance of his presence at the meeting.

On the day of the meeting, Margaret searched for Georges. Even though the meeting wasn't for a few hours, she wanted to make sure he would attend, and she thought that perhaps she could even get him to change his mind before the call took place. Giselle told Margaret that he would be in the office soon and that she would remind him of the meeting.

As the 1:00 PM hour for the meeting approached, Margaret was frantic. She phoned Giselle and demanded to know where Georges was and when he would be in the conference room. Giselle responded that she didn't know where he was and that she really didn't care. When Giselle rudely hung up the phone, Margaret was convinced that Georges would not show up for the meeting. She decided, however, that she might be able to use this to her advantage.

The call from London came precisely at 1:00 PM, with just Margaret sitting in the Paris office. She explained to the people in London that Georges was not present and that she had no idea why he was not there. She went on to tell the London managers that she was not surprised by

Georges's behavior; he continually expressed contempt for her, and he had an apparent disregard for the welfare of EUROi. Margaret went on for over 30 minutes detailing Georges's shortcomings, when suddenly he entered the room with three other EUROi employees. Georges apologized for his tardiness but explained that he and the others had been across town working with marketing personnel from a very popular magazine targeted toward the 16 to 24 age group in Europe. Georges was very excited about what this "team" had accomplished, and he wanted the London managers to know the details.

The video call went on for another hour with the three EUROi employees explaining with charts and figures how the association with the youth magazine would be beneficial to the company. They proposed new creative advertising designs and an association with the popular magazine. The team appeared to have been well prepared for the meeting. Georges, who spoke with great confidence and enthusiasm, directed the entire presentation. From the questions asked by the London managers, it was clear that they felt Georges's plan was superior to the one proposed by Margaret. When the presentation was completed they thanked Georges and his team and quickly approved the plan.

At that point Margaret rose from her chair, red-faced and very angry. She appeared at first barely able to speak, but when she began, she angrily accused Georges of undermining her authority. Margaret called Georges a "sneaky bastard," and for the next five minutes vented her frustration at Georges, who sat quietly staring at the ceiling, smoking his cigarette.

Finally the most senior London manager interrupted Margaret and politely asked if Georges and his team could leave the room for a moment. Georges got up and began to leave, but before he left he stopped, smiled at Margaret, and said, "au revoir, *Mrs.* Williamson."

Discussion Questions:

1. What role does culture play in the interpersonal difficulties found in this case?

2. Who is more to blame; Georges or Margaret; for these difficulties?
3, What advice would you give a British expatriate going to France?

Sources: N. Joseph, <u>Passport France.</u> Novato, CA: World Trade Press, 1997; and J. Scarborough, <u>The Origins of Cultural Difference and Their Impact on Management.</u> Westport, CT: Quorum, 1998.

Case prepared by Charles A. Rarick

EXERCISE 12

HOFSTEDE'S CULTURAL
CLASSIFICATION MODEL
COUNTRY-RANKING EXERCISE

Purpose: To develop a better understanding of cultural differences and how they affect international management. This exercise uses the model developed by cross-cultural researcher Geert Hofstede and tests your knowledge of eight different cultures.

Procedure: Read the brief description of each element of Hofstede's framework and individually rank each of the listed countries from high to low on the four dimensions of the model. The country highest on a dimension receives a ranking of 1, and the country lowest on the dimension receives an 8. Assemble into groups and discuss your rankings. As a group, develop another ranking, again using 1 = highest and 8 = lowest. Finally, answer as a group the three questions at the end of the exercise.

Hofstede Model:

Working with IBM employees, Danish psychologist Geert Hofstede discovered four dimensions on which cultures differ. Although the sample was limited in terms of representation (employees of IBM), it was an extensive empirical study of individuals from many different cultures, and it stands as the most popular cross-cultural framework involving managerial issues. Hofstede discovered that cultures differ in terms of power distance, uncertainty avoidance, masculinity-femininity, and individualism-collectivism.

Power Distance:	The degree to which unequal power is accepted and valued by a society
Uncertainty Avoidance:	The degree to which a culture feels comfortable with uncertainty. In high uncertainty avoidance cultures, people do not value ambiguity
Masculinity/Femininity:	The emphasis a cultureplaces onvalues that have been associated with males and females. Masculinity is associated with aggression, materialism, and achievement. Femininity is associated with cooperation, compassion, and human development.
Individual/Collective:	The primary focus a society accords either the individual or the group. Individualistic societies value individual rights and responsibilities; collective societies value groupachievement and harmony.

Country Ranking

	PD	UA	M	I
USA				
Sweden				
Mexico				
Peru				
Costa Rica				
Japan				
Germany				
Australia				

PD = power distance
UA = uncertainty avoidance
M = masculinity
I   = individualism

Discussion Questions:

1. In which country do you feel a participative management style would have the greatest acceptance? Which country would be the least accepting? Explain.
2. In which countries would a company policy of financially rewarding individuals based on their performance be most effective?
3. In which countries would managers be expected to give precise directions to their employees?

PART EIGHT

INTERNATIONAL FINANCE, ACCOUNTING, AND TAXATION

Cases:

Wilson International
"Baa"d Pricing Policies
"Baa"st Transfer Price
Diving into a Tax Haven

Exercises:

Exercise in International Accounting
OECD

CASE 42

WILSON INTERNATIONAL: INTERNATIONAL CAPITAL BUDGETING

Wilson International is a chain of over 100 luxury hotels found mostly in developed countries. George Wilson, a former Chicago sales representative who frequently traveled internationally, started the company. As an international business traveler, Wilson found that hotel quality varied from country to country. He quit his very successful sales job and started a hotel in Dublin, Ireland, a country known for its extensive bed-and-breakfast industry. Wilson felt that business travelers needed a greater selection of hotels in Dublin, particularly in the higher-priced market. The Wilson of Dublin was an immediate success with business travelers and, with the help of a venture capitalist, George was able to expand his hotel concept to 20 countries.

Wilson has always sought hotel opportunities in more developed countries in Europe and Asia. George and his associates felt that the problems found in less-developed countries presented too much risk for his company; thus they avoided most countries of the world. Because the countries in which Wilson operates are considered politically stable and present little political risk, the investment decisions are normally made on the basis of revenue projections using a net present value approach. The firm's cost of capital is used as a means of discounting expected cash flow. If the net present value (NPV) of the investment is above zero, the hotel is constructed. This approach has worked well for the company over the years.

With the possibility of market saturation beginning to rise, George is considering an opportunity to expand into other markets. He has been approached by a trade representative of St. Charles, a small and moderately industrialized island in the Caribbean, who proposes that Wilson International build a business hotel in the capital, Dominic. The trade rep has assured George that an additional hotel is needed in the capital due to the country's expanding industrialization. St. Charles has always enjoyed a brisk tourist trade, and now the country is diversifying its economy into light manufacturing.

Multinationals from the United States and Europe have established customer service operations on the island, and a number of garment manufacturers have begun operations there as well. The trade representative tells George that managers from these companies frequently visit the island, and they need a more luxurious hotel in which to stay. The hotel would certainly be profitable, reasons the trade rep.

Financial analysts for the company have created a report indicating that, using the present financial model, a small hotel would be a good investment. Data included in the model can be seen below.

**Wilson International – St. Charles Operation
Preliminary Financial Analysis**

Yearly Expected Cash Flow from Operations: $750,000US
Expected Life of the Investment   25 years

Wilson International Cost of Capital   12%
Investment $5,000,000US

Basic Financial Model: (12% PVF of 7.84314)

(Present Value of Cash Flows – Investment) = NPV (5,882,355 –
5,000,000) = $882,355

Some Wilson analysts argue, however, that a higher discounting factor than cost of capital should be used. It is proposed by some that a more appropriate discounting factor would be 15% (with a PVF of 6.46415), due to the higher risks associated with the investment environment.

George is uncertain about the proposed investment. While he sees the need for the company to find new markets, he is also troubled by reports he has read about increasing social unrest on the island. Although George and his associates do not consider St. Charles to be a high-risk country, they are concerned about recent increases in petty street crime and social unrest. It has been reported that citizens have resorted to violent street protest to express their displeasure with the increasing prices of some consumer goods. The currency of St. Charles, the Caribbean dollar, has been devalued against most hard currencies of the world and, as a result, imported goods have increased in price. On the other hand, St. Charles has no currency or foreign direct investment restrictions, and allows for full repatriation of company profits. In recent years, the government has been attempting to promote the island as an attractive location for foreign investment.

With declining opportunities in more stable environments, George must consider the feasibility of this opportunity, and the necessary change of strategic direction it would mean for Wilson International.

Discussion Questions:

1. What additional information might be useful to consider before making this investment decision?
2. Can an international company avoid all political risk? Explain.
3. Would you recommend that Wilson International build a hotel on St. Charles? Are there any alternatives to consider other than building the hotel or staying out of the country? Explain.

Case prepared by Charles A. Rarick

CASE 43

"BAA"D PRICING POLICIES

Tara Grant looked out at the rugged landscape of the Australian Outback. The young controller took a sip of coffee and thought about how drastically the view differed from the green pastures of her native home in Boston. Even after spending four years in Australia, she was still amazed by the contrasts. The "change of pace" of the Australian Outback had influenced her decision to accept the accounting position with Outback Woolworks, a wholly owned subsidiary of the United States - based Celtic Sweaters, Inc., after completing college.

Outback Woolworks is a large sheep ranch that had been owned by the Young family until five years ago, when it was incorporated and subsequently sold to Celtic Sweaters for cash and Celtic common stock. Two brothers, Aron and Joe Young, still managed the flock of sheep and oversaw the shearing, combing, and spinning activities necessary for production of worsted wool. During the 1990s, the Australian wool industry faced a depressed market with limited demand. In mid-1999, the Wool International Privatisation Act was passed by the Australian Parliament to deregulate the wool industry, and the following year, wool growers were given the opportunity to vote on future industry practices in the historic Wool Poll 2000. Both brothers were instrumental in the sweeping statutory reform and remained actively involved in various adhoc groups formed to address issues such as ongoing demand building, trade access, risk management, self-regulation and industry leadership, and wool contamination.

As a U.S. company, Celtic Sweaters, Inc. was required to comply with the Wool Products Labeling Act, a 1939 U.S. law requiring that all fabric containing wool carry identification indicating the percentage of wool in the cloth, as well as the appropriate legal description for the fiber according to category (i.e., new, reprocessed, reused wool). Therefore, Celtic purchased only new (or virgin) wool, importing over 75% of the virgin wool produced on the ranch for the manufacture of hand-knit sweaters and tweed jackets. The remaining virgin wool, as well as reprocessed wool made from scrap fibers or mill ends, was sold locally.

Tara headed back to her desk to review some paperwork for an upcoming meeting with J.R. Wolf, the controller of Celtic Sweaters, Outback's parent company. He was interested in the details of Australia's sweeping new tax reform. The country's previously high corporate tax rate was gradually being reduced from 36% to 30%, and a Goods and Services Tax (GST) was being introduced. Fortunately, the GST would not apply to the wool being exported, so Outback's overall tax liability would decrease. This was probably what J.R. wanted to discuss; the extent of the change in tax expense. Tara recalled that J.R. was always concerned with budget preparation and "increasing the bottom line." This was especially true during the past two years, when Outback's lower earnings had mirrored those of the entire Australian wool industry, which is the world's largest producer of raw wool.

The next day, J.R. arrived at the small, administrative offices of Outback Woolworks dressed in a navy-blue suit and tie. Tara recalled her college seminars on "Dress for Success" and smiled. J.R. would be right at home at a high-level corporate meeting on Wall Street, but he looked out of place on the ranch, where all the employees dressed in jeans. She was well aware of the fact that the ranch workers called the business executives from corporate headquarters "the Suits."

After presenting an overview of the changes to the tax law, Tara asked if J.R. had any questions. He quickly turned the conversation to pricing issues. Given the new tax laws, corporate headquarters wanted to increase the price that Outback was charging Celtic for wool purchases. The executives were considering a 30% increase in the transfer price between the entities. At first Tara was puzzled. She had expected J.R. to ask her for an estimate of the effect of the tax legislation on the "bottom line." Changing Outback's sales price (and revenue) would only increase Celtic's costs - the net effect would be zero after the two companies' financial statements were consolidated. Then the real reason for the price change request occurred to her, and she felt her cheeks turn red. J.R. wanted to change the transfer price of the wool to decrease taxes paid in the United States, where the corporate tax rate was 35%, by shifting income to Australia, where the rate would decrease to 30%. To put the facts in their proper perspective, Tara prepared the following projected numbers for the upcoming year, before the price change (amounts in millions of U.S. dollars):

Outback (Sales to Celtic)		**Celtic (Parent Before Consolidation)**	
Sales revenue	$100	Sales revenue	$320
Operating expenses	- 90	Operating expenses	-240
Income before taxes	10	Income before taxes	80
Tax expense (30%)	- 3	Tax expense (35%)	- 28
Net Income	$ 7	Net Income	$ 52

After the proposed 30% transfer price increase (amounts in millions of U.S. dollars):

Outback (Sales to Celtic)		**Celtic (Parent Before Consolidation)**	
Sales revenue	$130.00	Sales revenue	$320.00
Operating expenses	- 90.00	Operating expenses	- 270.00
Income before taxes	40.00	Income before taxes	50.00
Tax expense (30%)	- 12.00	Tax expense (35%)	-17.50
Net Income	$ 28.00	Net Income	$32.50

While the potential tax savings looked appealing, Tara's mind raced. She knew that the Australian Competition and Consumer Commission (ACCC) has been given special powers by the Australian government to oversee wool prices during the transition to the new tax law. She excused herself and located the relevant information. ACCC guidelines noted that wool prices were expected to fall as producers passed tax savings onto purchasers. In fact, the ACCC literature noted penalties for price exploitation of up to $10 million for corporations, and $500,000 for individuals.

Later that day, having produced the appropriate documents, Tara was sure that J.R. would agree that the price increases were out of the question. Instead, he appeared somewhat agitated and simply replied, "Well Tara, how you structure and explain the price increase is up to you, but we'll be looking for higher sales prices beginning next quarter. I guess you'll just have to be creative. Besides you are not the only one who feels pressured by this scenario. Can you imagine how the middle managers at Celtic are going to react when I have to inform them that their profit margins are going to be reduced due to higher product costs?" When Tara boldly asked him what the pricing scheme for domestic sales or wool sales to other customers would look like, he reluctantly agreed that a price increase similar to the one proposed for Celtic would not be warranted. Then he added with a sly grin, "See, Tara, you'll still be in compliance with the ACCC guidelines. Just reduce the sales prices to all other customers to a competitive level; this should bury the inflated transfer prices charged to Celtic. The Aussie regulators don't care about the international business; they'll be happy to get some extra tax revenue from an American company. Heck, they should be glad to have our business!"

As Tara tossed and turned that night, she remembered from her college cost accounting and tax classes that the U.S. Internal Revenue Service (IRS) had transfer-pricing guidelines. The next morning, she located some information on the Internet and learned that the IRS regulations were specifically targeted at reducing U.S. corporate tax evasion. Transfer prices between related organizations should be comparable to market price, if available, or an "arms-length" transaction between two unrelated organizations. She also learned that transfer-pricing regulation dated back to the 1920s, but had been updated frequently. In fact, Congressional hearings in 1990 addressed perceived inbound transfer-pricing abuses and further expanded the IRS regulations. Thus, it appeared as though transfer prices were regularly monitored. Under U.S. tax law, tax agents have the authority to redistribute income to reduce tax evasion or properly reflect income. Violation of the IRS regulations could result in a 20% penalty on the additional assessed tax amounts.

Given diminished retail demand, an emphasis on increasing demand for the Australian wool industry, and the upcoming tax rate cuts, the market prices of Australian wool would be declining. Tara realized that any pricing test that compared the transfer price proposed by J.R. to market or "arms-length" Australian wool prices would clearly draw attention to the higher price charged to Celtic.

While she personally would not be in trouble with the IRS because that was a corporate headquarters issue, she did not want to be involved in this pricing "scheme." Also, if the pricing issue were discovered, the negative publicity could prove devastating to Aron and Joe, who were so involved in the Australian wool industry. Finally, the fact that her meeting with J.R. was private could leave her as the "fall guy," since there was no paper trail. With that thought, Tara headed out to the barn to confer with the Young brothers, who both owned millions of dollars of Celtic Sweaters, Inc. common stock from the ranch's sale.

Discussion Questions:

1. How would a 30% increase in the transfer price affect the net income figures for Outback Woolworks and Celtic Sweaters? How would it affect the overall consolidated net income?
2. Generally, what are the pros and cons of increasing the transfer price for both companies' stakeholders, that is, investors, creditors, employees, and citizens?
3. How might the increased transfer prices affect the managers' morale at Celtic, if the managers are eligible for profit sharing based on income from domestic operations? What if the managers hold stock options?
4. What should Tara do?

Case prepared by Suzanne Lowensohn and Lawrence Hudak

CASE 44

"BAA"ST TRANSFER PRICE

[Note: This case is a follow-up to the previous *"Baa"d Pricing Policies* case. Here the primary character (Tara Grant) must be a problem-solver rather than a whistleblower. Environmental and economic changes enable transfer prices to be adjusted to permit overall tax savings within a consolidated corporate group. The challenge is by how much, at what "cost" to whom, and could the "cost" be minimized among stakeholders?]

Tara Grant looks out the rain-soaked window of her airplane as it landed at Logan International Airport on a dreary April morning. Exhausted after the long flight, and excited about the opportunity to visit family and friends after spending the past five years in the Australian Outback, she prepared to deplane. Tara had been summoned to corporate headquarters in Boston to confer with her new boss, Alec Young, about a very important issue. Alec is the baby brother of the Young family, the previous owners of Outback Woolworks, the large sheep ranch where Grant is employed as controller. Six years ago, when Outback was acquired as a wholly owned subsidiary of Celtic Sweaters, Alec agreed to join Celtic's management team. Alec had requested that Tara come to the States to help devise an optimum transfer price for the virgin wool produced by her subsidiary company (Outback) and sold to his parent company (Celtic) that would *legally* reduce the combined taxes paid to the Australian and American governments, and thereby maximize consolidated earnings.

Tara was very anxious to make a good first impression with her parent company's top executives, because it was just one year ago that she had "blown the whistle" on her former boss, J.R. Wolf, who subsequently was asked to resign due to his unethical practices. Then she felt a sudden calm come over her as she was greeted at the gate by a familiar face and a warm, "good day mate." Alec, the newly promoted controller of the United States - based Celtic Sweater, Inc., Outback's parent company, took time out of his busy schedule to personally meet Tara at the airport. After exchanging a warm hello, Tara quickly filled in Alec about what his two older brothers were up to back on the Australian sheep ranch.

As the conversation shifted to business, Tara's anxiety level began to increase. Before dropping her off at her hotel, Alec cautioned her that his predecessor, J.R. Wolf, still had numerous friends at corporate headquarters that were not too happy that he had been forced to resign. This potentially hostile environment could make the task at hand for Tara and Alec even more formidable. So they agreed to meet early the next morning to sort out the facts, prior to the afternoon meeting with Celtic's top management. Since Celtic's corporate culture can be best described as a participatory management, consensus building among key executives is crucial to obtaining the necessary approval for business decisions.

The next morning, Tara exited her hotel, beaming with confidence, as she was greeted with bright sunshine and a rainbow, to hail a cab for her meeting with Alec at Celtic headquarters. Despite the typical hustle and bustle of the city, she smiled as she spotted a robin sitting in a tree, thinking about her fond memories of springtime in the Northeast. While riding in the cab, she double-checked her briefcase's contents to make sure she had the critical data about the projected prices of virgin wool and her watch to make sure she would arrive on time.

Upon entering Alec's office, Tara is introduced to Kaylee Ann Wright, a CPA tax consultant, who specializes in related party transactions within consolidated groups. After exchanging pleasantries, Alec informs Tara that Kaylee was hired to provide technical assistance to make sure their transfer price strategy is in compliance with the U.S. Internal

Revenue Code and related Treasury regulations. "What a pleasure to meet you, Kaylee!" exclaims Tara. "I feel so much better about the whole transfer-pricing issue knowing you will review the intercompany transactions. In my opinion, transfer pricing is a complex issue that requires an expert opinion."

Kaylee smiles and replies, "Well, thank you for your vote of confidence, Tara. I tend to agree that these issues are important. In fact, Celtic's 100% ownership of Outback (a foreign subsidiary) requires us to file the IRS Form 5472. This form includes information about all intercompany transactions, such as Outback's sale of wool to Celtic Sweaters. Hence, information about transfer pricing between related parties is red flagged.

"Furthermore, the Internal Revenue Code Section 482 and the related Treasury Regulation 1.482 offer specific guidance about 'appropriate transfer prices' for related parties. The most appropriate transfer-price is a comparable uncontrolled sales price, if available; for example, the price Outback charges unrelated customers for virgin wool. If a comparable uncontrolled sales price is not readily available, then the next best transfer price is cost-plus when the parent performs substantial processing; for example, converting raw virgin wool into clothing. This method examines the selling price of Celtic's finished goods (wool clothes) and allows for a 'reasonable' gross profit (industry average) in determining an 'acceptable' cost of goods sold. Since cost of goods sold consists of direct labor and overhead costs incurred by Celtic, plus the 'unknown' cost of raw materials (virgin wool), the transfer price for wool is a plug number to arrive at an 'acceptable' cost of goods sold amount. Finally, any attempts to evade U.S. corporate income taxes through extremely high transfer prices may result in severe penalties ranging from 20-40% on the additional tax assessments."

Given the relevant tax rules, Tara proposes two transfer-price options, as approved by key executives from Outback. Under the first scenario, the selling price of wool would be increased to reflect market changes, and this cost increase would not be absorbed in the selling price of wool clothing (i.e., consumers would not pay a higher price for a Celtic sweater). According to Aron Young (Alec's oldest brother and vice president of production at Outback), environmental conditions, specifically a devastating "mad sheep" disease in Europe and the

Americas, have drastically reduced the world's supply of virgin wool. The limited supply is projected to cause Australian wool prices to rise by up to 50% without any objections from the Australian Competition and Consumer Commission (ACCC). Furthermore, Outback plans to increase its prices for virgin wool across the board by 40% to all its unrelated customers, if there is any excess product not purchased by its parent company. [However, due to the worldwide shortage, it is doubtful that there will be any excess.] Tara demonstrate the impact of a 40% increase with the following projected numbers, presented before and after the change (amounts in millions of U.S, dollars):

Outback (Sales to Celtic)		**Celtic (before consolidation)**	
Sales revenue	$100	Sales revenue	$320
Operating expenses	-90	Operating expenses (incl. wool)	-240
Income before taxes	10	Income before taxes	80
Tax expense (30%)	-3	Tax expense (35%)	-28
Net Income	$7	Net Income	$52

After the proposed 40% transfer price increase (amounts in millions of U.S. dollars):

Outback (Sales to Celtic)		**Celtic (before Consolidation)**	
Sales revenue	$140	Sales revenue	$320
Operating expenses	-90	Operating expenses (incl. wool)	-280
Income before taxes	50	Income before taxes	40
Tax expense (30%)	-15	Tax expense (35%)	-14
Net Income	$35	Net Income	$26

Under the second scenario, the selling price of wool would be increased to reflect market changes, and this cost increase would be absorbed in the selling price of wool clothing (i.e., consumers would pay a higher price for a Celtic sweater). According to Joe Young (the middle brother and vice president of marketing at Outback), a combination of environmental and economic conditions should justify higher prices for wool products. Unseasonably cold weather around the world for the past few years and major fashion designer preferences create a very strong demand for wool products despite cost increases in raw materials. Unlike the first scenario, Joe's analysis (based on a thorough market research study) assumes that consumers will accept price increases equal to 31% for fine wool clothing. Hence, clothing manufacturers such as Celtic may be able to preserve gross profit margins, while absorbing significantly higher costs for raw material (virgin wool). Under this second scenario, the projected numbers for the upcoming year before the price increase are (amounts in millions of U.S. dollars):

Outback (Sales to Celtic)		**Celtic (before consolidation)**	
Sales revenue	$100	Sales revenue	$320
Cost of goods sold	-50	Cost of goods sold*	-160
Gross profit	50	Gross profit	160
Other expenses	-40	Other expenses	-80
Income before taxes	10	Income before taxes	80
Tax expense (30%)	-3	Tax expense (35%)	-28
Net Income	$7	Net Income	$52

*Where Celtic's cost of goods sold = $100 raw materials + $60 direct labor and overhead.

Furthermore, the industry average is very similar to Celtic's gross profit margin of 50%. After the proposed 31% price increase for wool clothing, Outback will be able to increase its transfer price to Celtic by 50% (amounts in millions of U.S. dollars):

Outback (Sales to Celtic)		**Celtic (before consolidation)**	
Sales revenue	$150	Sales revenue	$420.0
Cost of goods sold	-50	Cost of goods sold**	-210.0
Gross Profit	100	Gross Profit	210.0
Other expenses	-40	Other expenses	-80.0
Income before taxes	60	Income before taxes	130.0
Tax expense (30%)	-18	Tax expense (35%)	-45.5
Net Income	$42	Net Income	$84.5

** Where Celtic's cost of goods sold = (100 + 50) for wool + 60 for direct labor & overhead.

Alec noted, "Either of these *legal* options seems reasonable to me." Both women nodded in agreement. "However, before claiming victory we had better consider how the rest of the Celtic key executives might interpret the proposed price change." He was referring to the "old boy network" that is prevalent among Celtic's top executives, especially since his predecessor, J.R. Wolf, has two influential friends on the executive board: Sylvester (Sly) Fox, vice president of marketing, and Sam Coyote, vice president of operations. The two labored long and hard over the dismissal of their long-time friend, but finally agreed it was best that J.R. be "offered an early retirement." The real reason Sly and Sam did not support their friend was because they were fearful that his proposed scheme to increase the transfer-price of wool from Outback to Celtic by 30% (to illegally evade U.S. income taxes one year before) would hurt their profit-sharing bonus. "Can you image how these two will react when a 40-50% increase is proposed one year later?" added Alec.

After careful consideration, the team agreed that for the new transfer prices to be accepted by Celtic's executives, the "self-interest factor" had to be addressed. In addition to making a rational presentation about the legitimate price increase, something must be done to offset the price increase's effect on profit sharing. Hence, Tara suggested replacing the executives' profit sharing bonus (based on Celtic's domestic income) with a stock-option plan. Her logic was that the overall income tax savings should be reflected in higher stock prices in the future. Since the option would provide executives with the opportunity to purchase stock at a fixed lower price, they should be pleased with the new arrangement. Both Alec and Kaylee agreed. Alec congratulated Tara on her stock-option suggestion, especially considering that Celtic has plenty of authorized, but un-issued shares of common stock to cover the stock-option plan. They all left the office feeling adequately prepared for the upcoming big meeting.

Discussion Questions:

1. How would each of the proposed options regarding the transfer price for wool affect the net income figures for (a) Outback, (b) Celtic, and (c) the consolidated group?
2. Generally, what are the costs or benefits of increasing the transfer price for the following stakeholders under each scenario: (a) Outback's creditors, (b) Celtic's production employees, (c) Australian citizens, (d) Celtic's investors, (e) Celtic's executives, (f) Celtic's customers, and (g) American citizens? Be sure to identify which option each group would prefer.
3. What transfer-price increase for virgin wool would raise the least amount of controversy with respect to the two countries' government regulators, i.e., (a) the ACCC and (b) the IRS? Why?
4. In the spirit of consensus building, if scenarios # 1 and # 2 were to be combined, complete the following analysis by calculating (a) the appropriate sales revenue and (b) the increase in wool clothing prices. [Hint: Assume the 40% increase in virgin wool would be passed onto Celtic customers in order to preserve Celtic's gross profit margin of 50%. The gross margin is equal to gross profit divided by sales revenue.]

Outback (Sales to Celtic)		**Celtic (before consolidation)**	
Sales revenue	$140	Sales revenue	$(a)
Cost of goods sold	-50	Cost of goods sold ***	-200
Gross profit	90	Gross profit	200
Other expenses	-40	Other expenses	-80
Income before taxes	50	Income before taxes	120
Tax expense (30%)	-15	Tax expense (35%)	-42
Net Income	$35	Net Income	$78

*** Where Celtic's cost of goods sold = (100 + 40) for wool + 60 for direct labor and overhead.

(b) The increase in wool clothing prices = [(a) less $ 320] divided by $320 = ____% .

5. What is a "whistleblower"? If Tara did the appropriate thing by exposing J.R. Wolf's unethical scheme, why does the decision still affect her a year later?
6. While discussing the anticipated reactions of top management to the price changes, Alec, Kaylee, and Tara touched on the "self-interest factor." What were they referring to, and how does it affect business decision making?

Case prepared by Lawrence Hudack, and Suzanne Lowensohn

CASE 45

DIVING INTO A TAX HAVEN: SHOULD WESTERN CALIFORNIA LIFE MOVE TO BERMUDA?

Dan Richardson, CEO of Western California Life Insurance, is an avid SCUBA diver. He often dives in the waters off his home state of California, and he frequently travels to the Florida Keys to engage in his favorite sport. Dan is now in Bermuda, diving a number of famous shipwrecks. While in Bermuda he has discovered that many insurance companies have established operations on this island off the East Coast of the United States. Bermuda, the Bahamas, the Cayman Islands, Belize, San Marino, and other countries are often referred to as tax havens, since they do not tax income or profits. Technically, the IRS considers any country with a lower tax rate than the U.S. a tax haven; however, certain countries (many in the Caribbean) are specifically known for their lack of taxation. Tax-haven countries earn revenue for their treasuries by assessing licensing fees. Although tax havens have existed for many years, they have recently become a more popular means of avoiding personal and corporate taxation.

Approximately 1,500 insurance companies operate on this tiny island of 57,000 residents. Bermuda is a self-governing British colony with an above-average GDP of over $26,000US per capita. The residents of Bermuda speak English, and the political environment is considered stable. The Bermuda dollar is pegged at parity to the U.S. dollar (1 Bermuda dollar = 1 U.S. dollar) and is freely convertible. One can reach the island quickly and easily from many cities along the East Coast, including New York City. Dan has been told that he can establish a corporate presence in Bermuda in 24 hours for only a few thousand dollars. Insurance companies frequently channel investment income to their subsidiaries in Bermuda, in the form of premiums paid for reinsurance in order to avoid taxation.

Dan reasons that if his small California insurance company relocates, or establishes a subsidiary in Bermuda, he would have a greater opportunity to further enjoy his diving hobby. The fact that the company would be able to avoid taxation is also appealing. As Dan boards his flight back to California, he is excited about the prospect of establishing an operation in Bermuda, but he wonders if he should consider other tax-haven countries. While on board, Dan reads in the newspaper that the Organization for Economic Cooperation and Development (OECD) has recently listed 35 countries as possessing unfair tax practices. The Paris-based organization accuses the 35 tax-haven countries of "poaching" tax revenue from other countries, and has asked for world pressure to be brought on these countries to end their policies. The tax-haven countries respond that they, as sovereign nations, have the right to make their countries attractive to foreign investment, much the same as other countries have done through other incentives.

Dan feels worried; however, he is somewhat reassured as he reads that Bermuda has not been placed on the list because government officials in Bermuda have agreed to share financial information with the OECD. As Dan heads back to California, he begins to plan for a Western California Life subsidiary in Bermuda, although he is not completely certain that it is the right thing to do.

Discussion Questions:

1. Do you feel that it is ethical for a company to channel income to a tax haven in order to reduce or eliminate taxation? Explain.

2. Are there any disadvantages to Western California Life in establishing a subsidiary in Bermuda? Explain.
3. What should Dan Richardson do?

Sources: D. Perry, "Lax on Tax Bermuda Causing Uproar in U.S." <u>Minneapolis Star Tribune</u>, April 14, 2000; B. O'Keefe, J. Burgess, "35 Countries Named as Unfair Tax Havens." <u>The Washington Post</u>, June 27, 2000; D. Mitchell, "OECD War on Low-Tax Countries" <u>The Washington Times</u>, August 20, 2000; "Havens Can Wait." <u>Fortune</u>, October 30, 2000; A. Pascual, "Taxing Times for Tax Havens." <u>Business Week</u>, October 30, 2000; "Organization for Economic Cooperation and Development (OECD) Web site (<u>www.oecd.org</u>); U.S. State Department Web site (<u>www.state.gov</u>).

Case prepared by Charles A. Rarick

EXERCISE 13

EXERCISE IN INTERNATIONAL ACCOUNTING: CONSOLIDATED FINANCIAL STATEMENTS

Purpose: To better understand how the financial operations of a foreign subsidiary affect the financial condition of the parent company.

The following are selected amounts from the separate financial statements of a parent company (unconsolidated) and one of its foreign subsidiaries:

	Parent	Subsidiary
Cash	$180,000	$80,000
Receivables	380,000	200,000
Accounts payable	245,000	110,000
Retained earnings	790,000	680,000
Revenues	4,980,000	3,250,000
Rental income	0	200,000
Dividend income	250,000	0
Expenses	4,160,000	2,960,000

Parent owes subsidiary $70,000
Parent owns 100 percent of subsidiary.
Subsidiary paid the parent $250,000 dividend during the year.
Subsidiary owns the building that parent rents for $200,000.
During the year parent sold inventory to subsidiary for $2.2million.
The inventory had cost the parent $1.5 million.
The subsidiary sold the inventory for $3.2 million to a third party.

Procedure: Using the financial information above, determine the following:

1. The parent's (unconsolidated) net income.
2. The subsidiary's net income.
3. The consolidated profit on the inventory that the parent originally sold to the subsidiary.
4. The amounts of consolidated cash and receivables.

Exercise prepared by Charles W. L. Hill. Used with the permission of the author.

EXERCISE 14

WEB-BASED EXERCISE:
ORGANIZATION FOR ECONOMIC CO-OPERATION AND DEVELOPMENT (OECD)

Purpose: To gain an understanding of the basic objectives and functioning of the Organization for Economic Co-operation and Development (OECD) and the organization's position on international tax evasion.

Procedure: Visit the Web site of the OECD (www.oecd.org) and answer the questions listed below.

Questions:

1. What is the Organization for Economic Co-operation and Development and what does it seek to achieve?
2. How many member countries belong to the Organization and where is it headquartered?
3. Explain the position of the OECD on tax havens and transparency.
4. In your opinion, should countries be allowed to operate as tax havens? Explain your answer.

PART NINE

SOCIAL RESPONSIBILITY IN INTERNATIONAL BUSINESS

Cases:

Exercise

Case 46

MLB SWEATSHOP?
MAJOR LEAGUE BASEBALL
PRODUCTION IN COSTA RICA

A two-hour drive from the capital of San José, Costa Rica, sits the small community of Turrialba where mostly young workers sit and sew baseballs destined for Major League Baseball teams. Rawlings Sporting Goods Company moved its baseball manufacturing operations from Haiti in 1986 when the political landscape of the country began to change.

Rawlings selected the town of Turrialba due to the incentives offered the company by the Costa Rican government. Rawlings was awarded a free-trade zone in which the company would be allowed to operate duty-free in the country. Rawlings pays no import tariffs on the goods it imports to manufacture its baseballs, and the finished product can be shipped duty-free into the United States under the Caribbean Basin Imitative. The Turrialba region was hard hit economically in the 1980s when a major highway from the capital bypassed the town. Since travelers no longer stopped in Turrialba, the Costa Rican government wanted to develop the local area through foreign investment. Rawlings found the potential workforce better educated, and more disciplined than its workers in Haiti. The country was also well known for being very politically stable. With few employment opportunities in the area, Rawlings had no difficulty in securing dedicated and motivated employees. Although Costa Rica is the wealthiest country in Central America, per capita income is still only about $4,200 a year. Costa Rica has an unemployment rate of 6.7% nationwide, however, the rate can vary from region to region. With the completion of the new highway and declining employment opportunities in the coffee and sugarcane industries, many local residents of Turrialba were eager to find stable employment.

Most Rawlings employees in Costa Rica are engaged in sewing operations. In the plant, 300 employees sit in rows of high back chairs and sew baseballs. Many employees break the boredom of the work by listening to music on their headphones. The plant employs a total of 575 workers. At one time Rawlings employed approximately 1,900 workers at the Costa Rican plant, however, employment fell when the company shifted production of its lower quality baseballs to China. The Rawlings plant takes a baseball core and wraps it in yarn. The product is then covered with cowhide and sewn by hand. Baseballs must be sewn by hand in order to achieve the quality level demanded by the Major Leagues. Each worker sews 108 perfect stitches using a long needle and thread. The balls are then inspected, cleaned, and stamped with the MLB logo and the signature of the commissioner of baseball. The balls are then packed and shipped to the port city of Limón where they are loaded onto a ship bound for Port Everglades, Florida. The baseballs are then trucked to Rawlings' Springfield, Missouri facility, and then onto Major League teams or retail stores. Rawlings has been the exclusive supplier of baseballs to the Major Leagues since 1977. The Costa Rican facility produces approximately 2.2 million baseballs a year, with 1.8 million of those going to Major League Baseball. The remaining balls are sold to minor league and college baseball teams, or sold to the public through retail stores or the websites of MLB and Rawlings. While Rawlings refuses to disclose the price of the baseballs paid by MLB, the baseballs retail on the Company's website for $12.99 per unit.

Employees are paid $1.21 per hour and receive the value of 67 cents an hour in benefits, or about thirty cents per ball produced. Workers can go home early in the week if they complete their production quotas.

Rawlings workers earn about 14% above the Costa Rican minimum wage. In addition to their wages, Rawlings employees in Costa Rica must be paid for eleven holidays, receive two weeks of paid vacation a year, and receive a Christmas bonus equal to one month's pay. The Company must also pay into a retirement and medical plan and provide four months of maternity leave when needed.

A 2004 *New York Times* article questioned the pay and working conditions of the Rawlings plant in Costa Rica. The article accused Rawlings and MLB of running a sweatshop in Costa Rica where workers were underpaid and worked in an unhealthy environment. Consumer advocate Ralph Nader joined in the criticism by writing a letter to Bud Selig, MLB Commissioner and the Executive Director of the MLB Player Association. In the letter Nader condemned the two men for allowing baseballs to be manufactured in what he considered to be poor conditions. Portions of the letter follow:

> *"Your respective organizations must not ignore their roles in this exploitation and abuse of worker rights committed under Major League Baseball and Player Association product sourcing and licensing agreements."*

> *"American consumers and baseball fans currently have no guarantee that any licensed Major League Baseball products are not being made under sweatshop conditions that violate basic human and worker rights standards."*

Major League Baseball consumer products vice president, Howard Smith, responded to the rising complaints by stating: *"I can assure you that there is no company we do business with that knowingly goes into a factory with sub-par working conditions."* Not everyone agrees with Mr. Smith.

Maribel Alezondo Brenes worked at the Rawlings plant for seven years before her doctor told her to stop working there for health reasons. Carpal tunnel syndrome has been noticed in the Rawlings employees due to the repetitive nature of the work. Dr. Carlos Guerrero who worked at the Rawlings plant as company physician says that up to 90 percent of Rawlings employees may have experienced pain from the work, from minor cuts to disabling injuries. Others feel that the plant has been a good addition to the region, including Warny Gomez, who worked at the Rawlings facility for four years and made enough money to attend college and to become a teacher. With average pay for Major League Baseball players close to $2.3 million a year, some Rawlings employees feel that their compensation is unjust. Many, however, feel like Alan Cascante, an eight-year employee of the baseball factory: "We can live on that (Rawlings wages). We never made that working in the fields." Plant manager, Ken West agrees with Cascante, by saying "The best thing's the pay. We're a good place to work."

The debate over pay and working conditions of employees who supply MLB with its products appears to be growing in some quarters. People like Kenneth Miller; a self-appointed champion of sweatshop workers takes his message to the fans by camping outside ballparks. He tells potential consumers of MLB products that the baseball player bobble head doll they are about to purchase was made by a Chinese worker who works 20 hour shifts for very little pay. Miller states that he often finds indifference among consumers. Some tell him: "Why are you trying to interrupt our nice day at the ballpark?" Miller and a handful of others are pressuring MLB to take greater control over the working conditions of its suppliers, such as Rawlings.

As the debate continues in the United States over the working conditions and pay of the Costa Rican employees and others, baseballs are sewn in Turrialba with pictures of Alex Rodriquez, Mike Piazza, and other baseball players hanging on the walls of the factory. Rawlings' employees, however, are too busy sewing baseballs for the millionaire players, to even notice the pictures hanging above them.

Discussion Questions:

1. In your opinion, is Rawlings exploiting its Costa Rican employees? Explain your answer.
2. Is it fair to compare the salary of Major League Baseball players to that of employees who sew baseballs?

3. If you were the CEO of Rawlings Sporting Goods' parent company (K2, Inc.) what action would you take, if any, given the present situation?

Sources: Hersh, P. (2003). *The sport of baseball has little popularity in Costa Rica, but big-league baseballs are produced here.* Chicago Tribune, July 15; Jones, D. (2004). *Baseball assailed for using sweatshops.* Pittsburgh Post-Gazette, October 16; Moore, C. (2004). *Baseball striking out in human rights league.* Western Catholic Reporter, March 1; Sloane, G. (2003). *Babe Ruth organizers eye world series try.* AM Costa Rica, February 17; Weiner, T. (2004). *Costa Rica: Low wage workers make baseballs for millionaires.* New York Times, January 25; www.state.gov. Country background notes – Costa Rica. Accessed on May 13, 2005.

Case prepared by Charles A. Rarick

CASE 47

DOING BUSINESS IN NIGERIA

Sitting at the desk in his office in Atlanta, Stew Morrison was elated by the contents of an envelope that had recently arrived from Africa. The envelope contained a letter and supporting documentation from a contact Stew had established in Nigeria and was promising to provide many new customers for Stew's company. Stew Morrison was the CEO of a company called, e-Future; a company that specialized in the sale of education vouchers for the developing world. The letter from Nigeria indicated that a number of businesses, and the government of Nigeria were very interested in purchasing the education vouchers. The letter invited Stew to come to Nigeria and meet with these important prospective customers. Stew was confident that the business was finally beginning to turn around and he was excited about the prospects awaiting him in Nigeria.

Begun with limited capital from a few wealthy investors in 2002, e-Future was a company with a dream. That dream was to bring education to the developing world. Stew Morrison, a former professor of education, had developed the idea of offering a simple means for potential students to pay for higher education and technical training through the use of electronic vouchers. Individuals could purchase the vouchers themselves, or the vouchers could be purchased by governments for their citizens. It was also assumed that businesses may offer them as incentives to their employees. The vouchers could be used in a number of universities and technical schools in Africa, Asia, and in Latin America. In addition, an on-line university created by e-Future offered a number of courses and would accept the voucher as payment. The voucher concept reduced the cost of a course significantly, as universities and schools deeply discounted their tuition under the program. The business concept, first developed by Morrison found its way to Jay Nettlehouse, who in turn convinced other private investors to fund startup of the organization. Nettlehouse became Chairman of e-Future and continued to provide financial support for the company. While the private investors hoped to profit from the business, they also hoped that their money would be used to help develop the poorer countries of the world. Unfortunately, sales of the vouchers proved to be more difficult than anticipated. The company had yet to make a profit and the private investors had to make additional contributions to keep the business operational.

While Stew had never to been on the African continent, he had no concerns with the upcoming trip to Nigeria. Doing some research Stew learned that Nigeria had gained its independent from Britain in 1960 and that political instability had ensued up until 1999 when a democratic government was established. He discovered that Nigeria is a diverse country with over 250 ethnic groups. The country is divided by religious identity with the north being mostly Muslim and the south being mostly Christian. The political boundaries of present day Nigeria came into being when the British gained control of the area in the late 1800's and established the area as a colony. During World War II, Nigerians fought with the British and shortly thereafter gained some autonomy, and a constitution. Stew learned from his investigations that democracy has not been the norm during Nigeria's short existence. Due to differing religious and ethnic identities, a series of coups and dictators had exercised power during most of Nigeria's history. With democracy once again in place, Stew felt that perhaps e-Future could help Nigeria in its nation building effort. Stew was encouraged by the fact that Nigeria is a leading supplier of crude oil to the world and is the most populated country in Africa with over 90 million inhabitants. Stew also was happy to learn that English was the official language of Nigeria. While Stew felt that Nigeria offered great promise to e-Future, he also had some concerns about the level of corruption found in the country.

He had read that corruption was a problem, and that some foreigners had been victims of various scams.

When Stew arrived at the Lagos airport he was overwhelmed by the sights and sounds he was experiencing. The airport was very noisy and crowded and being tired from his long journey, he felt as if he was too confused to find his way past immigration and get his luggage. As he wandered towards the immigration area he saw a sign being held up by a rather small, middle-aged man. The sign read "Welcome Mr. Stew Morrison". When he approached the man with the sign he realized that it was his contact in Nigeria, Bimbola Ogunk. The two men exchanged greetings and Bimbola took Stew's handbag and escorted him towards immigration. When Stew asked Bimbola if he would have any trouble passing through immigration Bimbola told him not to worry. He reminded Stew that he had connections and asked if he had acquired a Nigerian visa. Stew replied that he had not, as previously instructed by Bimbola, and Bimbola said "no problem." The two men proceeded to a separate line at the immigration stop and Bimbola told the official "this is my special friend." The official looked at Stew and waved the two through immigration. To Stew, it did appear that Bimbola had connections. Stew retrieved his luggage and the two men headed for the exit. Bimbola had arranged for Stew to stay at a hotel where he had further connections. Stew at that point just wanted to get to the hotel as quickly as possible and sleep. Unfortunately the traffic of Lagos would keep Stew from his room for another two hours. The two men chatted on the way to the hotel with Bimbola constantly reassuring Stew that he had connection in the government, and connections with education officials, and industry leaders. Stew would be meeting some of those officials later in the week, he was told. Bimbola also told Stew that he wanted to take him on a trip first; a trip he would "surely enjoy." Stew checked into his hotel to get some sleep.

Early the next morning the telephone in the hotel room rang and it was Bimbola. He told Stew that he was in the hotel lobby and ready to take him on a special tour. Stew arranged for a quick breakfast before leaving with Bimbola for a trip to Benin. The long trip, over 200 miles, allowed Stew the opportunity to get to know Bimbola better. The two men discussed many things, however, Bimbola seemed unable or unwilling to provide any details as to how he was going to arrange for the sale of large quantities of e-Future vouchers. He frequently told Stew not to worry and that he, Bimbola, would handle everything. When pressed, Bimbola told Stew that he had arranged for a meeting with Dr. Kema Agaguelu, Minister of Education and that she was very interested in the educational voucher system offered by Stew's company. While not much business was discussed on the trip to Benin, Stew did learn much about the ancient walled city and about the once great kingdom. He was grateful to Bimbola for taking him to see the impressive sights.

... night was taken up by the trip ... anxious to return to his room ... austed, he hardly slept due to the ... ng morning he awoke to the sound ... ola greeting him good morning. ... estaurant and Bimbola explained ... Agaguela was going to take place ... told Stew that he should get his ... the education minister. Bimbola ... offices were in the capital, Abuja, ... in Lagos and that it would not be ... eet her. ... ous and it took hours to reach the ... rted Stew up the flights of stairs ... the minister. They arrived on the ... of any marking to find a middle- ... looking at some papers. Bimbola ... lucation and Stew began to make ... ny could offer Nigeria. He went ... government could advance higher ... gram, all the time Dr. Agaguelu ... r asked any questions, she seemed very interested in what Stew had told her, and she thanked him for visiting. Bimbola told Stew that he had made a very good impression on her and that she would certainly be recommending that the government purchase a very large quantity of vouchers. Stew felt a bit uneasy about the meeting but he was encouraged by what Bimbola was telling him. Stew began to press Bimbola for more details on other contacts but

Bimbola told him not to worry. Bimbola stated that it was time for Stew to purchase some gifts for his family back in America.

Bimbola took Stew to a large market for shopping. While Stew had no interest in shopping at this time, he felt it best not to insult his host. The market was unlike anything Stew had ever seen. It contained a mix of food and household items, along with crafts, animal skins, and skulls. The variety and unique nature of the market was overwhelming to Stew. He managed to purchase some craft items and a special type of woven cloth recommended by Bimbola. It was approaching dinnertime and Bimbola told Stew that he had arranged for Stew to meet his family that evening. Bimbola took Stew to a restaurant where Bimbola's wife and many adults were waiting. The group represented Bimbola's immediate family as well as members of his extended family. Although the group was rather large, Stew enjoyed his meal and the company of this quite lively group of people. One of the dinner items Stew especially enjoyed was jollof rice, a Nigerian specialty. He was impressed when told by one of Bimbola's brothers that Bimbola's grandmother had invented the national dish. Some of the previous apprehensions Stew felt about Bimbola were beginning to be eased. When the waiter brought the restaurant bill to Stew, the moment was a bit uneasy. The bill was quite high and he wasn't sure who was expected to pay, but he reasoned that he would pay the bill since Bimbola had been so kind in taking him to Benin as a cultural side trip. The evening ended well and it appeared to Stew that Bimbola's family had enjoyed the meal. Bimbola took Stew back to the hotel and told him to "expect great things tomorrow."

Once again it was a night without much sleep for Stew. He was dragging during the day and awake most of the night. He hoped that he would be able to soon adjust to the time difference and get a good night's sleep. He was also uneasy because he still was not able to call home and speak to his wife, as the hotel's international telephone line was not working. As the telephone rang in his room, Stew knew that it Bimbola and he was looking forward to those great expectations promised by Bimbola. Bimbola told Stew that he had very good news for him and to come down to the hotel restaurant and they would discuss it. Over breakfast Bimbola had a hard time containing his happiness. He finally told Stew that he had heard from the Minister of Education and that she was arranging for the government of Nigeria to make an initial purchase of $500,000US e-Future education vouchers. Stew was excited about the news and thanked Bimbola for helping to arrange the meeting that produced these results. Bimbola told Stew that all that was needed now were three things. First, Bimbola would need the bank account number of e-Future in order to wire the funds, secondly, Stew would need to make a small payment of $10,000US to the education minister for her help, and lastly, e-Future would need to pay Bimbola a $50,000US finder's fee. Stew was taken aback by these requests. He asked Bimbola to explain more but all that Bimbola would tell him was that this is the way business was conducted in Nigeria. Bimbola told Stew that unless he wanted to lose this large contract, he would need to meet those three conditions. Stew told Bimbola that he was not sure if he would be able to do what was requested and that he would have to check with someone back in Atlanta. Bimbola told Stew that time was critical and that if he waited, he would certainly lose the contact.

Without the matter being resolved, Bimbola proceeded to tell Stew that he was going to meet with very high-level industry officials who were interested in hearing about the education vouchers for use with their companies. They were going to meet for lunch and so Stew needed once again to gather his presentation material and come along for a ride across town. On the drive across town Bimbola explained how many Americans are surprised by the way business is done in Nigeria but that "once they realize this they are able to acquire very good contracts and earn much money." Bimbola told Stew that "Nigeria is a good place to do business."

At lunch, Stew met with four men who were introduced by Bimbola as the leaders of Nigeria's business community. One gentleman, Segun Adelaja was introduced as Prince Segun, head of the Nigerian National Petroleum Corporation. Each man gave Stew a business card indicating their association with various business groups in Nigeria. In addition to the oil industry, the men represented textiles, agriculture, and manufacturing. The six men ate lunch and discussed many things including their love of "football" but not much attention was directed towards business, or e-Future's product. Stew felt very tired and his patience was getting thin. He asked to speak to Bimbola alone and expressed his concerns with the lack of business substance. Bimbola explained that in Nigeria it was customary for people to get to know each other first before they discussed business. Bimbola told Stew that he would provide the opportunity for Stew to present his business ideas before the group left. After many hours of entertaining, Bimbola finally told the group "Mr. Morrison has a plan that is of great value to each of you." Acting on this cue, Stew proceeded to tell the men how e-Future could help their industries, and Nigeria in general. The men seemed very interested and asked a number of questions. Stew felt encouraged and continued to discuss product features at great length. After more than five hours of eating, drinking, and discussing, Bimbola told the group that Mr. Morrison had to get back to his hotel and that that they should contact him, Bimbola, if they were interested in having their companies buy the vouchers. He told the group that he strongly recommended that they take advantage of this opportunity. Once again Stew was presented with a rather large bill from the restaurant.

Bimbola drove Stew back to his hotel and explained that these men represented the best opportunity for Stew to sell thousands of vouchers. He told Stew that millions of dollars were at stake and that it was necessary that Stew completely trust Bimbola to make the deals. All that would be required was for Stew give Bimbola his normal ten percent fee, along with a retainer of "a few thousand dollars, today." Stew felt as if he was being played by Bimbola and told him that he needed to rest before making any decisions. Stew felt that it was time to make a call to Jay Nettlehouse back in Atlanta. At the hotel Stew once again experienced difficulties making an international call. His frustration level was rising and he was unsure of what he should do. While he was worried that he might be taken advantage of by Bimbola, he didn't want to miss out on the opportunities that may emerge from the relationships Bimbola provided. Stew decided to try and find another way of calling America. Stew sat on his bed watching television, resting, worrying, and wondering what his next move should be.

When the telephone rang in his room Stew hoped that it would be someone from e-Future calling. It was Bimbola who told Stew that he was coming over to the hotel for dinner and that he was bringing Stew "something that would make him very happy." When pressed as to what the surprise was, Bimbola told him that it was a contract from the Nigerian government. Stew decided to rest a bit before dinner and was hopeful that perhaps something was finally developing.

Bimbola arrived for dinner with Stew and brought along Dr. Agaguelu who presented Stew with a three-page document. The document was a government contract for $500,000US and included many seals and official stamps. It had already been signed by the President of Nigeria and the Minister of Education. Dr. Agaguela explained that the government was receiving much oil revenue and that in an effort to develop support from the people of Nigeria, the President had decided to spend some of the money to expand the educational opportunities of its citizens. Bimbola explained that it was important that the contract be signed by Stew and that the necessary payments be made immediately. When Stew asked about how he could pay the necessary "fees" Bimbola told him that he could wire the funds into a bank account, or better yet, Stew "could get cash from his American Express card and be done with it." Bimbola stressed how important he and Dr. Agaguela were in getting this contract, and that many more could follow if Stew took care of them.

Sitting at the table, confused and totally exhausted, Stew wondered what he should do, as he looked at the smiling faces of Bimbola and Dr. Agaguela.

Discussion Questions:

1. What mistakes did Stew Morrison make in his Nigerian business trip?
2. Do you think Bimbola is trustworthy? Explain.
3. What should Stew do now?

Sources: Blauer, E. and J. Laure. (2001). <u>Nigeria</u>. New York: Scholastic; Nnoromele, S. (2002). <u>Nigeria</u>. San Diego: Lucent; www.countrywatch.com

Case was prepared by Charles A. Rarick

CASE 48

THE GLOBAL PROBLEM OF E-WASTE

A growing problem in the developed economies of the world is what to do with outdated or unusable electronic equipment. Electronic waste, or e-waste, is created when people discard old computers, monitors, printers, televisions, and other electrical equipment. E-waste contains hazardous materials such as lead, mercury, and cadmium. Public landfills generally prohibit the disposal of such hazardous materials due to the potential to cause harmful environmental conditions. Toxic chemicals from the discarded e-waste can seep into underground water and contaminate drinking supplies. With millions of electronic devices such as old computers, cell phones and television monitors, discarded each year in the United States alone, a strong need exists to find a place for these potentially harmful devices.

Computer recycling requires that low wage employees disassemble old computers by extracting the valuable and working parts for reassembly. The so-called "white box" computers are reassembled computers that are sold in developing countries at a much lower price than new ones. By reusing existing computer parts, resources are saved and consumers who might not otherwise be able to afford a computer can purchase one.

Given the labor cost differences between the United States and third world emerging countries, much of the e-waste from the U.S. is shipped to India and China where the cost of recycling is one-tenth the cost of the United States. Unfortunately, the low cost comes at a high price. Safety regulations and worker protection are generally not available in these countries. Workers in the major recycling centers of Guiyu, China and Delhi, India report health-related issues such as respiratory problems and skin irritations. In addition to removing usable parts from old computers, the recycling industry literally burns circuit boards in order to recover valuable silver and gold used in their manufacture. Wiring is dipped into acid vats to remove the plastic covering to salvage the commodity value of the wire. Much of the work is done by women and children from the rural areas, who come to seek work in the cities of China and India. Both of these groups are especially vulnerable to the hazards of toxic substances such as lead. Lead, found in computer monitors and televisions in heavy concentrations can cause led poisoning in children and often harms an unborn fetus. Compensation for such toxic work is low. Given other employment opportunities, few people would choose to do such work; however, it is often not an option for these workers.

Disposal of e-waste is a lucrative business in the United States, and is expected to increase with even more electronic products being sold each year. In addition, the move to a completely digital television broadcast will produce large quantities of unusable analog sets which will become e-waste. While an old television may be nearly worthless in the United States, a 40 foot container filled with e-waste is worth approximately $5,000 in Hong Kong, the preferred port of entry for such disposables. In order to sell e-waste abroad, U.S. companies must get Environmental Protection Agency (EPA) approval, and the approval of the receiving country before legally shipping their cargo. Enforcement of EPA regulations is, however, is difficult. According to one source, "ninety percent of electronics recyclers are cheaters." The United States is one of the few countries in the world that has not ratified the Basel Convention (Basel Convention on the Control of Transboundary Movements of Hazardous Waste) which regulates the movement of hazardous materials, especially from developed to less developed countries.

One proposed solution to the problem is to require electronics manufacturers or retailers to charge a disposal fee at the time of purchase to cover the cost of safely disposing of the product at the end of its usefulness. Or similarly, a recycling fee could be assessed and refunded when the device is returned. As commodity prices drop globally, there is increased pressure to reduce the cost of processing e-waste to extract the precious metals and other components. With an overflowing stock of old computer monitors and other electronic devices in developed countries and a growing population in developing countries needing employment, the hazardous work of recycling is expected to continue to grow.

Discussion Questions:

1. Who do you feel is most responsible (consumers, manufacturers, American recyclers, foreign governments) for the e-waste problem? Explain your answer.
2. Is it fair for rich countries to dump their e-waste in poor countries? Explain your answer.
3. Do you think a recycling fee or deposit will solve the e-waste problem? Do you have another possible solution?

Sources: B. Elgin, B. Grow, and E. Gibson. *The dirty secret of recycling electronics.* Business Week, November 27, 2007; *Growing concerns over India's e-waste.* BBC News, November 8, 2008; *Heavy metal.* Forbes, October 27, 2008; www.basel.int.

Case prepared by Kasia Firlej

PATAGONIA: CLIMBING TO NEW HIGHS WITH A SMALLER CARBON FOOTPRINT

"There is no business to be done on a dead planet."

David Brower, Sierra Club Founder

A recent United Nations' Intergovernmental Panel report on the environment indicated that the earth's climate is changing quite rapidly. The report stated that global temperature is without a doubt rising, and there is a very strong chance that the reason for the temperature change is man-made pollution in the atmosphere. The eleventh warmest years ever recorded have occurred in the period of 1995 to 2006, with 2006 being the warmest year on record in the United States. The suspected cause of this global warming is the rise in carbon dioxide which traps solar heat and keeps it form radiating out of the atmosphere. Atmospheric levels of carbon dioxide have risen since the dawn of the industrial revolution and correlate with increases in global temperature. Still, not everyone is convinced that carbon dioxide is the cause of global temperature increases, and some argue that warming is part of the earth's natural cycle of changing temperature. An additional debate can be found in the appropriate human response to rising global temperatures. Some have argued that effort should be directed towards reducing the effects of global warming, such as building sea defenses and shifting agricultural production. This argument proposes that attempts to reduce greenhouse gases are simply too expensive and will take too long yield any significant gains. While the debate on the causes of global warming, and the appropriate response to it continues, many activists and politicians have found the issue worthy of their attention and they almost universally argue that global warming is a man-made event.

In recent years it has become fashionable to show concern for the environment. With increased concerns about global warming a number of celebrities, politicians, and companies have become outspoken about the perceived harm human beings are doing to the planet. Celebrities such as Brad Pitt, Leonardo DiCaprio, Susan Sarandon, and many others have staked a claim to environmental friendliness. Former Vice President Al Gore has devoted himself to the reduction of greenhouse gases and other harmful byproducts of industrialization, and has produced a popular documentary on the subject. A number of companies have also begun taking account of their impact on the environment and taking corrective action to reduce negative environmental externalities. One company that has risen above others in its concern for the environment is Patagonia.

Patagonia manufactures and sells apparel and equipment for rock and mountain climbing, surfing, paddling, fishing, and running. The company traces its beginnings back to a garage in Burbank, California where a young outdoor enthusiast named Yvon Chouinard began forging three inch metal strips used for rock climbing. Chouinard sold the strips for $1.50 each out of his car. From his parents' garage he moved the operation to Ventura, California, married, and began to branch out into outdoor clothing and accessories. With his wife as partner, the couple pledged that they would only sell quality goods produced in a socially responsible manner. Today Patagonia is a $270 million privately-held company, known for high-quality outdoor clothing and equipment and a social conscious.

Chouinard is the author of *Let My People Go Surfing: The Education of a Reluctant Businessman;* the story of his company and its philosophy. Chouinard, who states that he never really wanted to be a businessman, extols a different, and some would say kinder approach to business. The company was an early adopter of progressive employment practices such as flexible working hours and family-friendly practices including day care and after school programs. The company will also provide a sabbatical leave of up to two months with pay for employees who want to engage in environmental activities. Patagonia receives about 900 applications for every job opening. Many of Patagonia's 1,275 employees are like Scott Robinson, who with two MBA degrees and significant European internship experience decided to work for Patagonia stocking shelves, just to be part of this company. Robinson had read *Let My People Go Surfing* and decided that he wanted to work for an organization that was "driven by values" even if it meant less money and prestige. Patagonia encourages its employees to be creative and to be responsible citizens of the world.

One of the early environmental activities the company began was the promotion of organically grown cotton. Patagonia decided a number of years ago to reduce the environmental damage caused by cotton growing when traditional methods are used. Since the company's products at the time used much cotton, this move would be a major step in making the organization more environmentally friendly. Traditional methods of growing cotton, although more efficient, use pesticides and defoliants to increase plant yield. Organically grown cotton is more expensive to produce but avoids these environmentally harmful practices. The use of organic cotton raises the price of the finished product. Likewise, Patagonia has developed a more environmentally friendly wetsuit for surfers that replaces petroleum-based neoprene with recycled polyester and organically produced wool. The price of the Patagonia wetsuit is $470, compared to competitors with neoprene suits priced from $99-175. In addition to being better for the environment, the Patagonia wetsuit is considered warmer than competitor's products and does not have the typical wetsuit smell some find unappealing. Patagonia now conducts an environmental assessment of all the material it uses for its products.

It has created a fleece jacket made in part from used plastic soda bottles and encourages its customers to return old clothing so that it can be recycled. Patagonia discourages its customers from using overnight shipping of its products because this requires that the goods be sent by air, a higher carbon producing mode of transportation. The company's catalog is produced on recycled paper. The company also makes as much use as possible of solar and wind power for its energy needs. Recently Patagonia was awarded the Gold level certification in Leadership in Energy and Environmental Design from the U.S. Building Council for its distribution facility in Reno, Nevada. Patagonia's distribution center is only the second center to be certified at this level by this organization. The facility uses renewable energy for all its energy needs, used recyclable materials for construction, and has a greatly improved water conservation program in its operation.

Patagonia has established or supported a number of environmental projects including the Conservation Alliance and 1% for the Planet, and gives environmental grants to grass root level groups. The Conservation Alliance is a group of firms in the outdoor activities supply business that work together to support environmental causes. The organization, 1% for the Planet, is a group of firms that have agreed to give one percent of annual revenue to environmental organizations. Patagonia has also given over $20 million to environmental groups for projects that other donors have rejected. For 2006-2007, Patagonia's environmental campaign was "to investigate the connection between the vitality of human life and marine environment." Patagonia said it wanted to understand how "the vast schools of tuna are like herds of buffalo," or "how bottom trawling is like clear-cutting an entire forest to get a single tree."

Some feel that Patagonia could grow even faster if it were to go public. The company has experienced annual revenue growth in the range of 3-8% and Chouinard feels even this may be too much growth. "We could grow the business like crazy and then go public, make a killing. But that would be the end of everything I've wanted to do." Patagonia is slowly increasing its group of devoted customers, and its higher prices have allowed the company to realize operating margins above the industry average. An argument could be made that if Patagonia were to go public and grow sales at a higher rate the company could do even more good for the environment.

While companies such as Patagonia have promoted themselves as environmentally friendly companies, many other firms have become actively engaged in sustainability issues, yet have not promoted themselves as "green firms." Anheuser-Busch for example has reduced industrial waste and energy consumption by focusing on its production processes, and has developed a lighter and more efficient aluminum can, however, A-B is seldom seen as an environmentally friendly company. Some feel that the green image may not be a selling point for all consumer groups. It is clear that Patagonia isn't concerned about appearing to be "too green," and the company takes the quote from David Brower (There is no business to be done on a dead planet) seriously. This quote is etched on the front door of the company's headquarters and the message is manifested throughout the company in its practices and policies.

Discussion Questions:

1. Is green business good business? Explain. Why aren't all companies green businesses?
2. What is the difference between green marketing and green business?
3. Can a corporation be environmentally sensitive and still be responsible to shareholders? Is this easier for a privately held company?
4. Do you think all businesses should follow Patagonia's lead in its environmental practices? Explain.

Sources: Artz, N. (2007). *What does it mean to be an environmentally sustainable company?* MaineToday, March 20; Casey, S. (2007). *Eminence grace.* Fortune, April 2; Hamm, S. (2006). *A passion for the planet.* Business Week, August 21; Harvey, F. (2007). *Urgent call to adapt to climate change.* Financial Times, April 7; Holland, J. (2007). *How green is your dollar? Diligent consumers have many ways to check out a company's true colors.* Knight Ridder Tribune Business News, January 28; Kanter, L. (2006). *The eco-advantage.* Inc. Magazine, November; Kluger, J. (2007). *What now: Our feverish planet needs a cure.* Time, April 9; http://www.hoovers.com. Accesed on March 15, 2007; http://www.patagonia.com. Accessed on March 15, 2007.

Case prepared by Charles A. Rarick and Lori Feldman

CASE 50

FAIR-TRADE COFFEE

Most of the coffee production in the world takes place in elevations from sea level to 6,000 feet, in a 25-degree latitude belt on either side of the equator. Arabica grows best in higher elevations, while Robusta grows best in lower elevations. Moderate sunlight is desirable (tree shade or side of mountains that obscure the sun for part of the day), high humidity, and constant temperatures are most favorable. Major coffee-growing regions include countries in South America and the Caribbean, in Central America, in Africa, and in Asia. For many of these countries, coffee exports are a crucial source of employment for small farmers and farm workers and a vital means of procuring hard currencies. In 1997-1998, the largest producer was Brazil, followed by Colombia. Today, Brazil remains in first position with 35% of world production, but Vietnam has captured second place with 12% of world production through modernization and development of its coffee industry, in part due to international subsidies.

Since World War II, world coffee prices have been regulated by producer countries, organized under the auspices of the United Nations. They allocated export quotas among themselves to maintain a steady world supply and guarantee each producing country a certain share of the world market. The International Coffee Agreement was first signed in 1962 and renewed in 1968, 1976, and 1983. Member nations failed to agree on a new coffee agreement in 1989. Since then, the price of coffee has fluctuated on the world commodity market, according to climactic events that would favor or shrink world supply.

Untimely frosts in Brazil, the producer of over a third of world production, would drastically affect the market price. Brazil attempted to regulate the world price by building inventories of coffee beans in plentiful years to be depleted in leaner years. In the 1990s, Vietnam significantly increased the world supply through the fast development of its low-cost, modern coffee industry. Coffee prices can vary significantly. In 1998 coffee sold for over $180 per sack, while by 2002 the price had dropped to below $60.00. By 2008 the price of a sack of coffee was around $150 per sack. World coffee prices apply to "conventional" coffee, meaning coffee that is not "farm identified." Conventional coffee is bought and sold in bulk without regard to grower, or even to country of origin. The principal purveyors of such coffee are the three major coffee companies: Philip Morris (Kraft Foods' Maxwell House Coffee), Procter & Gamble (Folgers Coffee) and Nestle. Specialty coffee represents a very small share of world production; this refers to coffee that is "farm identified." The identification of the farm of origin may focus on the ownership of the "farm" (estate or cooperative), or on the harvesting practices (organic coffee and/or shade-grown coffee), or on the economic system under which the coffee is purchased (fair-trade coffee). Specialty coffee commands a price premium.

The fair trade movement focuses on commodities that constitute a large share of a developing nation's economy: coffee, tea, cocoa, bananas, sugar, lumber, and the like. Its goal is to organize farmers in fair trade cooperatives that eliminate the middlemen and to establish an economic system under which the product is produced and distributed. Certification agencies guarantee the integrity of the production/ distribution chain and authorize a fair-trade label for products in compliance. The premise is that world trade is good for consumers and producers, depending wholly on how goods are made and sold. The activists feel they are using free-market economies to implement social change.

In the case of coffee, the roasters must purchase fair-trade coffee from fair-trade cooperatives at a guaranteed minimum base price that represents a "livable wage" for the farmer, regardless of world conditions.

The cooperatives grant their members credit and advance payment to tide them over adverse economic conditions. Members are encouraged to adopt production methods that protect the environment and the health of consumers. Members are also encouraged to plow profits back into their community for daycare, medical care, schools, and the like. Certification agencies in Europe and in the U.S. inspect the cooperatives, the importers, and the roasters to guarantee the integrity of the fair trade coffee label. Social consciousness campaigns ensure that socially aware consumers pay a premium at the retail level for fair-trade label coffee with the intent of helping small farmers and their families attain a decent standard of living. The fair trade coffee movement was created in 1988 in the Netherlands. There are now 17 importing countries involved and 300 growers' cooperatives across 21 countries. In the U.S. (the world's largest coffee consumer), the movement is quite recent. The monitoring agency that certifies fair-trade coffee is Transfair USA, a not-for-profit organization established in 1996 under the auspices of the Ford Foundation.

Fair-trade coffee roasters are paying a price floor of $1.26/lb to fair-trade growers. They pay an additional premium of 0.15/lb for organically grown coffee. Roasters have the highest profit margin in the production chain, and they are encouraged to absorb a portion of the cost of fair trade; consumers absorb the other portion of the cost. Transfair USA has targeted specialty retailers and large grocery store chains to persuade them to sell fair-trade coffee. Under threat of boycott, chains such as Peet's Coffee and Starbucks offer whole bean fair-trade certified coffee on their shelves next to their own brands, but they haven't changed their own basic buying policies.

The demand for specialty coffee appears to be price insensitive. Starbucks' fair-trade coffee, for example, retails at $13.45/lb, while its own house blend retails at $9.95/lb. The typical U.S. consumer of fair-trade coffee lives on the West Coast or in the Northeast and is young, female, educated, urban, socially conscious, quality conscious, and able to pay a higher price to support fair-trade practices. Market studies in the United States reveal that 78% of adult consumers declare a willingness to buy a product associated with a cause they support, and 54% declare themselves willing to pay more for such a product.

Discussion Questions:

1. Do firms such as Starbucks and other roasters truly bear any cost for supporting the fair-trade label?
2. Is fair-trade fulfilling its objectives?
3. Do consumers in wealthy countries have a responsibility to the producers in poor countries?

Sources: F. Robles, "Ground Down by Debt - Low Prices Hurt Coffee Growers." Miami Herald, April 7, 2001; "Coffee Falls More Than 3% as Growers Start Selling." Miami Herald, April 20, 2001; "Decline of the Coffee Republic." The Economist, April 21, 2001; www.transfairusa.org; www.globalexchange.org; www.virtualcoffee. com; www.realcoffee.co.uk; www.nationalgeographic.com; www.guardfoods.com/ coffee.

Case prepared by Martine Duchatelet

EXERCISE 15
THE CHILD LABOR QUESTION

Purpose: The purpose of this exercise is to explore the universalist argument for ethical standards, and to develop a better understanding of the ethical dilemmas faced by international managers.

Procedure: Read the background note that follows and then assemble into small groups. Your task to develop a reasoned argument which either attacks or defends child labor.

Background Note:

The International Labor Organization (ILO) estimates that over
250 million children are employed throughout the world, with ages ranging from four to fourteen. A large percentage of these children are employed full-time and do not attend school. Child laborers can be found in large numbers in Africa, Asia, and Latin America. One country known for its child labor is Pakistan. In Pakistan, carpet master, Sadique, recruits boys ages seven to ten to weave his carpets. Sadique states: "They make ideal employees. Boys at this stage of development are at the peak of their dexterity and endurance, and they're wonderfully obedient." The carpet master can hire a child for about one-fourth the cost of an adult carpet weaver.

Critics of child labor, which includes many international organizations, argue that these children are exploited by their employers, forced to work long hours in poor and dangerous conditions, and are deprived of an opportunity for a better life. They argue that a universal standard should be agreed to by all nations that ensures that no child will be subjected to full-time employment before the age of fourteen.

Others argue that while child labor is never a country's first choice, it is necessary for the survival of some less developed countries. Critics of international standards argue that what is unethical in one country may not be unethical in another. This relativist perspective maintains that child labor standards cannot be applied globally because the economies of the world are not equal. While prosperous countries can afford to keep children in school for a long time, it is necessary that children work in poorer countries. They point out that rich countries today, such as the United States, had children working during their less prosperous times. It is further argued that without employment, many of these children would be homeless and subject to even greater exploitation on the streets. The families of the working children depend on them in many cases for money for food. The question is not education or work, but rather, work or starvation.

The carpet master in Pakistan quote is from J. Silvers, The Atlantic Monthly, February, 1996.

LaVergne, TN USA
14 March 2010
175842LV00001B/133/P